Giorgio Bonsanti

CARAVAGGIO

SCALA

New revised edition, 1991
Translation: Paul Blanchard
Editor: Karin Stephan
Layout: Fried Rosenstock
Photographs: SCALA (M. Falsini, N. Grifoni, M. Sarri), except: 87 (Banca Commerciale Italiana S.p.a., Milan); 35, 43, 44, 48 (Bildarchiv Preussischer Kulturbesitz, Berlin); 64 (Cleveland Museum of Art, Cleveland/Ohio); 47 (Colorphoto Hans Hinz SWB, CH-Allschwil); 10 (Founders Society Detroit Institute of Arts, Detroit); 26, 31, 32 (Istituto Centrale per il Restauro, Rome); 85 (Kimbell Art Museum, Fort Worth/Texas); 62, 67 (Kunsthistorisches Museum, Vienna); 7, 86 (Metropolitan Museum of Art, New York); 83 (Musée des Beaux-Arts, Nancy); 40, 41, 42, 66 (National Gallery, London); 78 (Patrimonio Nacional Editorial, Tesoro Artístico e Inventarios, Madrid); 65 (Photo Ellebé, Rouen); 55 (Salmer, Barcelona); 80 (Shickman Gallery, New York); 84 (Soprintendenza per i Beni Artistici e Storici, Rome); 45 (State Museum of Eastern and Western Art, Odessa); 8 (State Museum Hermitage, Leningrad); 15 (Thyssen-Bornemisza Collection, Lugano); 9 (Wadsworth Atheneum, Hartford/Connecticut); 52 (William Rockhill Nelson Gallery of Art, Kansas City)
Produced by SCALA
Printed in Italy by Amilcare Pizzi S.p.A. - arti grafiche
Cinisello Balsamo (Milan), 2002

Back cover: David with the Head of Goliath
cm. 125x100
Rome, Galleria Borghese

Certain figures in the history of civilization give a special impetus to the course of events. They stimulate technological or cultural advances that otherwise would have taken much longer to achieve. With regard to the Western artistic tradition, for instance, Giotto and Masaccio come to mind (just to limit our discussion to painting). After them, Caravaggio alone, perhaps, can be considered part of this very special elite, possibly together with Paul Cézanne. Caravaggio, as we shall see, was such a forcefully innovative painter that his mark remained deeply impressed on the entire course of Western painting.

When Caravaggio began to work independently, at the beginning of the 1590s, the prevailing artistic style, in Italy as elsewhere, was late mannerism. This term is generally applied to most sixteenth-century art, which was concerned with developing and varying the styles of the great masters of the first quarter of the century (Raphael, who died in 1520; and Michelangelo, who painted the Sistine Ceiling between 1508 and 1512) according to a formula that, although it was initially innovative and anticonformist (Pontormo, Rosso Fiorentino), later became tired and sterile, generating a conventional approach to painting that promised little in the way of important developments. After 1575 a few leading painters began to react against late mannerism. In Florence Santi di Tito and Lodovico Cardi, called Cigoli, sought a simpler, more direct way to express feelings and emotions. In Bologna the Accademia of the Carracci championed the necessity of reestablishing a direct relationship with the great masters of the beginning of the century, especially Raphael, in order to propagate a classical style — a style that would have more than just incidental value and that would adapt painting to noble and lofty ideas. These Emilian artists (Annibale Carracci, Domenichino, Guido Reni, Giovanni Lanfranco, and Guercino) all worked in Rome, where their artistic principles were widely accepted.

Caravaggio's painting style also arose as a reaction to mannerism. It offered a new and promising path for the future that led in the direction of naturalism, as Caravaggio declared and as his biographers and contemporary theorists clearly recognized. Thus the specific solution he found, and not only his general role as an innovator, relates him to Giotto and Masaccio, two artists who had discovered a way out of a stylistic impasse through the direct study of objective reality. This of course does not mean that Caravaggio was out of step with his times, independent of other stylistic tendencies, or disdainful of the study of the art of earlier masters. Unlike his contemporaries, who saw only the innovative aspect of his art (and in some cases even judged it negatively), we perceive in Caravaggio's paintings the influence of such artists as Raphael and Michelangelo. But we are surprised by the intelligence with which he used what he drew from the great art of the past, in accordance with his own very personal principles.

Caravaggio's naturalistic outlook had important, if incomplete, precedents that are closely related to the region where he was born and trained as an artist. Michelangelo Merisi (this was Caravaggio's real name) was born, to Fermo Merisi and Lucia Aratori, in 1570 or 1571. Whether his precise birthplace was Caravaggio, or Milan, as recent research suggests, is uncertain. The town of Caravaggio is not far from Treviglio, in an area of Lombardy that is closer to Bergamo than to Milan. Michelangelo's father died a young man. What he did for a living is unknown, but it seems he was an architect, or at least a master builder, and that his family was fairly well to do. In 1584 the young Merisi entered the workshop of the mediocre Milanese mannerist painter Simone Peterzano. Judging from his contract, he stayed there for four years; a document of 1589 shows that he was again at Caravaggio. When he moved to Rome, in all likelihood in the second half of 1592, he was already more than twenty years old, and he probably was not at the very beginning of his career.

So, Caravaggio was trained in Lombardy where he had as a model that peculiar realism characteristic of Lombard art, the essence of which has been recognized and defined by modern scholars. Even late Gothic art in Lombardy, from the end of the fourteenth century to the middle of the fifteenth, is distinguished by a particular attention to the results of direct observation of nature. This attitude was assimilated and developed by the great Renaissance master, Vincenzo Foppa of Brescia, of whose work it became a central feature. In the sixteenth century artists such as Girolamo Savoldo, Girolamo da Romano (called Romanino), Alessandro Moretto, Giovan Battista Moroni, and particularly the Venetian Lorenzo Lotto during his many years at Bergamo, showed a pronounced curiosity toward nature (not a dispassionate interest, but a participatory and sympathetic one, in the etymological sense). The relation between objects and natural and artificial light, and the ability of color to construct and define, are elements that Caravaggio assimilated from the local tradition (it is no coincidence that the artists mentioned above worked in

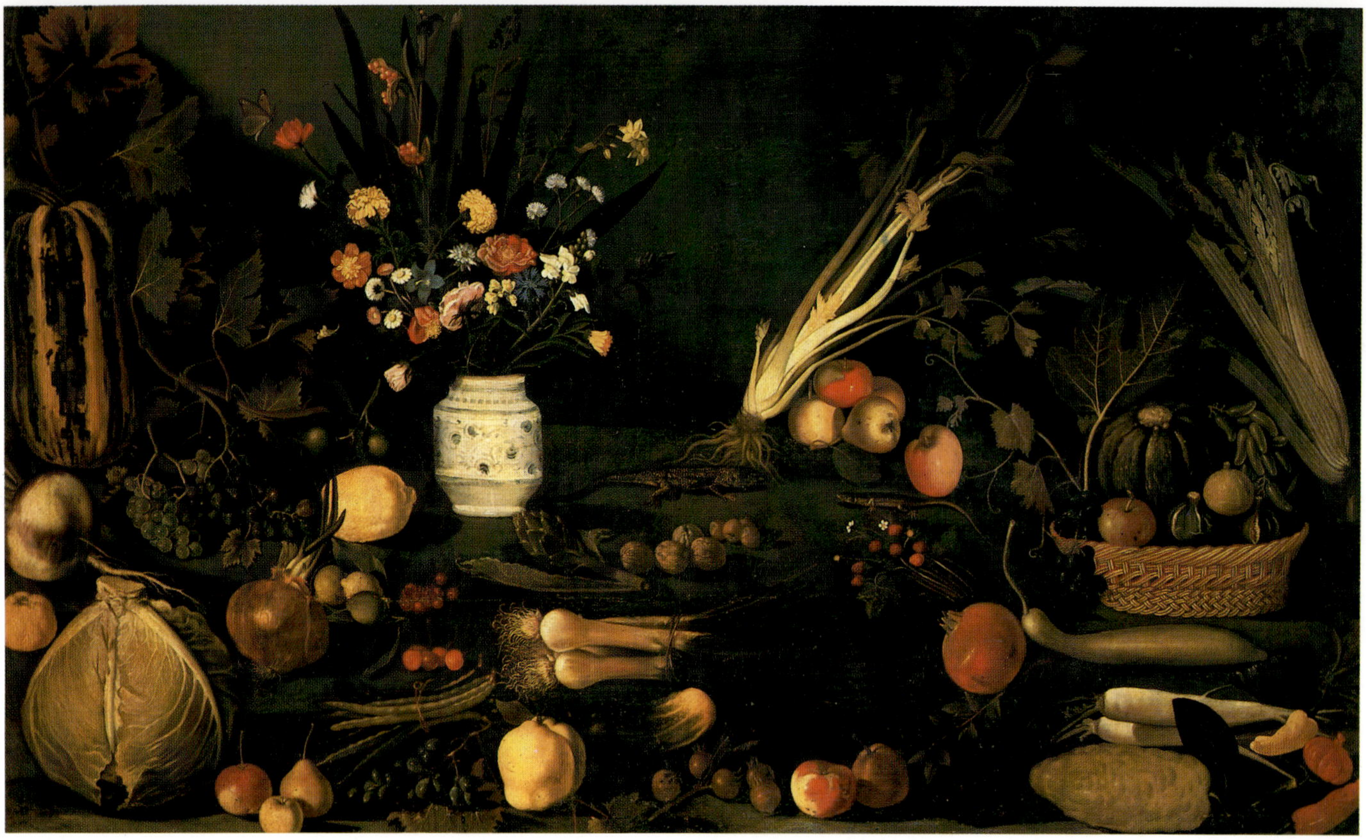

1

Bergamo and Brescia, half way between Milan and Venice), although he would dramatically develop them far beyond their foreseeable limits.

Caravaggio's first biographers (Giulio Mancini, Giovanni Baglione, and Giovan Pietro Bellori) say that he went to Rome when he was about twenty (in reality he was just a little older, as we have seen). They tell of a difficult initial period in which the artist had little to live on, and of his "service" with Cavalier d'Arpino, a famous late mannerist painter, for whom the young Caravaggio painted chiefly "flowers and fruit." Apparently the master immediately recognized the young painter's skill in this field, a skill that is also apparent in certain early works containing particularly handsome still-lifes. Recently scholars have even attributed to Caravaggio some highly innovative still-lifes (among the very first examples of this genre, which would later enjoy enormous success) formerly ascribed to his master. On the basis of an inventory made in 1607, when numerous paintings in Cavalier d'Arpino's workshop were confiscated (some of which have now been found, it seems), Federico Zeri has attributed to Caravaggio two still-lifes
1 (one of vegetables, the other of game) now in the Galleria Borghese. His proposal has yet to be closely examined by critics, but his argument is certainly convincing.

On the basis of what we know from Caravaggio's biographies and from the documents, it is possible to place with certainty the artist's first independent works before 1595. Two of these paintings are in the Galleria Borghese in Rome; they were given to the Borghese family by Pope Paul V after being seized from Cavalier
d'Arpino. The first, the so-called Sick Bacchus, is cer- 2
tainly a self-portrait, although the hypothesis, according to which Caravaggio painted it in the hospital after being kicked by a horse, has now been abandoned. We know that the artist was too poor to hire models, and so painted his own image in the mirror. In this first version of the theme the observer finds the immediacy of the image quite striking, especially if he or she is acquainted with the cultural climate of the period in which the picture was painted. The youth dressed as Bacchus is seen as through a window that opens on an image of reality objectively portrayed, without being interpreted or improved by the painter. The figure stands out in a directly perceptible manner made possible, in part, by a modern "point of view" that make us think, four centuries later, of a photograph. Of course the painting also contains meanings that are not immediately identifiable, or that demand an erudite interpretation; and this obliges us to recall what we said before, that Caravaggio's naturalism does not by any means imply that his art arises without deep cultural matrices.

The highly skilled rendering of the fruit and ivy that we find in the Sick Bacchus is merely an introduction to
the spectacular basket held by the youth in the other 3
Borghese painting from this early period. Here Caravaggio's capacity for the surface textures of the fruit and leaves appears straight-away as the most advanced of the art of his age. It is quite understandable that the

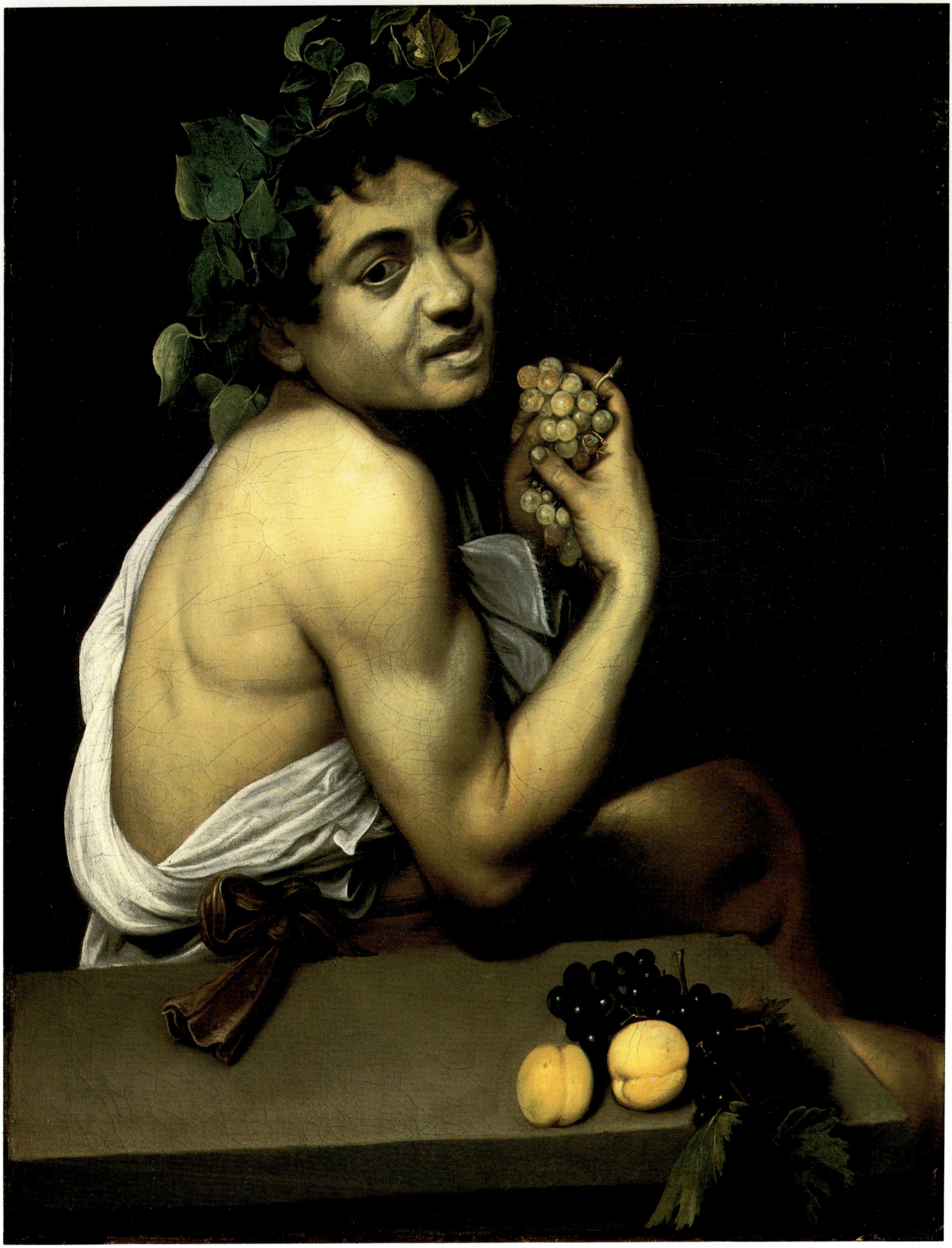

2

1. Still-Life with Flowers and Fruit
cm. 105x184
Rome, Galleria Borghese

2. Sick Bacchus
cm. 66x52
Rome, Galleria Borghese

3

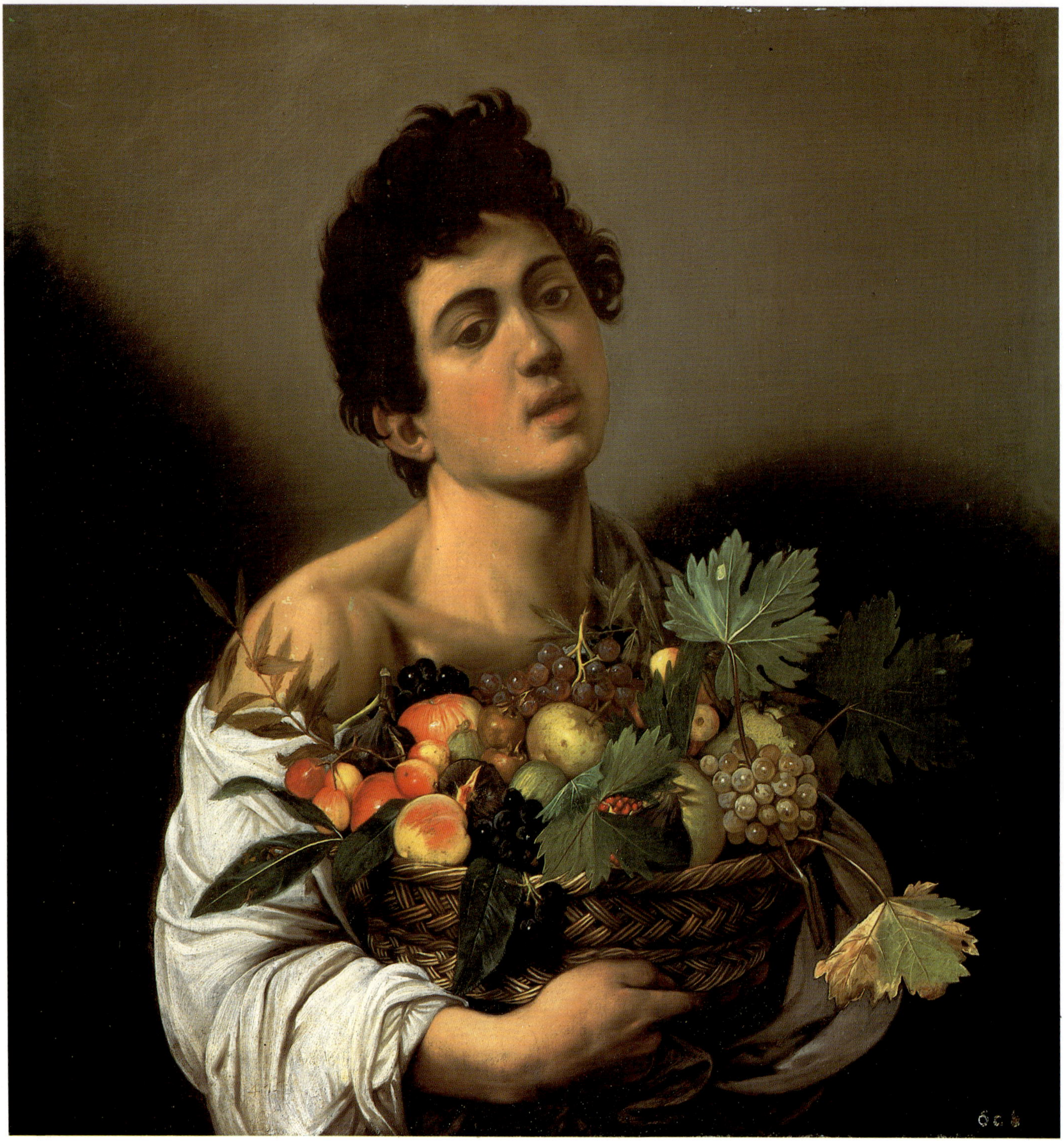

young Lombard's skill made a keen impression in Cavalier d'Arpino's workshop, and that it soon asserted itself in the city's learned circles. The youth with the fruit basket looks out at the observer with a velvety gaze, his lips parted in an inviting manner. It is an ambiguous expression that has led some scholars to hypotheses of dubious validity; but it is true in any event that the slant of the head and the direct gaze, which recall the Venetian portraits of Giorgione, introduce us here to a much more immediate and disturbing relation between the viewer and the object of the painting.

The same immediacy pervades the Youth Bitten by a Green Lizard in the Longhi Collection in Florence. Several copies were made of this picture, as of almost all Caravaggio's paintings, and this attests to the extraordinary success his works met with. The action is frozen in a fraction of a second, as in a snapshot. The virtuoso rendering of the fruit and flowers is accompanied (and we know that this was particularly appreciated by the artist's contemporaries) by that of the carafe of water in which the roses stand. A similar composition existed in another youth with a vase of roses. Unfortunately the

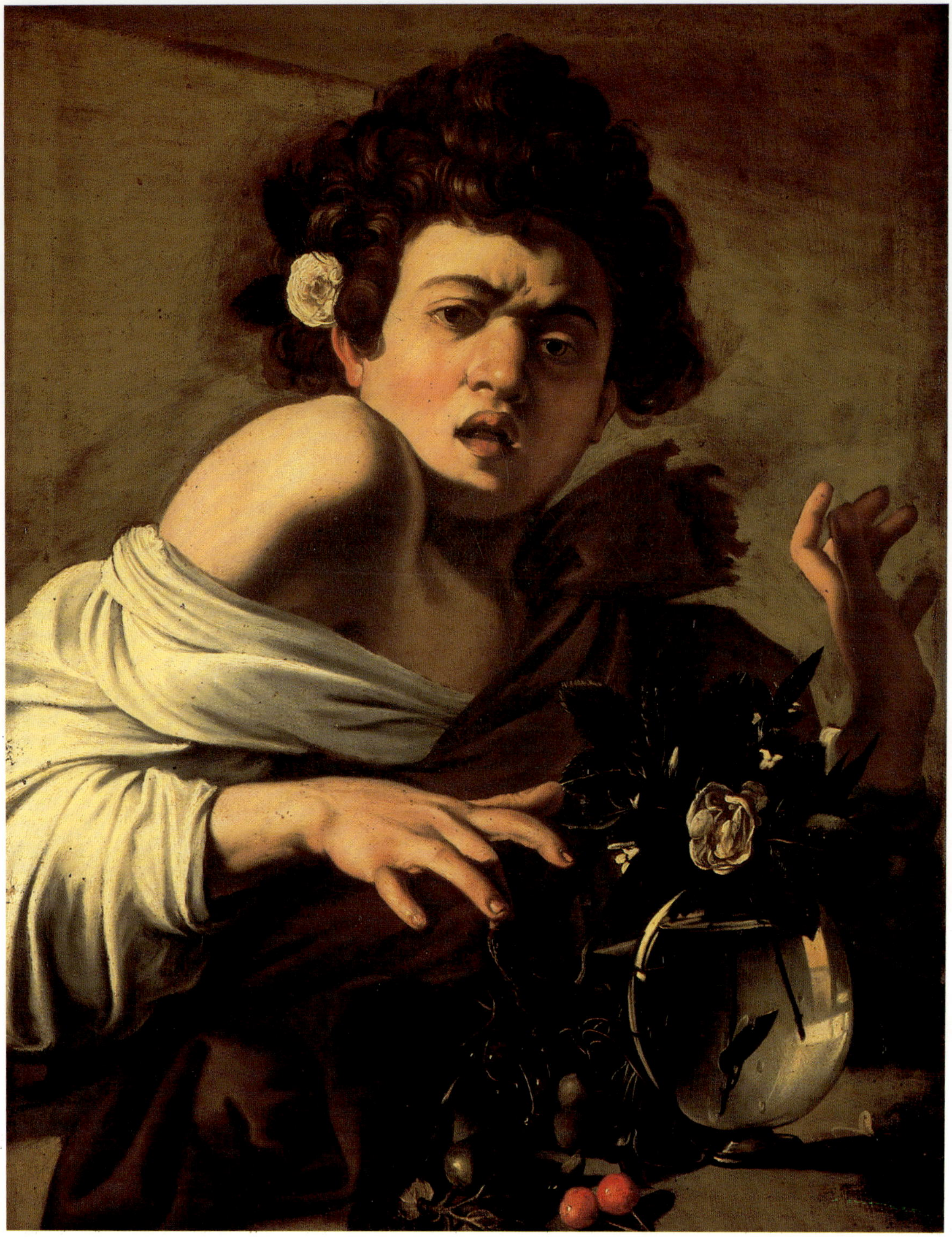

4

3. Youth with Flower Basket
cm. 70x63
Rome, Galleria Borghese

4. Youth Bitten by a Green Lizard
cm. 65.8x39.5
Florence, Longhi Collection

original has been lost; the best copy is in Atlanta, Georgia.

Caravaggio built his reputation on these early paintings, as we have said. The first collector of his works was the learned and influential Cardinal Francesco Maria Del Monte. An inventory of his collection, made after his death in 1626, includes eight paintings by Caravaggio, five of which can be dated to the early part of the artist's career, or at least before the end of the century. Thus we know that the young painter succeeded very soon in establishing a market for his highly novel

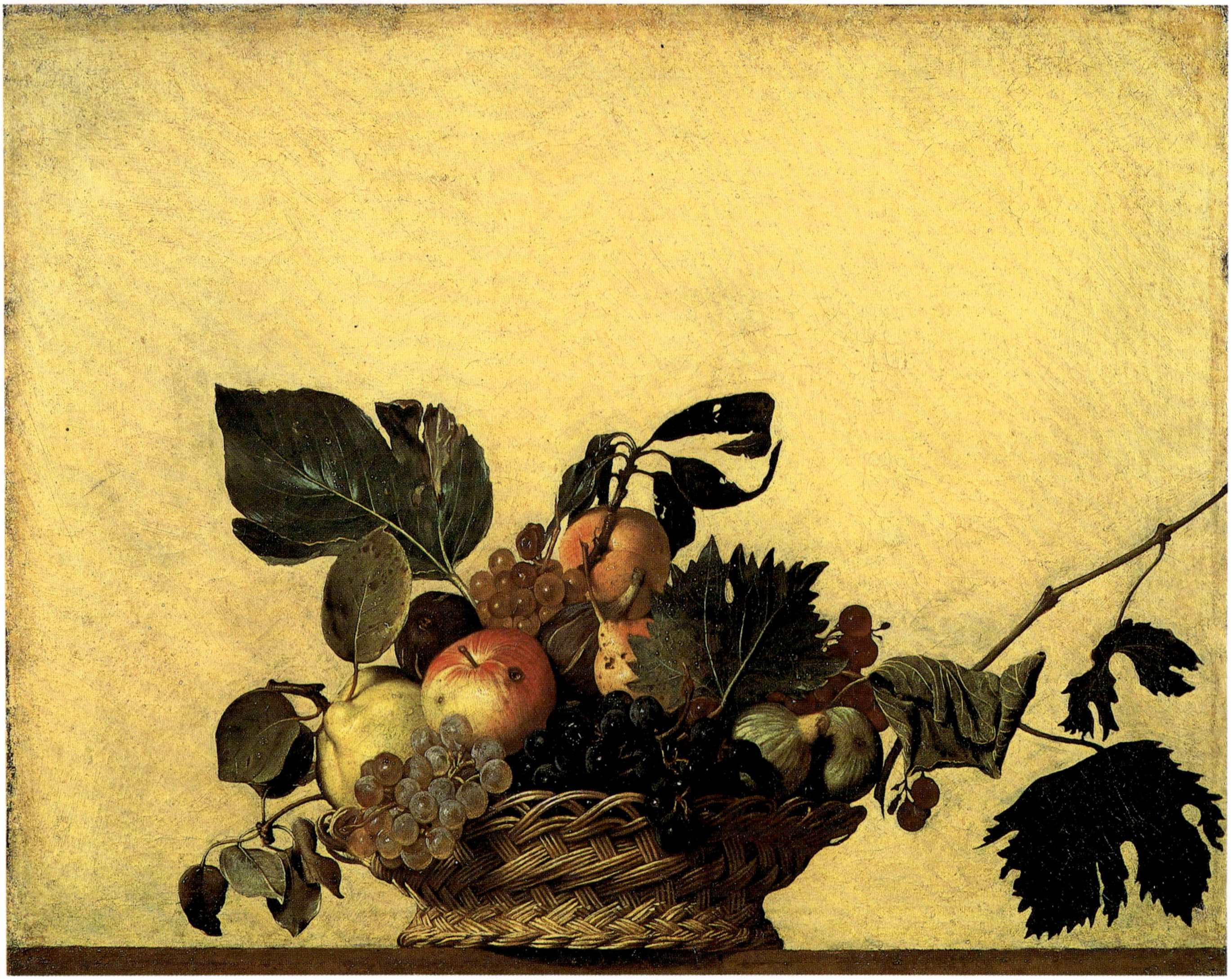

5

art. Moreover, that his early paintings were so greatly appreciated by one of the outstanding cultural figures of his milieu suggests that they contained, in addition to their ostensible meaning, allusions to deeper meanings that the collectors or the cultivated public of the artist's time recognized at a glance, and that are being redisco-
5 vered by modern iconologists. In the famous Basket of Fruit in the Ambrosiana in Milan (where the entire collection of Cardinal Federico Borromeo, to whom this painting formerly belonged, is preserved) the artist draws a deliberate contrast between healthy and sick fruit, between green and brown leaves. The work appears to make reference to the cyclical character of nature and to the coexistence in life of contrary principles. As a matter of fact, these themes come across so forcefully that this painting, which has been called the first still-life of the seventeenth century (and one should add, of the modern age), can be seen more as a melancholy existential meditation on nature than as a proud affirmation of her positive qualities.

The association of a single figure with a still-life re-
6 curs in the Bacchus in the Uffizi. This painting is also a self-portrait. Mention has been made of the dangerously tilted goblet that seems about to spill its contents, and the rippled surface of the wine — devices that give the image a sense of precariousness — as well as of the face skillfully reflected in the pitcher. But the important thing to notice here is the absolute newness of the invention, where one does not see a classically idealized Bacchus, but the image of a young man, almost a boy, whose features are hardly refined, and who is dressed — or perhaps it would be better to say disguised — as Bacchus, in a manner which today would be considered provocative. Caravaggio deliberately chose a model that could not be associated with the grotesque Bacchus or with the handsome young Bacchus of antiquity. Instead of Bacchus the god, he represents a common person brought in off the street and disguised as Bacchus. It appears as though, after posing for the painter, the model were about to stand up, throw off the drape, drink down the wine, and head off for the tavern.

A gang of friends animates the Concert in the 7
Metropolitan Museum in New York, from which all trace of irony, or parody, is missing. The two figures

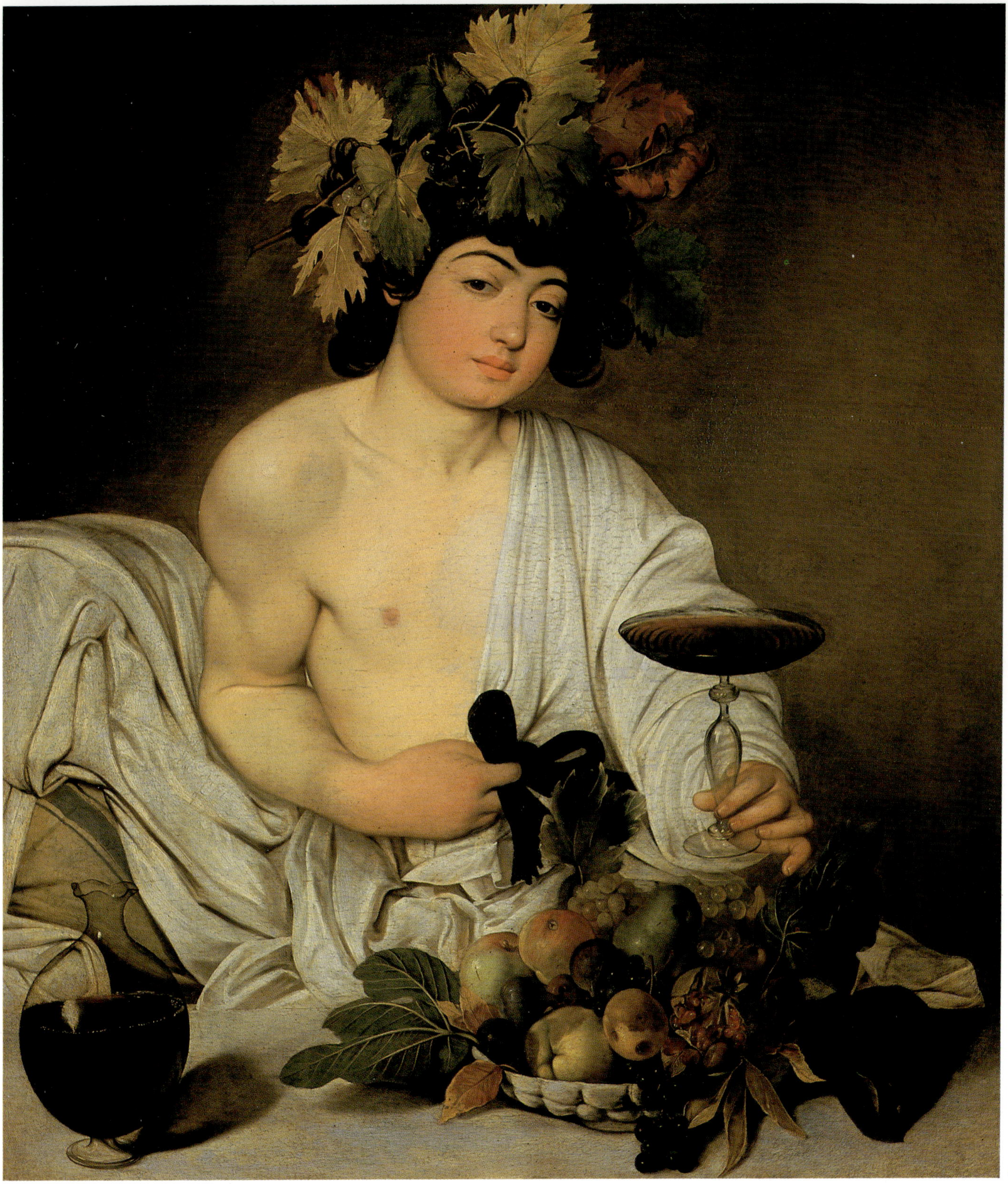

6

5. Basket of Fruit
cm. 46x64.5
Milan, Pinacoteca Ambrosiana

6. Bacchus
cm. 95x85
Florence, Galleria degli Uffizi

seen frontally are undoubtably portraits, and this fact disorients those who would like to make a conventional reading of the scene and concentrate on the noble, classical character of the composition, organized around the traditional opposition between the figure of the lute player and the corresponding figure whom we see from behind. The face between these two is Caravaggio's; the

7

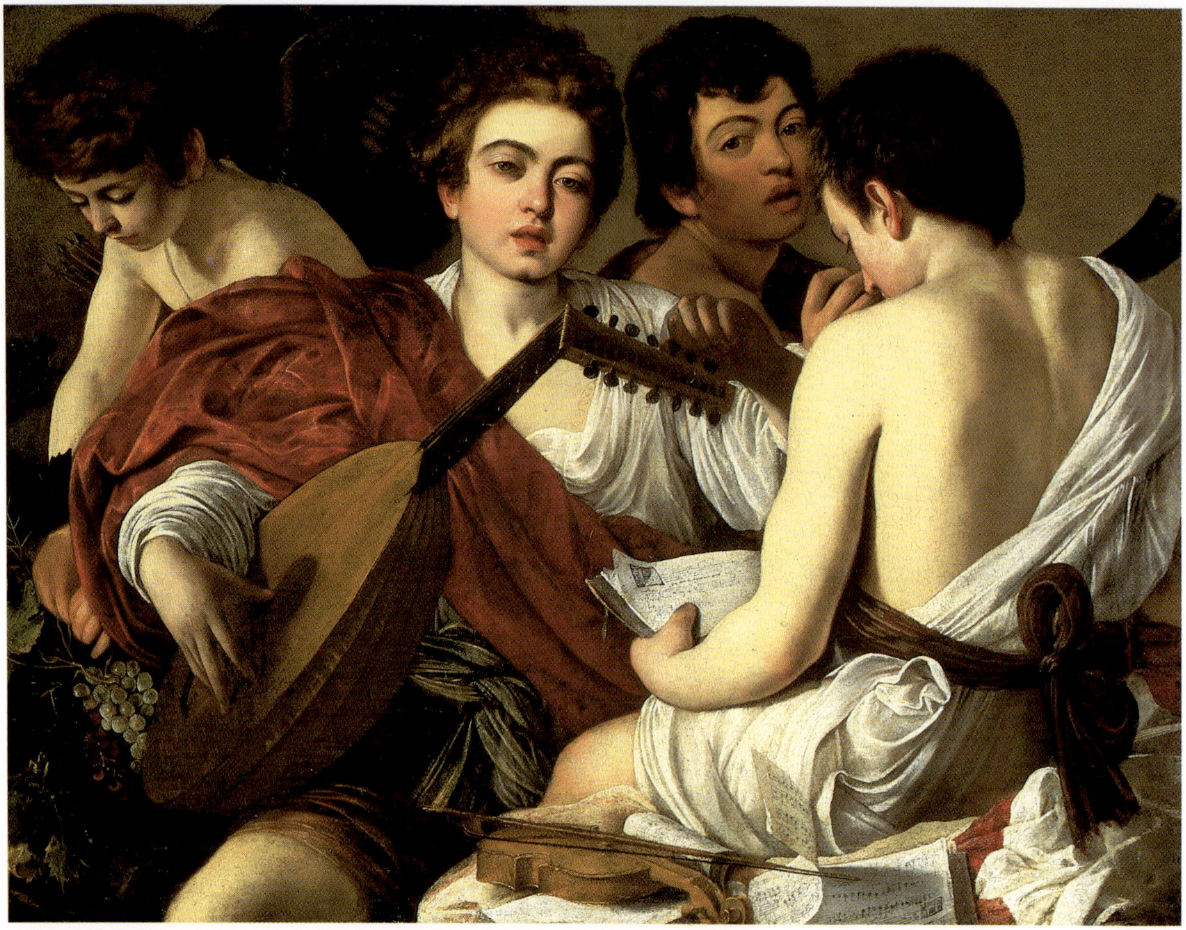

8

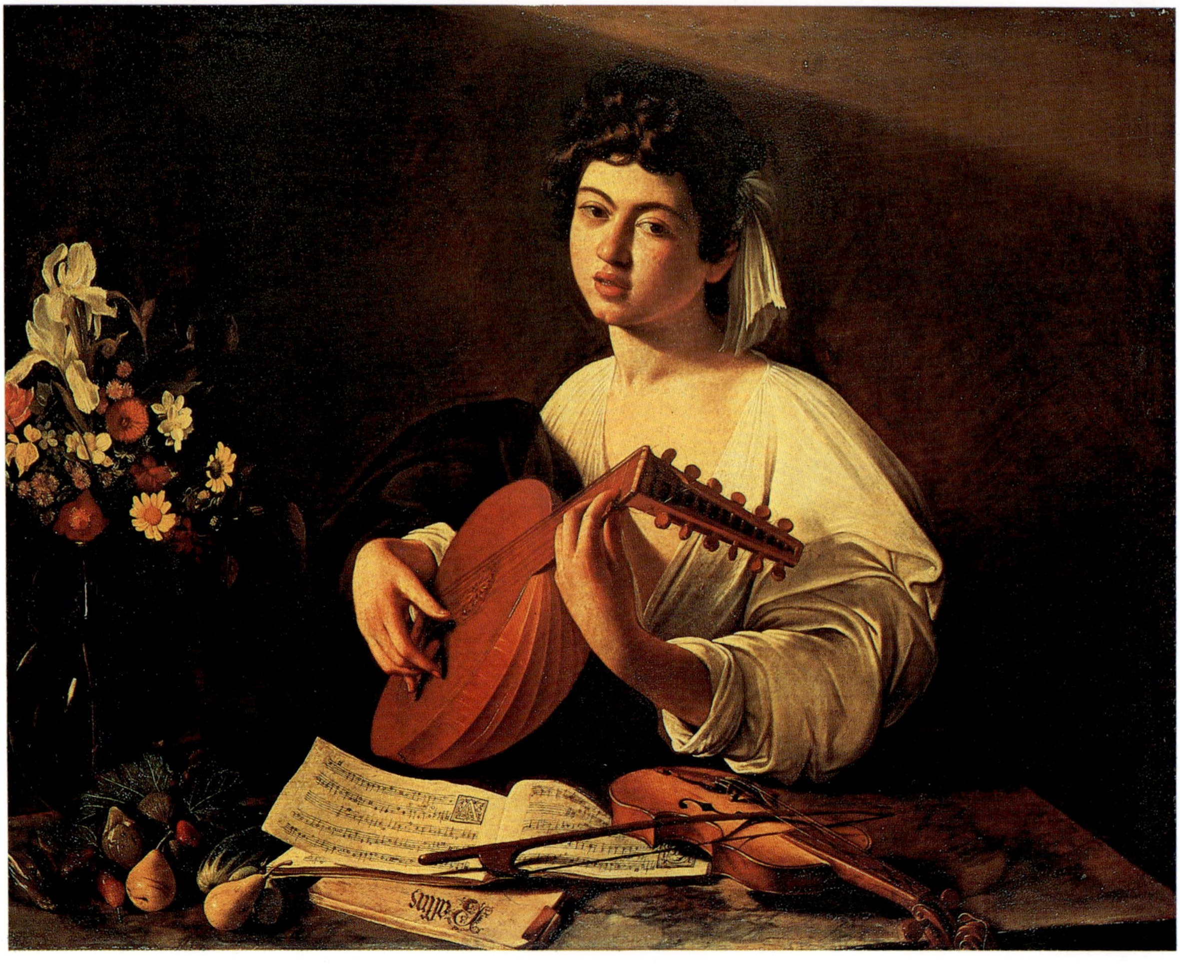

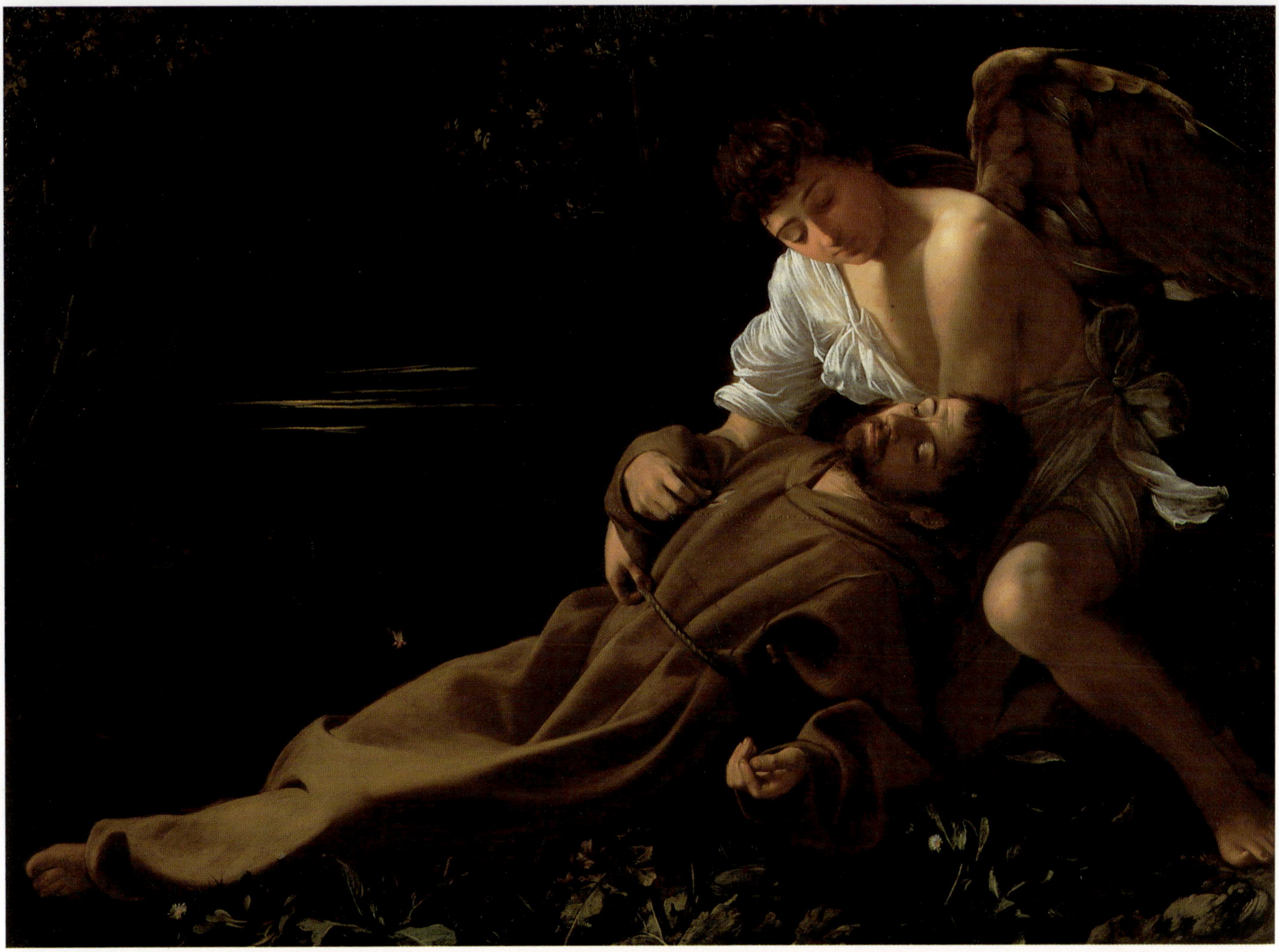

9

7. Concert
cm. 92x118.5
New York, Metropolitan Museum of Art

8. Lute Player
cm. 94x119
Leningrad, Hermitage

9. St. Francis in Ecstasy
cm. 92.5x128.4
Hartford (Connecticut), Wadsworth Atheneum

figure on the left is taken from an earlier composition, the Youth Peeling a Pear, which we know only from two copies. The broad play of drapery recalls the Lombard influences mentioned above, particularly the experiments of Girolamo Savoldo of Bergamo in rendering cloth and clothing.

Another painting with a single figure, the Lute 8
Player in the Hermitage in Leningrad, takes up the theme of music. In this extraordinary work the young Caravaggio's trademarks — the carafe with flowers and the fruit — mingle with sheets of music and the instrument in the foreground. The figure of the youth seems, as Giovanni Baglione (1642) notes, "real and alive." Here, beyond the traditional interpretation, one feels the repercussion of an immediately real presence.

During these early years in Rome, around 1595, Caravaggio dealt for the first time in his career with religious subjects and genre scenes. The former belonged to the most widespread tradition. The latter were quite new; thanks to him, they would enjoy immense success in seventeenth-century Europe.

The Stigmatization of St. Francis in the Wadsworth 9
Atheneum in Hartford, Connecticut, belongs to the first category. The painting was once in Trieste, and its subsequent passage through various collections is well

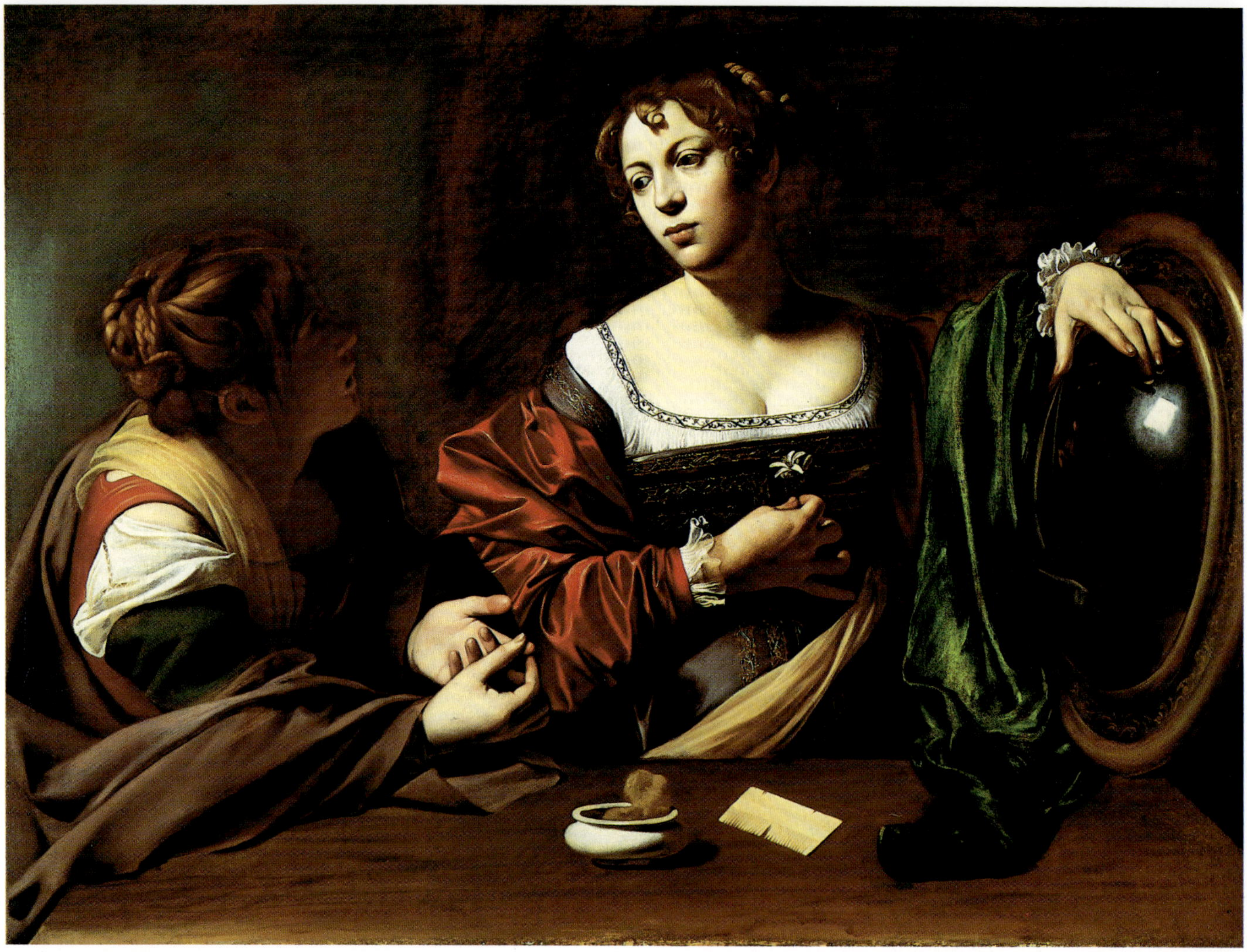

10

10. Martha and Mary Magdalen
cm. 97,8x132,7
Detroit, Institute of Arts

11. The Fortune Teller
cm. 99x131
Paris, Louvre

12. The Fortune Teller
cm. 115x150
Rome, Musei Capitolini

documented. Scholars agree in considering it one of the artist's first works. It has a perfectly Lombard air: The broad lines of the composition recall mannerist motifs like those of Peterzano, whereas the intimacy of the nocturnal setting brings to mind Savoldo and Lotto. But Caravaggio's characteristic approach to reality is already at work, and his brushstroke shows a magic that could be obtained only by a thorough analysis of Venetian painting. This he probably studied after his first years with Peterzano and before leaving his birthplace for Rome. The references to the art of Giorgione and to that of the young Titian (in addition to a meditation on Titian's later works, which Caravaggio would use only in subsequent paintings), were restricted for years by certain schools of art criticism in the attempt, at the time well founded, to emphasize the artist's substantial pertinence to the Lombard tradition. However even the better Lombard art owes much to Giorgione and Titian, and scholars have recently begun to take a more balanced view of the influence of Venetian painting on Caravaggio. His infallible ability to overcome the traditional dilemma of color and *disegno* by individuating optical reality as it really appears to the observer, is based on a conception of color as a structural element

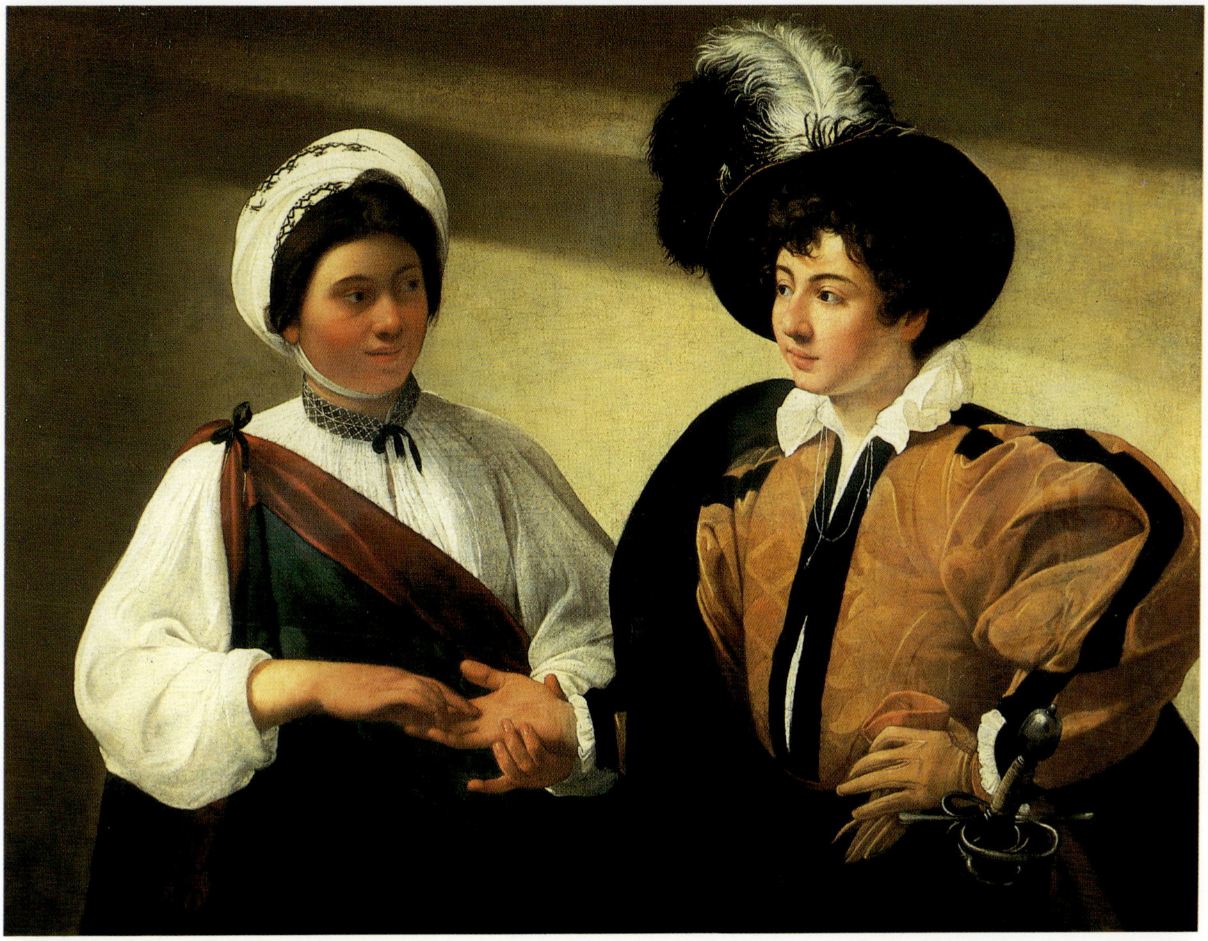

11

12

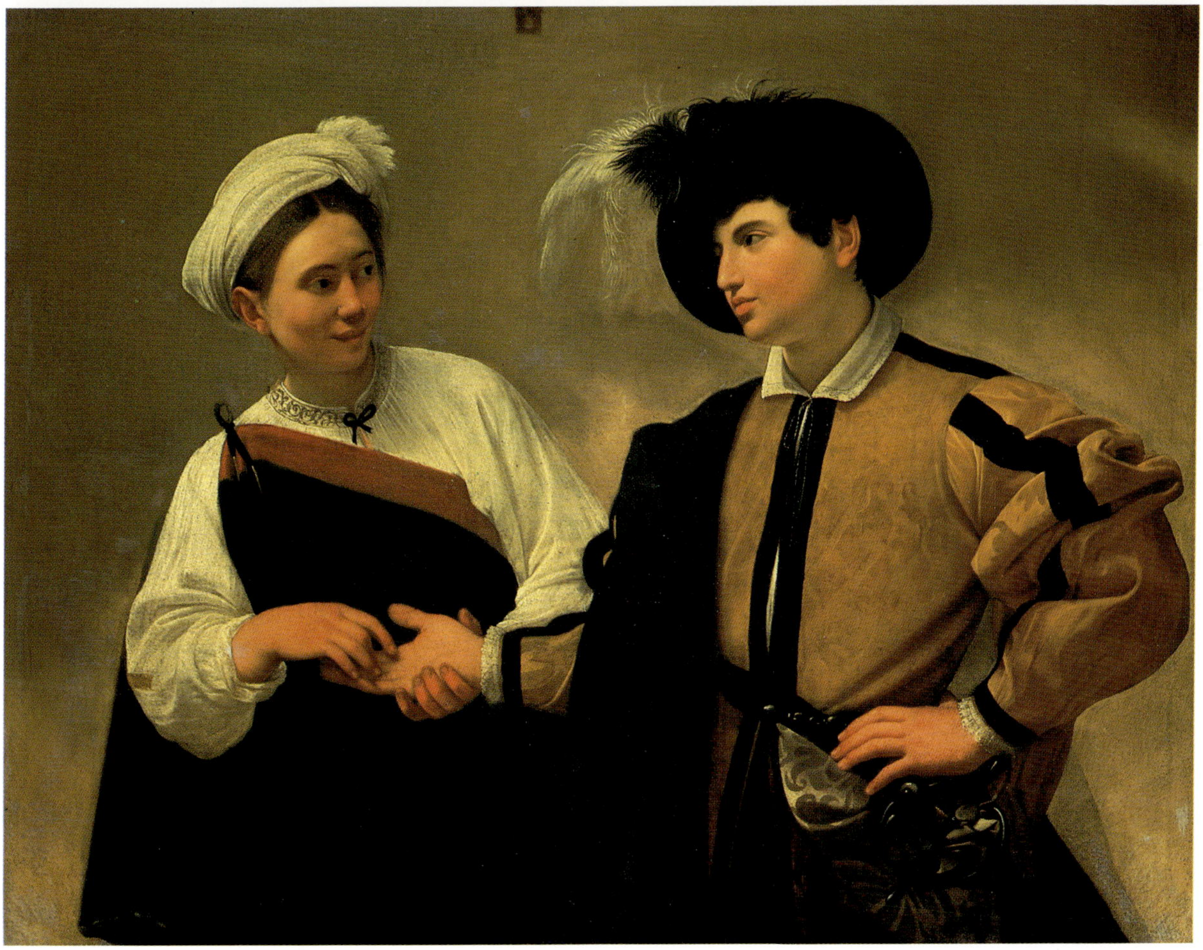

that is deeply indebted to Venetian art; and it would indeed be surprising if such an open-minded artist had not studied the Venetian masters of the early sixteenth century.

Caravaggio's portrayal of St. Francis receiving the stigmata in ecstatic rapture was revolutionary; as was his treatment of another, iconographically very unusual
10 theme. He showed Martha reproaching Mary Magdalen for her vanity, a subject that we know through a series of copies. One of these, now at the Institute of Arts in Detroit, has recently been recognized, probably correctly, as the original. As has already been pointed out, the religious theme is treated in a substantially profane manner. It is a pretext for making passages of highly intense painting and for constructing an image that, seen in the context of the usual dichotomy of Caravaggio's early years, is more of a genre scene than a religious one. The painting does not illustrate a precise subject, but merely alludes to it, moving toward another field of interest.

A genre scene may be defined as a conventional subject of a profane nature drawn from everyday life, but immediately removed from direct observation (which belongs to the initiators alone) to take its place in the current of conventional reproduction (which belongs to the more or less tight ranks of imitators). These paintings for private enjoyment fared very well with their public, and it is exciting to trace the origins of a form of figurative expression that later enjoyed such success. Two themes from Caravaggio's early years can be placed in the category of genre paintings. One, I Bari, represents a card game. It is known through several copies and through an original formerly in the Sciarra Collection in Rome, now unfortunately lost. It was a subject that Caravaggio must have been quite familiar with through personal experience, as we shall see.

The other theme, preserved in two paintings, both of which are probably originals, painted at a distance of several years, shows a Gypsy reading the palm of a youth
11 while skillfully removing the ring from his finger. The first example is in the Louvre; the second (which tecnical analysis recently confirmed as an autograph copy)
12 is in the Pinacoteca Capitolina in Rome. Contemporary sources tell us much about this composition. Indeed, Bellori (1672), a writer who was highly critical of Caravaggio (as we shall see better below), tells a particularly significant story: "Having been shown the most famous statues of Phidias and Glycon so that he could study them, his only response was to extend his hand toward a crowd of men, pointing out that nature had given him enough masters. And to lend authority to his words he called a gypsy that happened to be passing by in the street, and bringing her to his rooms, portrayed her in the act of forseeing the future, as these women of Egyptian descent are known to do. He made a young man with one gloved hand on his sword, the other, bare, held out to her, and she takes it and reads it; and in these two half-figures Michele translated the truth so purely, that it confirmed what he said."

This painting can thus be considered a precise illustration of Caravaggio's aesthetic creed. His attitude of dissociation with the past must have been difficult for his contemporary artists and connoisseurs to understand, and especially to share in. He maintained that the subject matter of painting should not be drawn from ancient or modern history, that is must not be celebrative or commemorative, laden with a moral lesson, or set up as an example. Furthermore, he believed that the study of famous old masters must not inspire the artist and form his technical training. Caravaggio's masters are not the mythical names of a more or less distant past, but men in general. His lesson is not drawn from history, but from life. According to his conception, the painter must be a careful observer of what lies around him, and not a student of preexisting technical and cultural traditions. Statements of this kind must have sounded thoroughly heretical in the context of late mannerism. As it turned out the artist's attitude did not meet with indifference, but with enthusiastic acceptance by a few sympathizers, and with opposition by most of the artist's audience, which, as always, tended to be conservative. Caravaggio's outlook became increasingly overpowering, however. It eventually influenced every artistic trend in Europe. Even his religious paintings became essential to the aesthetic and cultural climate of the cities they were located in (Rome, Naples, Messina and Syracuse). But we know from the sources, or we can guess, how heated the discussions that accompanied these works must have been.

Bellori, just before the passage we quoted, writes that Merisi "knew no master other than the model." Francesco Scannelli (1657) defines him "the first head of the naturalists." The Fleming Karel van Mander, writing at a very early date (1604), mentions "Michelangelo Caravaggio who does wonderful things in Rome," and says that he " is one who does not care much for the works of any master... he says... that all things are trifles, childishness, nonsense, whoever painted them, if they are not taken from life, and nothing can be good or better than following nature... and copying her in painting." In the transcript of a legal action brought against him by Baglione, Caravaggio tells the judge that a "skillful" painter is one who "knows how to paint and imitate natural things well." Finally, a letter written by the eminent patron of the arts, Marchese Vincenzo Giustiniani, confirms Caravaggio's indifference toward the traditional artistic hierarchies that see history painting as the highest genre. In reference to the difficulty of the various ways of painting, Giustiniani tells that "Caravaggio said that it took as much workmanship to make a good painting of flowers as of figures." This claim reveals Caravaggio's full revolutionary importance. In its origin-

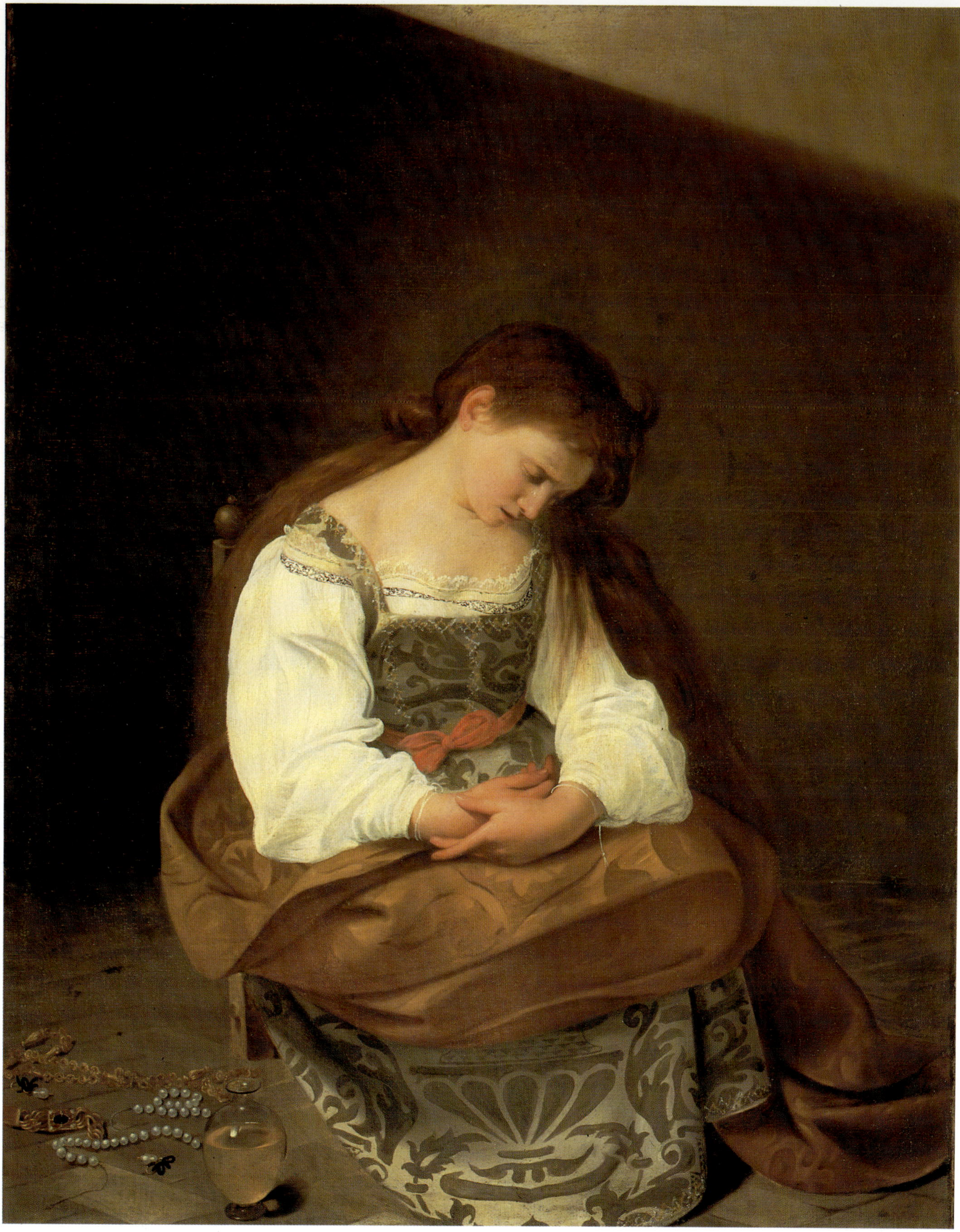

13

13. Mary Magdalen
cm. 106x97
Rome, Galleria Doria Pamphili

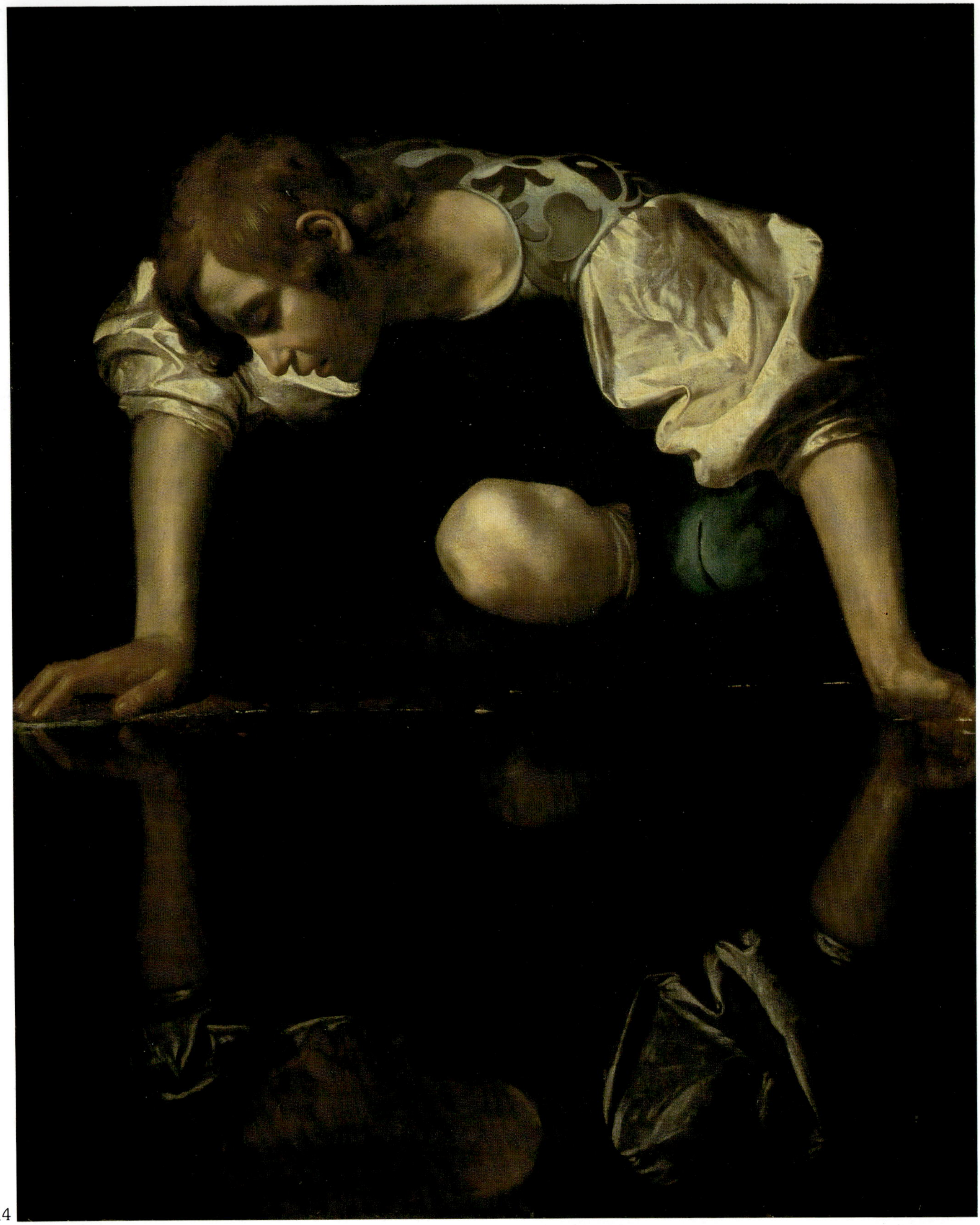

14

14. *Narcissus*
cm. 110x92
Rome, Galleria Nazionale di Arte Antica

15. *St. Catherine of Alexandria*
cm. 173x133
Lugano, Thyssen-Bornemizsa Collection

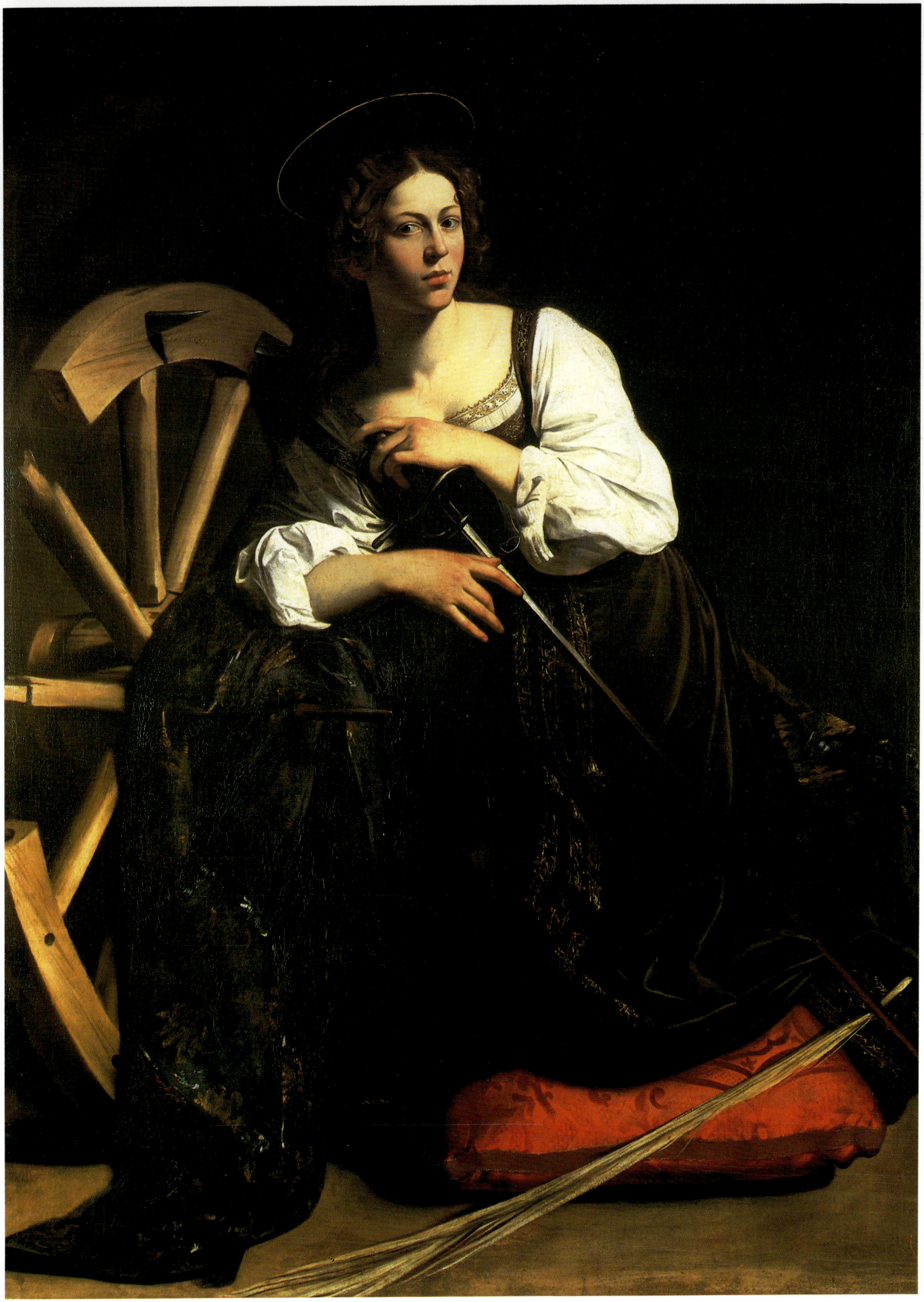

15

16

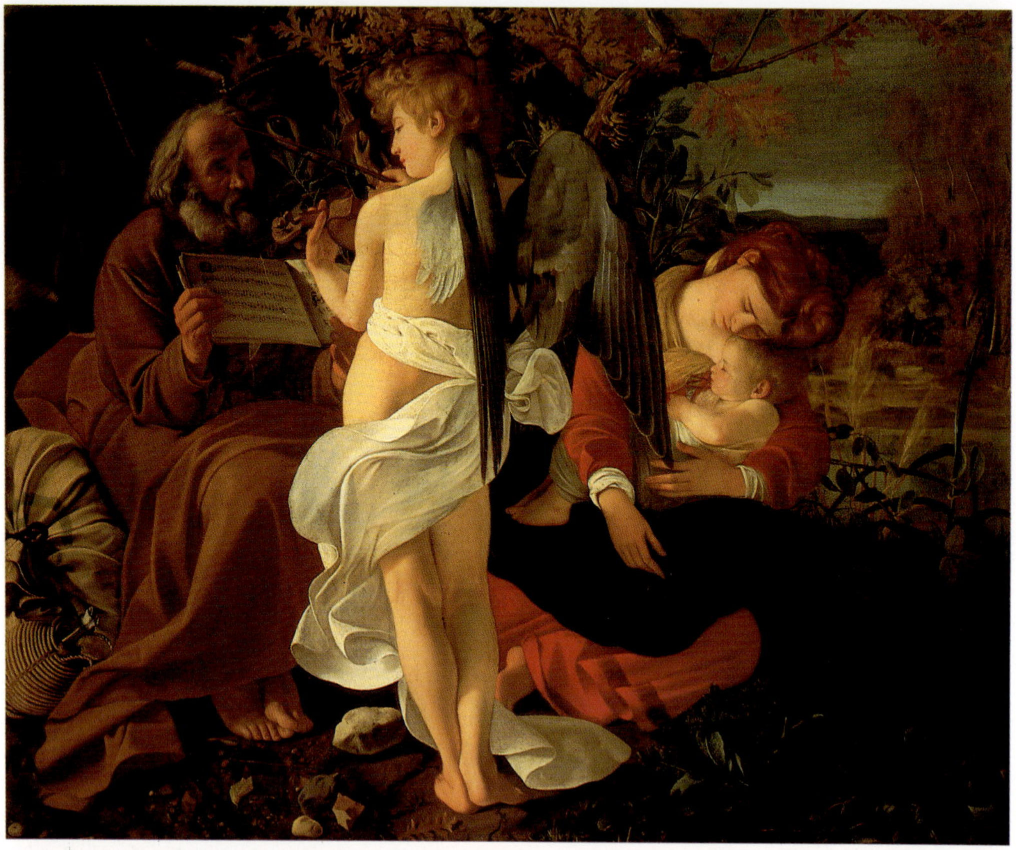

17

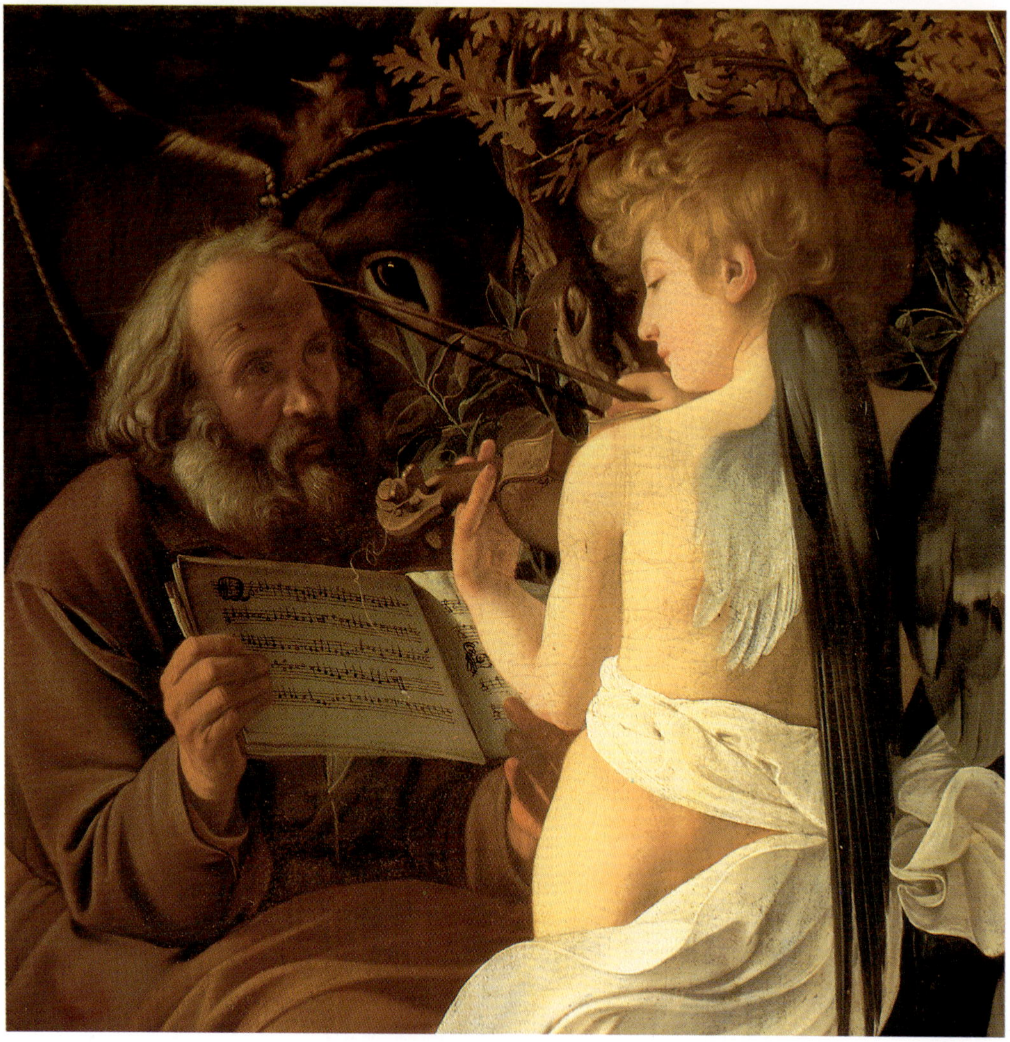

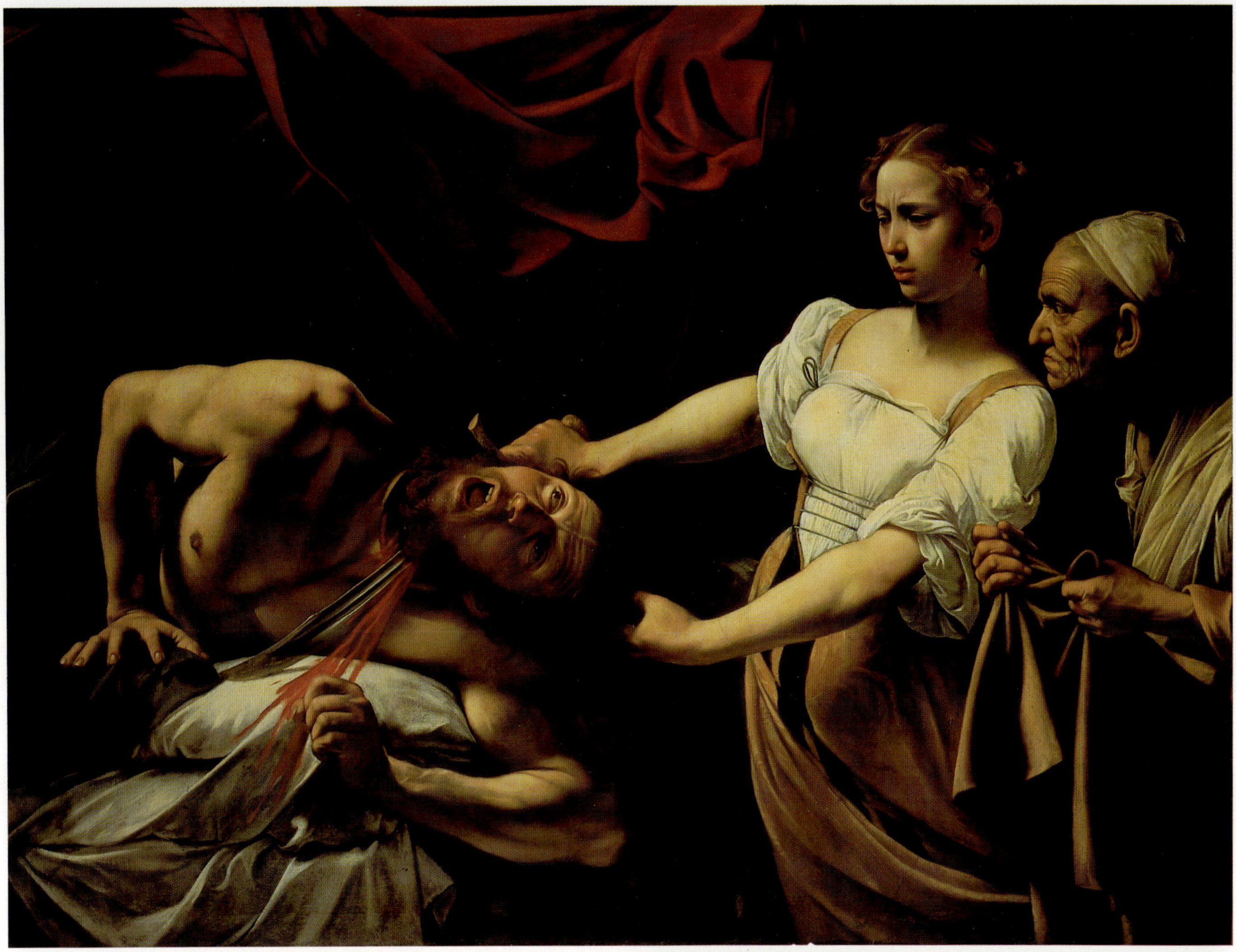

18

19

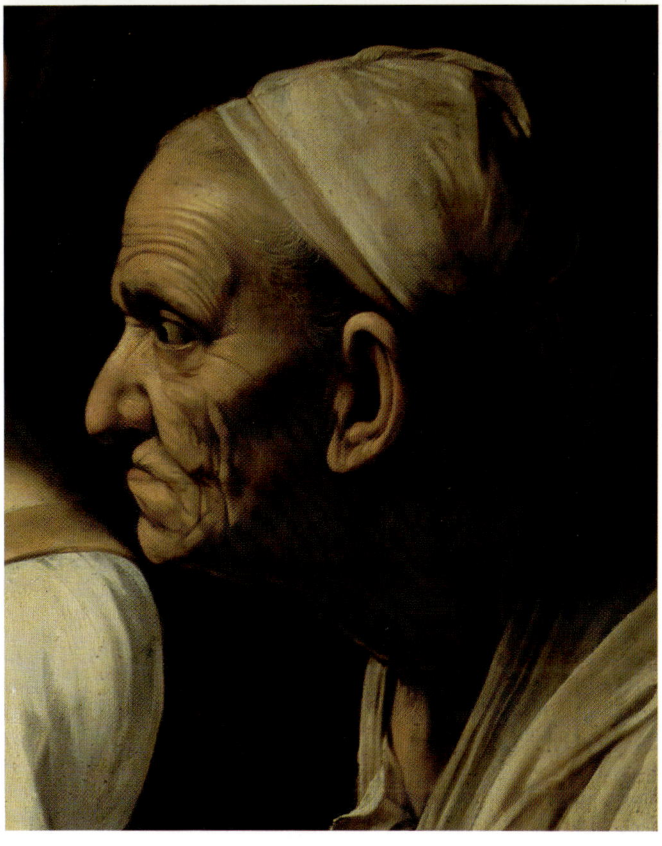

16. Rest During the Flight into Egypt
cm. 130x160
Rome, Galleria Doria Pamphili

17. Rest During the Flight into Egypt, detail of Joseph and the angel.
Rome, Galleria Doria Pamphili

18. Judith
cm. 144x195
Rome, Galleria Nazionale di Arte Antica

19. Judith, detail of the servant.
Rome, Galleria Nazionale di Arte Antica

20

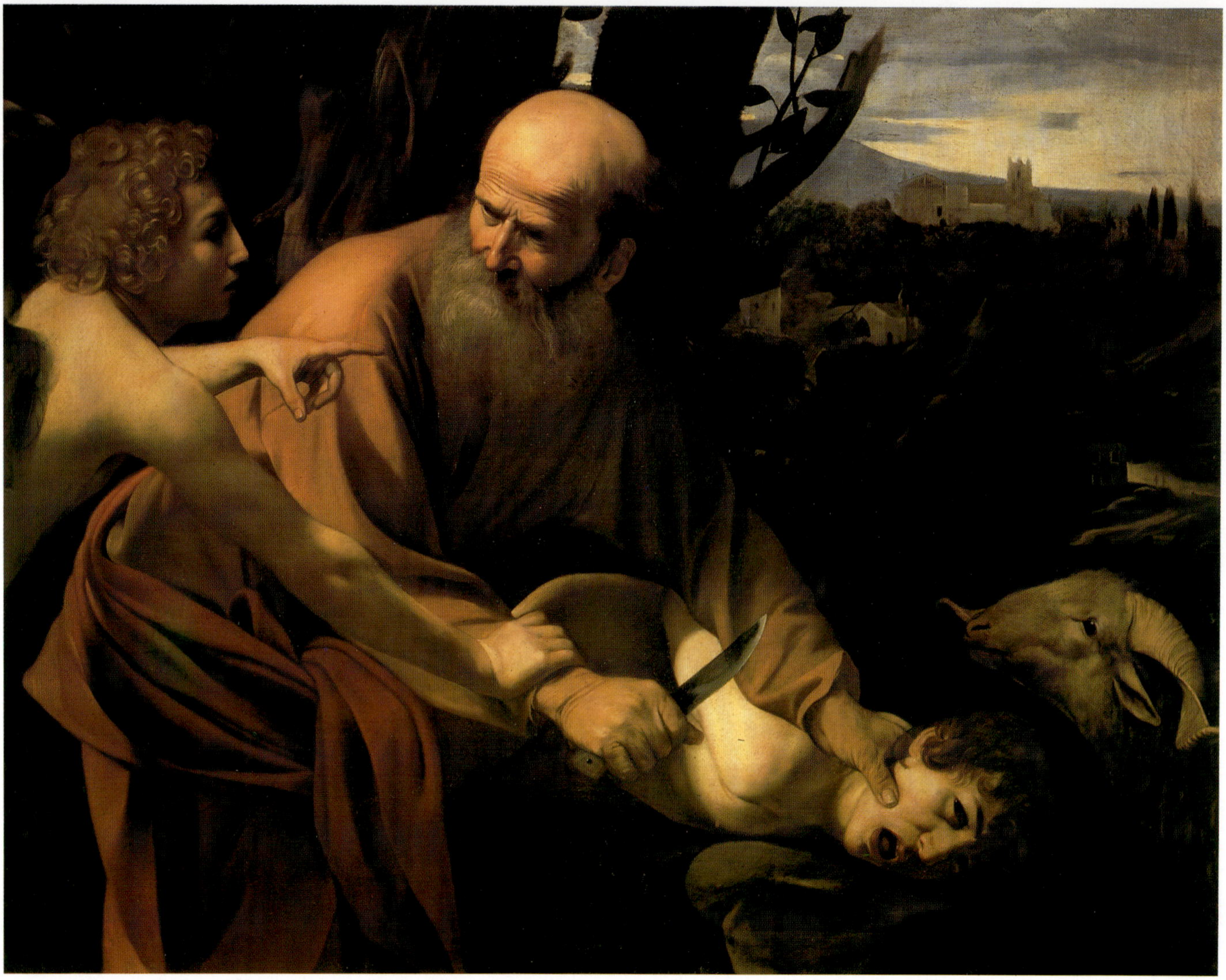

al context, it chiefly regards the question of technique; but it is not arbitrary to link Giustiniani's comment to Caravaggio's aesthetic principles as a genuine opening both in the direction of the still-life and in that of the genre scene.

This brings us to the last years of the sixteenth century. Caravaggio was gradually gaining acceptance among a select audience; his economic and social position was improving. At this time he made some of his most fascinating creations. Bellori magically describes
13 the Magdalen in the Galleria Doria Phamphili in Rome, seen earlier in the Pamphili home by Scannelli (1657), as follows: "he painted a girl on a chair with her hand in her lap, drying her hair; he painted her in an interior, and by adding an ointment jar and jewelry, he imagined her as the Magdalen." Bellori emphasizes how the painting is not planned from the beginning as an exemplary description of the biblical figure, but how the identification is almost made afterward, at the moment the artist adds the ointment jar and jewelry. The painting does not represent Mary Magdalen; it represents a girl who is "imagined" as Mary Magdalen. And this interpretation sticks, even when we recognize that the figurative sources of the painting include the sixteenth-century images of "Melancholia," including the famous engraving by Dürer. Again it must be pointed out that Caravaggio's attitude toward reality did not preclude familiarity with earlier figurative sources nor their use in his art. Besides, everyone felt — and feels — the discreet charm of this intimate image, whose domestic setting so clearly anticipates the central theme of seventeenth-century Dutch painting, that in looking for a close affinity for Caravaggio's painting we are obliged to turn to Vermeer.

A similar concentration on the expressive core of the composition, undiminished by superfluous elements, is
apparent in the Narcissus in the Galleria Nazionale 1
di Arte Antica in Palazzo Barberini in Rome. The attribution of this painting to Caravaggio has been discussed at length, and it is still questioned by some scholars. In this case there are no contemporary sources we can refer to (an inventory of the time mentions a Narcissus by Caravaggio, but there is nothing to prove that this is the painting referred to), and the attribution rests entirely on stylistic bases. It seems, though, that here as else-

20. Abraham and Isaac
cm. 104x135
Florence, Galleria degli Uffizi

21. Head of Medusa
cm. 60x55
Florence, Galleria degli Uffizi

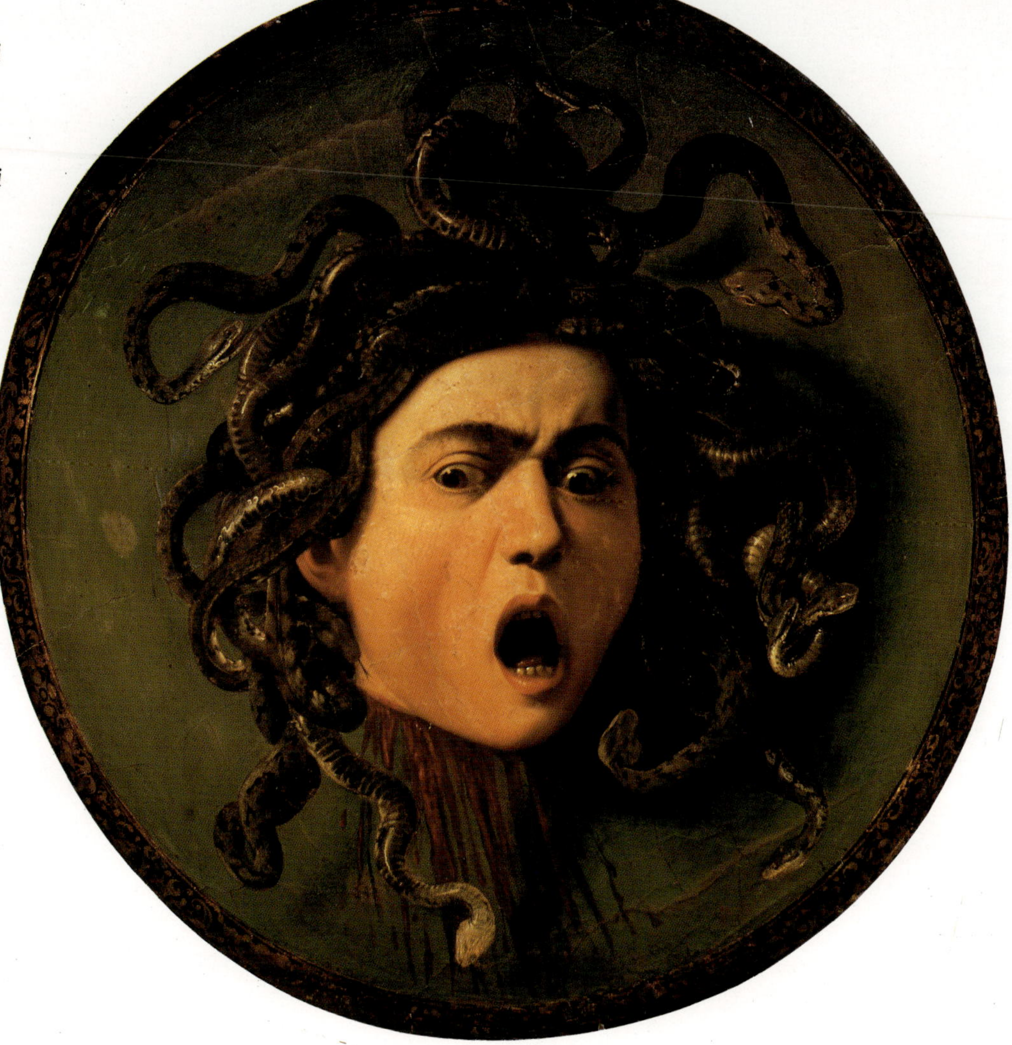

21

where the intuition of Roberto Longhi (who was the first to attribute the painting to Caravaggio) is correct, because of the very special mixture of sixteenth-century Lombard tradition and modern use of light, the way in which the material of the clothing is rendered, and the painting's inventive genius (although, because the numerous copies of Caravaggio's originals are often very good, the sole criterion of quality is not sufficient grounds for an attribution to the master).

15 The splendid St. Catherine of Alexandria formerly belonged to Cardinal Del Monte, one of the artist's patrons. It is now in the Von Thyssen Collection, which is located in Lugano, although the painting is not always in that city. Here we see a single female figure, as in the Doria Magdalen, in an interior devoid of architectural allusions. But the image appears with a different boldness and an immediacy that combine the nobility of the subject (St. Catherine was a king's daughter) with the almost plebeian pride of the model (no doubt a Roman woman of the people, possibly the same one who posed for a portrait formerly in Berlin and destroyed during the war). The breadth of conception and realization, and the perfect mastery of a very difficult composition (the figure and objects completely fill the painting, in a subtle play of diagonals) are striking. Caravaggio here chose a "grand" noble approach that heralds the great religious compositions he would soon do for San Luigi dei Francesi. The extraordinary virtuosity in the painting of the large, decorated cloth is absorbed as an integral part of the composition. This is something his followers would not often succeed in doing, for they frequently dealt with the single components of the painting individually, with adverse effects on the unity of the whole.

At roughly this same time, the artist made three paintings, of Old and New Testament scenes, showing actions carried out by several figures. In this way he experimented with complicating his compositions, gaining valuable practice for the great religious paintings mentioned in passing, above. These compositions with biblical subjects were intended for the private devotion of noble families, rather than for the decoration of public religious buildings. Just how much genuine devotion they inspired in their owners and in the guests who frequented their homes or private chapels, is unknown.

In the Rest During the Flight into Egypt in the Gal- 16
leria Doria Pamphili in Rome, the dominant feeling is

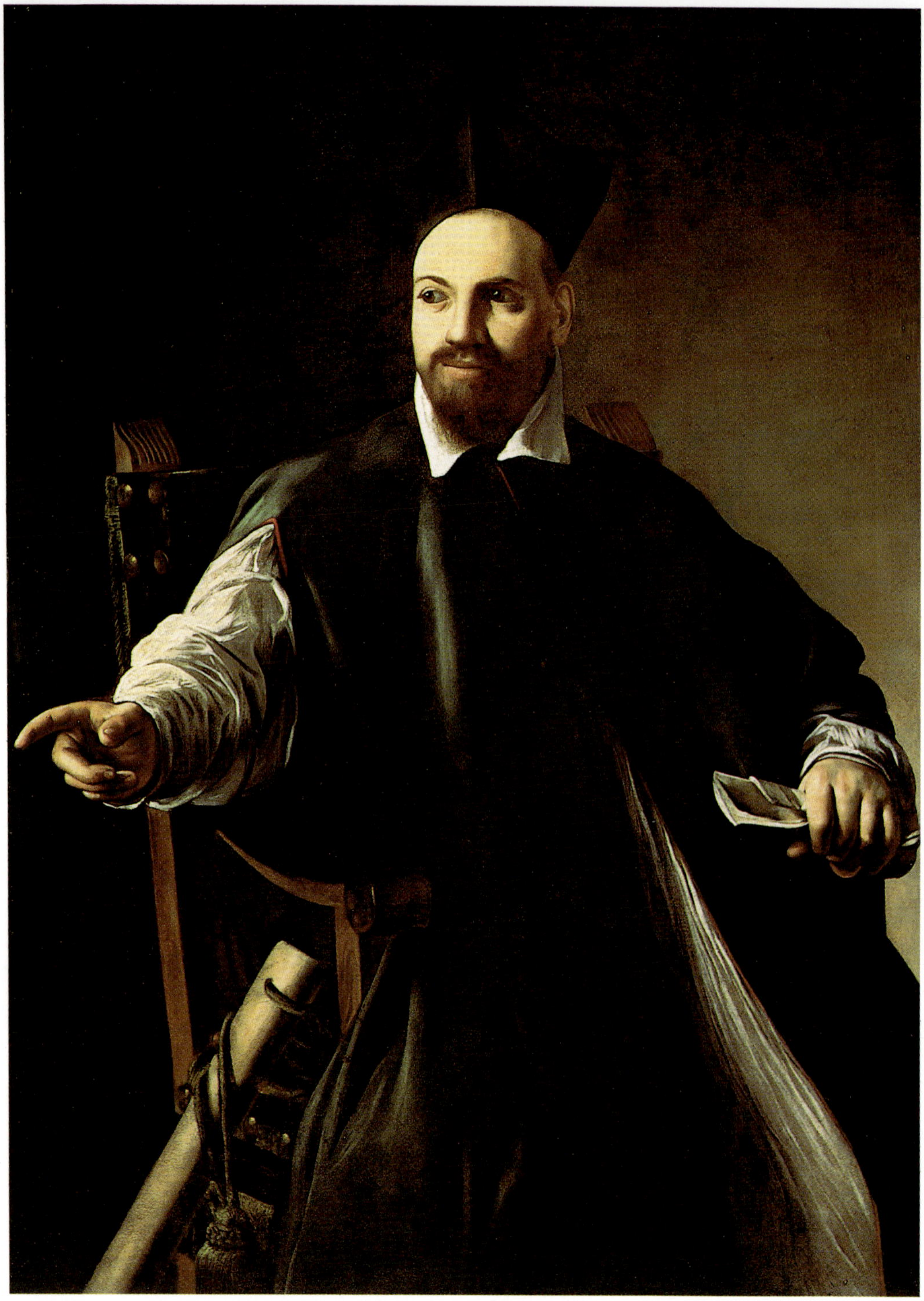

22

22. *Portrait of Maffeo Barberini*
cm. 121x95
Florence, private collection

23. *St. John the Baptist*
cm. 132x97
Rome, Musei Capitolini

24. *Calling of St. Matthew*
cm. 322x340
Rome, San Luigi dei Francesi

one of extreme gentleness. It is a miracle of peace and quiet. Beneath an oak tree, after removing the large sack with their few personal objects and the water flask
17 from the back of the mule, Joseph holds for the angel the score of the music that helped put to sleep the Christ Child and, it seems, his mother, too. In the quiet light, less violently defined than in the artist's other works, is set what with a classical term we may call an idyll, a small elegiac scene. The naturalistic rendering of the landscape, at the upper right, and of the plants, in the foreground, where artistic and scientific knowledge are combined, recalls the works of Leonardo da Vinci (who worked for many years in Lombardy). The angel is painted with great delicacy; its classical but subtly animated pose betrays the study of earlier models, and recalls in particular certain works of Andrea del Sarto, as in the Chiostro dello Scalzo in Florence (in all likelihood visited by Caravaggio on his way to Rome, but in any event widely known through drawings and prints).

The atmosphere of the other two paintings is entirely different. The Judith, recently acquired by the Galleria Nazionale d'Arte Antica in Rome, is surprisingly brutal. As early as the eighteenth century the writers Charles De Brosses and Joseph Lalande, who saw the work in the Palazzo Zambeccari in Bologna, were surprised by its extreme realism. But the painting had its

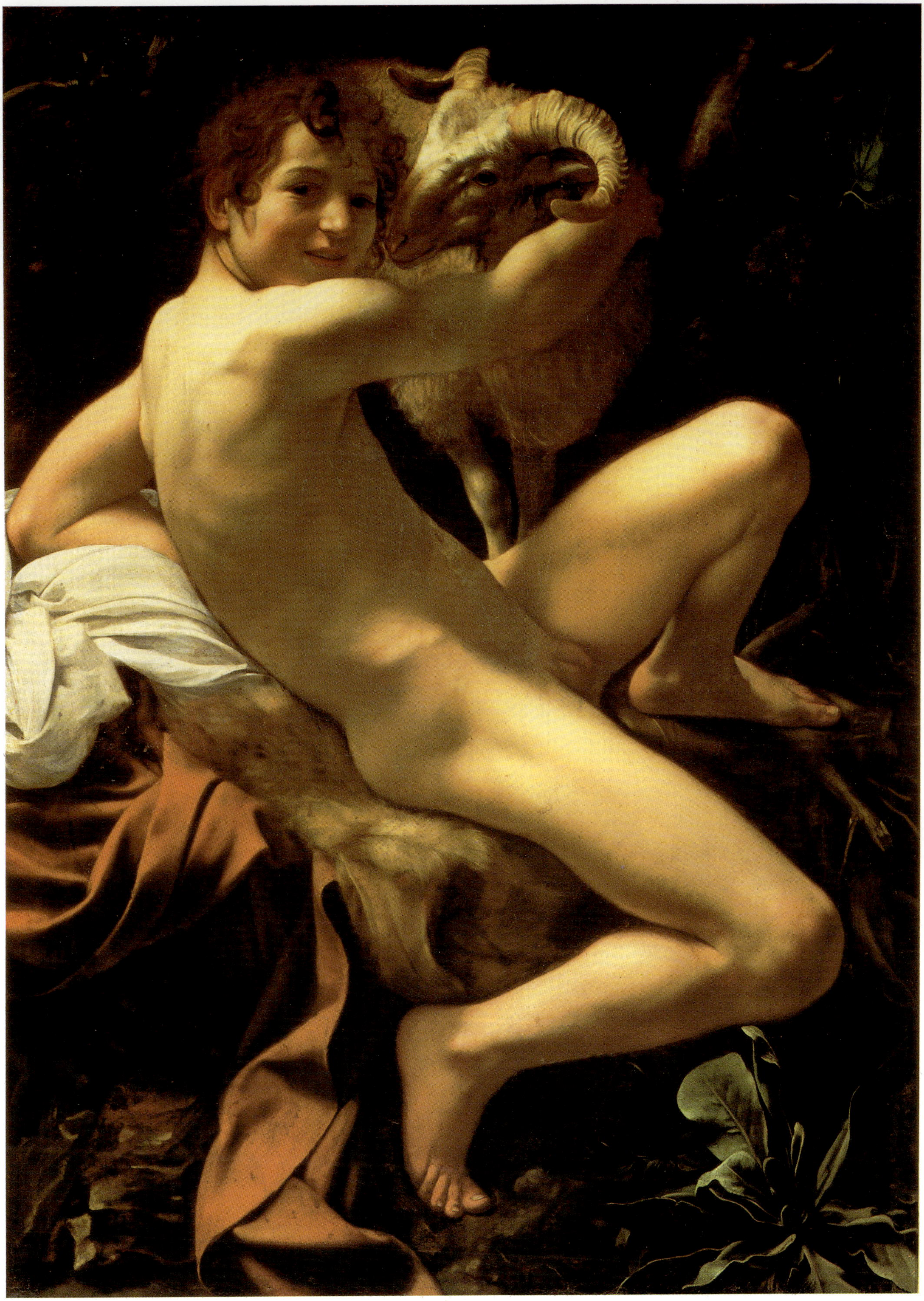

23

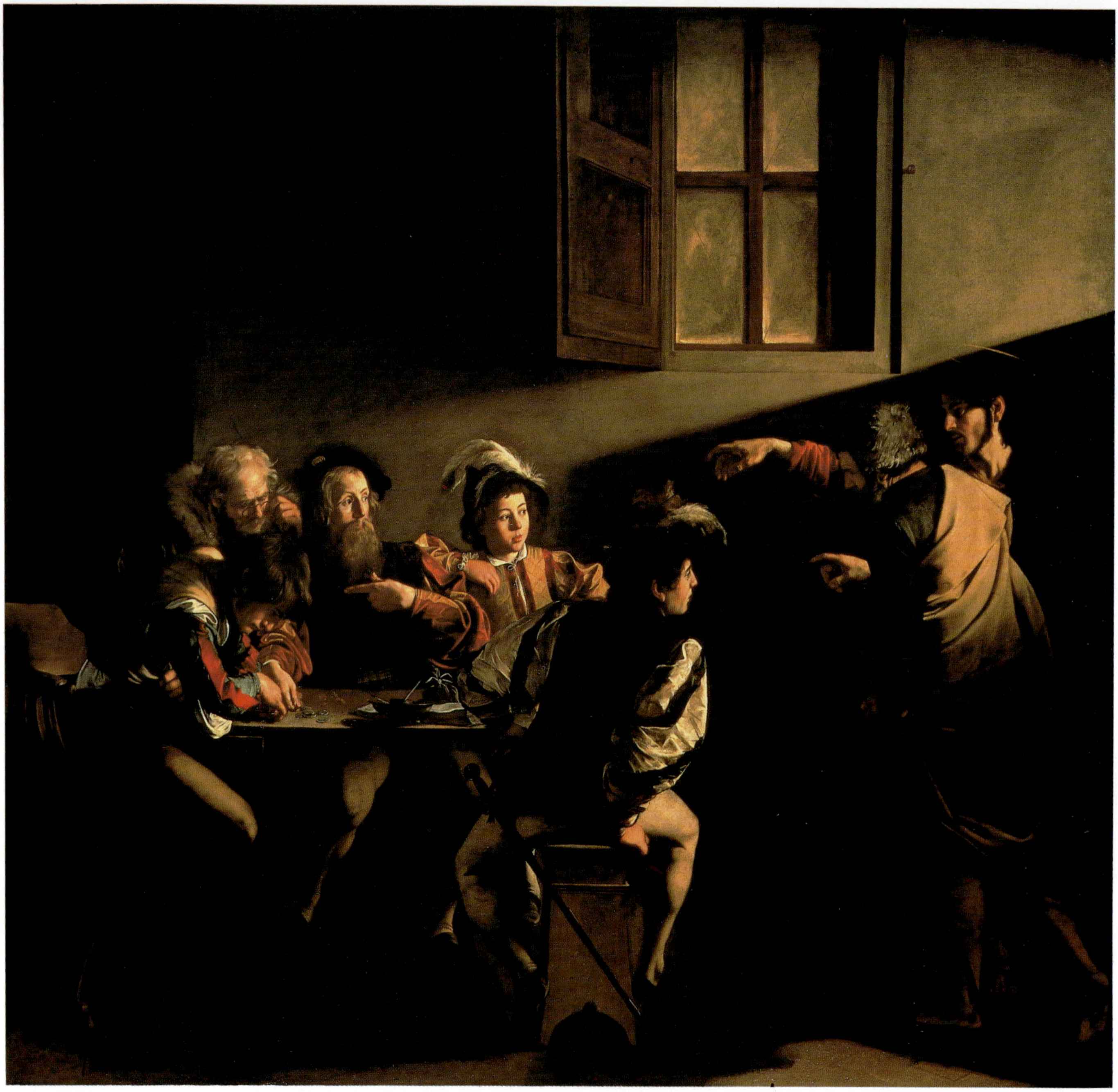

24

most tremendous effect on an English traveller, Lady Anne Miller, who saw it in 1770. She writes: "This picture is too well done; it struck me directly, that it must have been taken from life. The idea threw me into a trembling, and made me very sick; producing the same effects upon me, that perhaps I might have experienced from the presence of [a] real execution: the separation of the neck, the force she uses, the spouting of the blood from the divided arteries, and her contenance [*sic*], whilst she turns away her face from the dreadful work she is about, and which nevertheless expresses a fierceness and a sort of courage little befitting a woman, joined with the writhing convulsions of the body of Holofernes make it a picture quite improper for the inspection of those who have any degree of feeling: it is by Michael Angelo da Caravagio [*sic*]." So, the painting made its point. As for the presence of a real execution, there was certainly no lack at the time of cases for study. The genuine aggressiveness toward the viewer that Caravaggio sometimes shows, here reaches its peak, establishing a precedent that would be repeated by such artists as Jean de Boulogne, called Valentin, and Artemisia Gentileschi. Every element is carried to extremes: the
horror of the head of Holofernes; the red of the tent, 19
blood, and blade; the astonished expression of the servant, and even the sculptural severity of Judith, the true biblical heroine. I doubt that the painting is still as repulsive today as it was for eighteenth-century observers. Now it evokes a sense of extreme admiration, almost attraction, not because it sets in motion responses and secret sadisms; but because it is so full of skill, imagination, and manual quality — in short, of artistic power — that

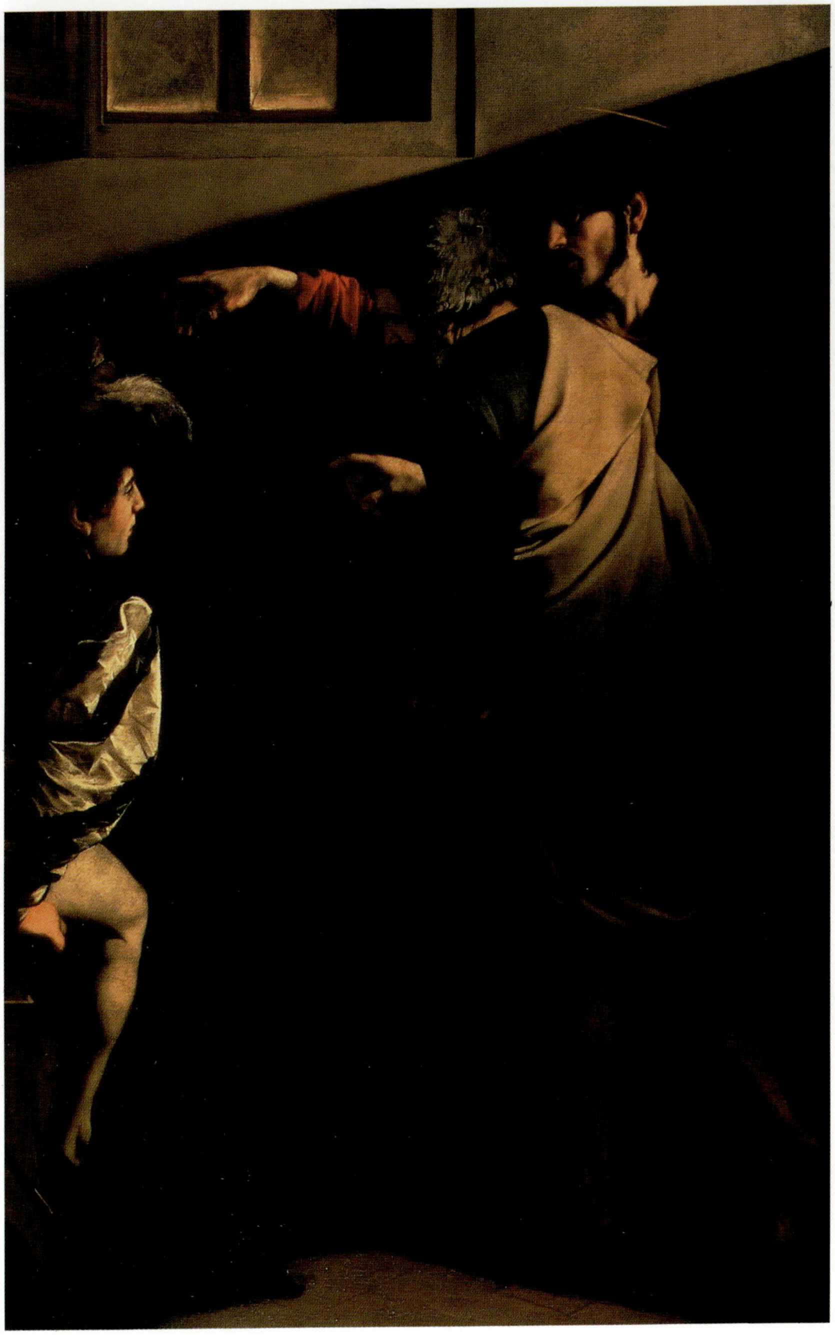

25

25. *Calling of St. Matthew, detail of Christ and St. Peter.*
Rome, San Luigi dei Francesi

26. *X-ray of the detail with Christ and St. Peter, showing the two different versions of Christ's arm and head. The drapery belonged to the figure of Christ.*

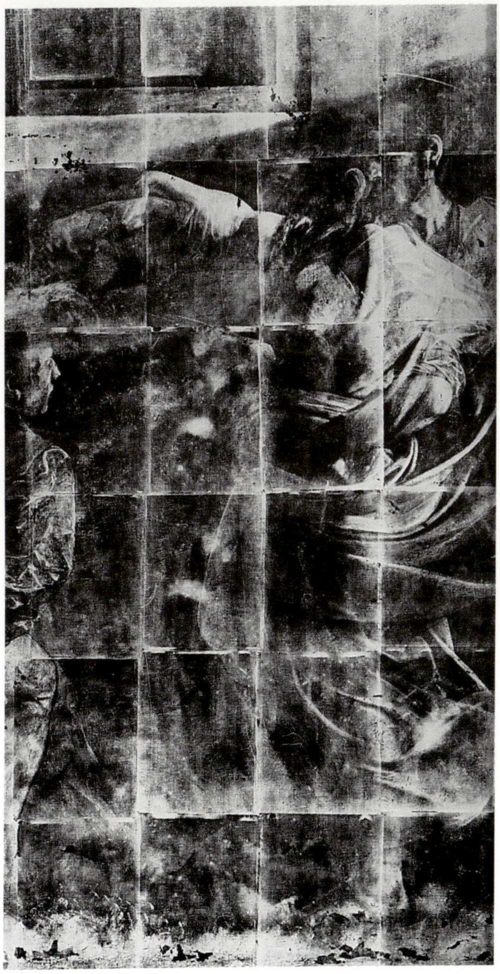

26

we are fascinated.

At the last possible moment, as we know from the biblical passage, Abraham's knife was diverted from his
20 son's throat. The Abraham and Isaac in the Uffizi, cited in the Barberini Inventory as early as 1608, is of uncertain date. Some critics place it at the beginning of Caravaggio's Roman sojourn, others as late as 1603. We prefer to include it at this point, toward the close of the century, considering it similar in theme, technique, and style to the Flight into Egypt and the Judith. Bellori (1672) offers an admirably synthetic description of the picture: "The sacrifice of Abraham, who holds the iron near the throat of his son who cries out and falls". The painting, organized around the diagonal that descends from upper left to lower right, represents an episode traditionally interpreted with reference to Christ, because of the obvious parallel between the son of Abraham and the Son of God, both innocent victims. Some scholars see a church with a baptistery in the background, a further allusion to the Redeemer. Notice, however, how little there is in common between Christ's attitude and that of Isaac, who "cries out" and does not seem at all willing, as he appears to be in many earlier representations, to be sacrificed. Notice also the landscape: its atmospheric quality and the way distant objects gradually fade into their surroundings constitute Caravaggio's clearest admission of his debt to Venetian painting and to Giorgione.

The "aesthetic of exclamation" by which the artist renders feelings with dramatic violence, as in the figures of Judith and Isaac, reaches its highest expression in the
famous Head of Medusa given to the Medici by Cardinal 21

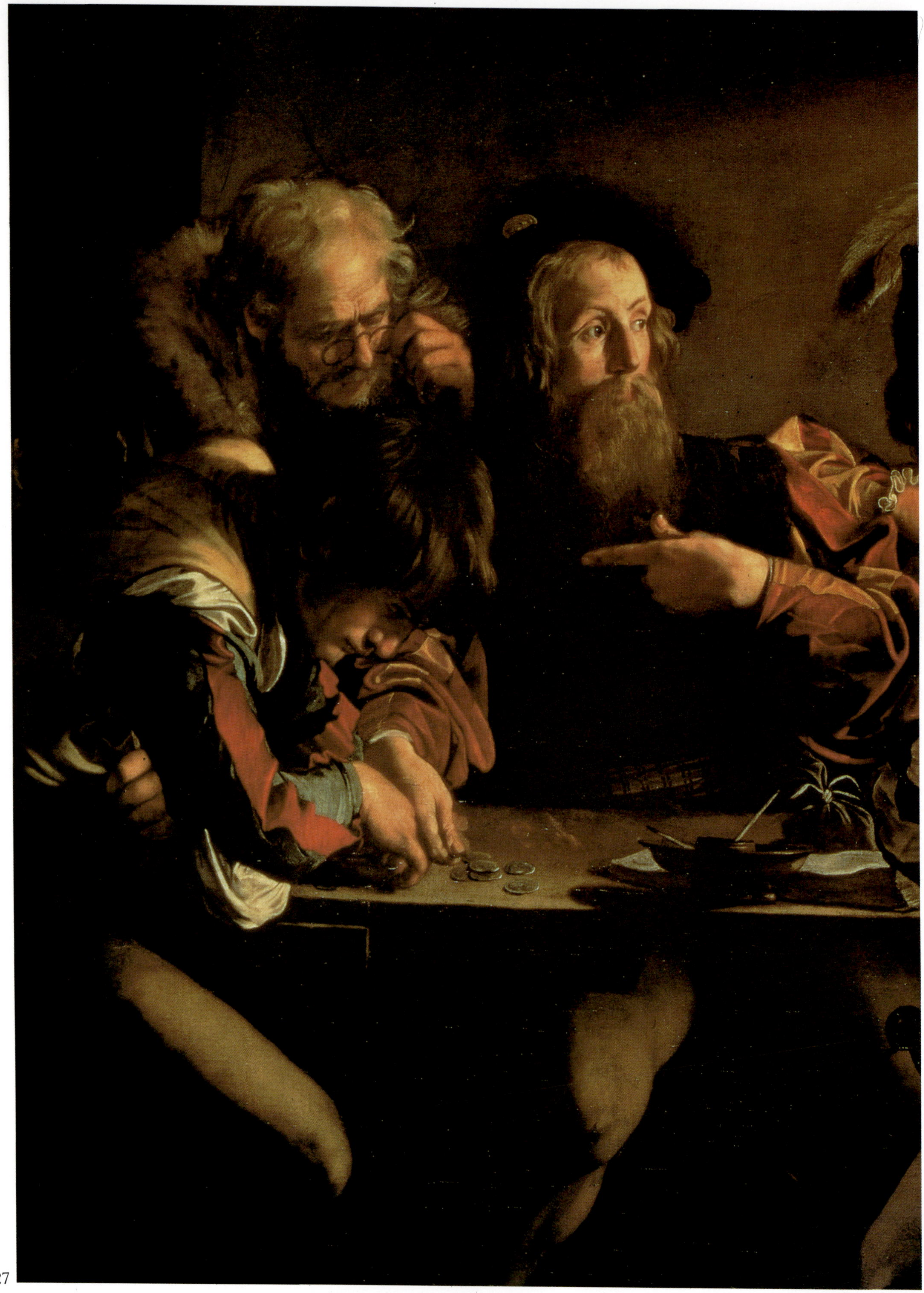

27

27. Calling of St. Matthew, detail with St. Matthew (figure on the right). Rome, San Luigi dei Francesi

28. Calling of St. Matthew, detail with the two central figures. Rome, San Luigi dei Francesi

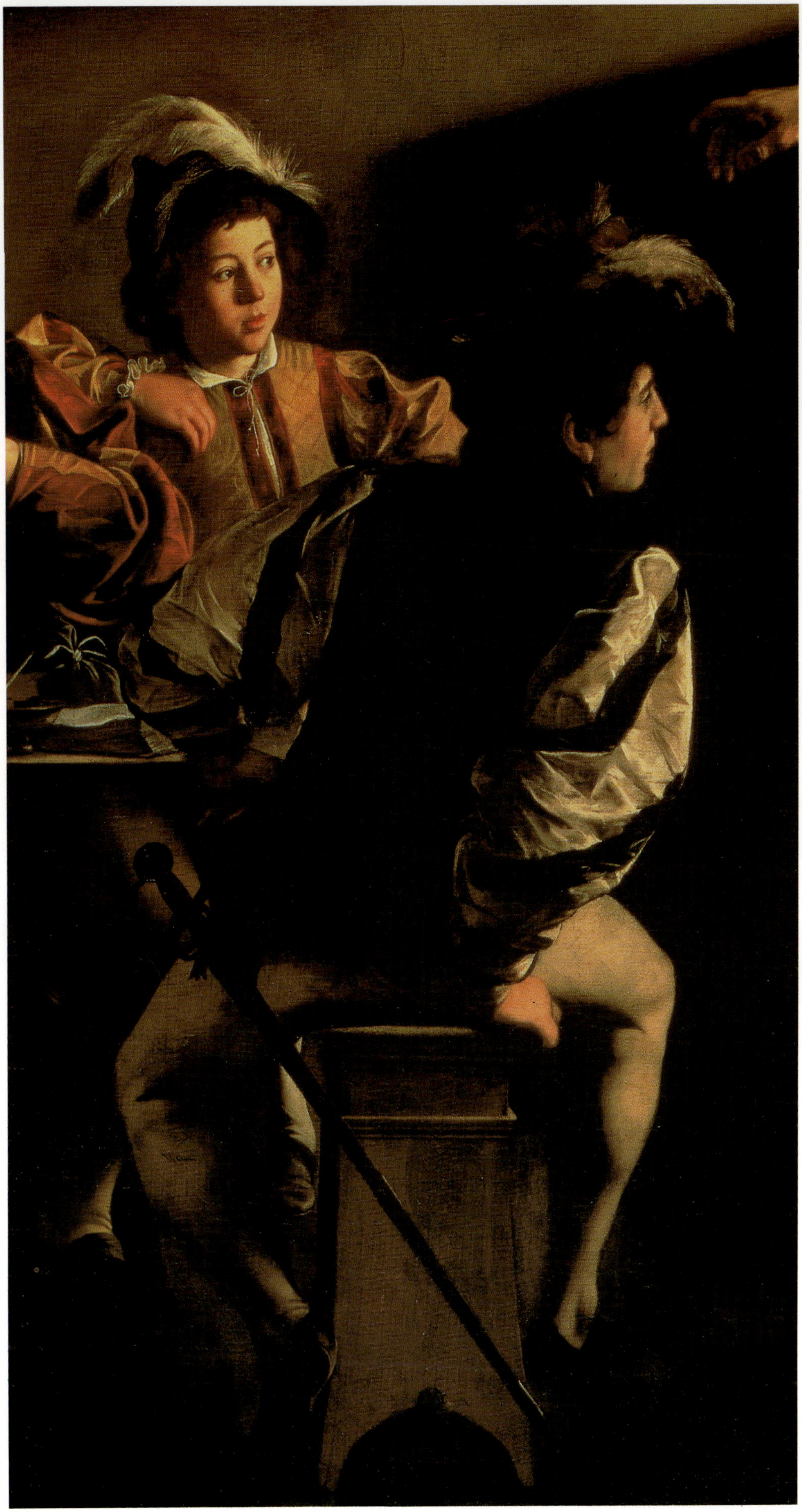

28

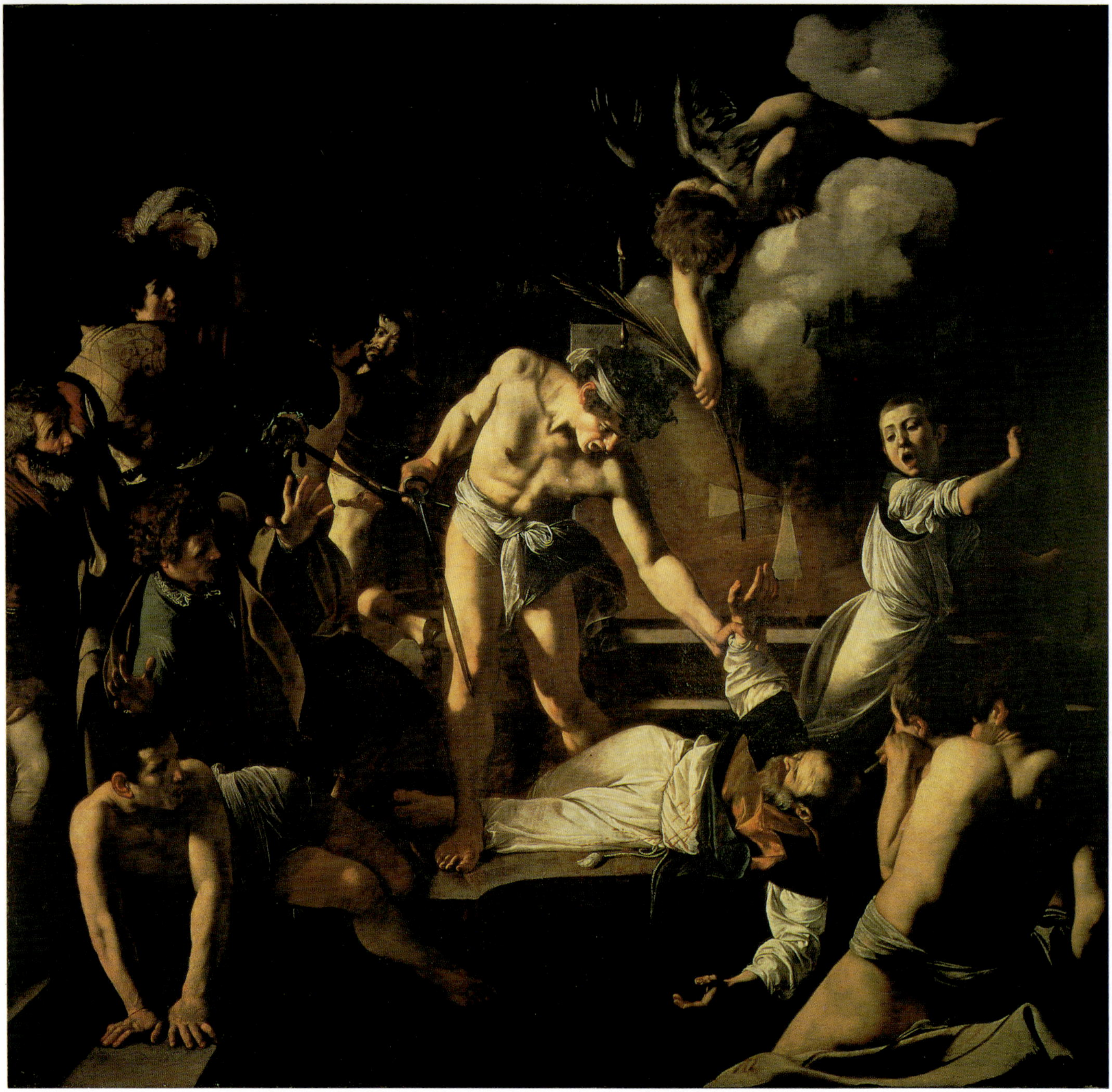

29

Del Monte and now in the Uffizi. This is a round shield (although it was obviously never used as such) that the artist's patron evidently desired to keep as a strange and unusual object.

There is a celebrated iconographical precedent for this painting (even though it is not extant) by Leonardo da Vinci. But it is unusual, and Caravaggio's treatment of the theme remains impressed in our memory by virtue of its inventiveness and absolute originality. The "serpent-covered" head (as it is called in a Medici inventory of 1631) is painted on a convex surface, an expedient already used by sixteenth-century mannerists to emphasize the metamorphism of the image (its property of subtly changing in relation to the way the light strikes it), or even to render reality in a deformed way. The convexity of the support helps project the head into real space, the space occupied by the viewer. Giovan Battista Marino, a poet who maintained that the goal of verse is wonderment, wrote (in 1513-14) of this painting, which he saw in the Gallery of the Grand-Duke of Tuscany: "That proud and ferocious Gorgon / horribly magnificent / in serpentine volumes / of frightening hair," and even earlier, in 1603, another poet, Gaspare Murtola, told of the "poisonous hair / armed with a thousand snakes."

The St. John the Baptist presents us with a much 23
more restful image. This painting exists in two versions, both of which are probably by Caravaggio (who frequently copied his own paintings, as we have seen with the Buona Ventura in the Louvre and the Pinacoteca

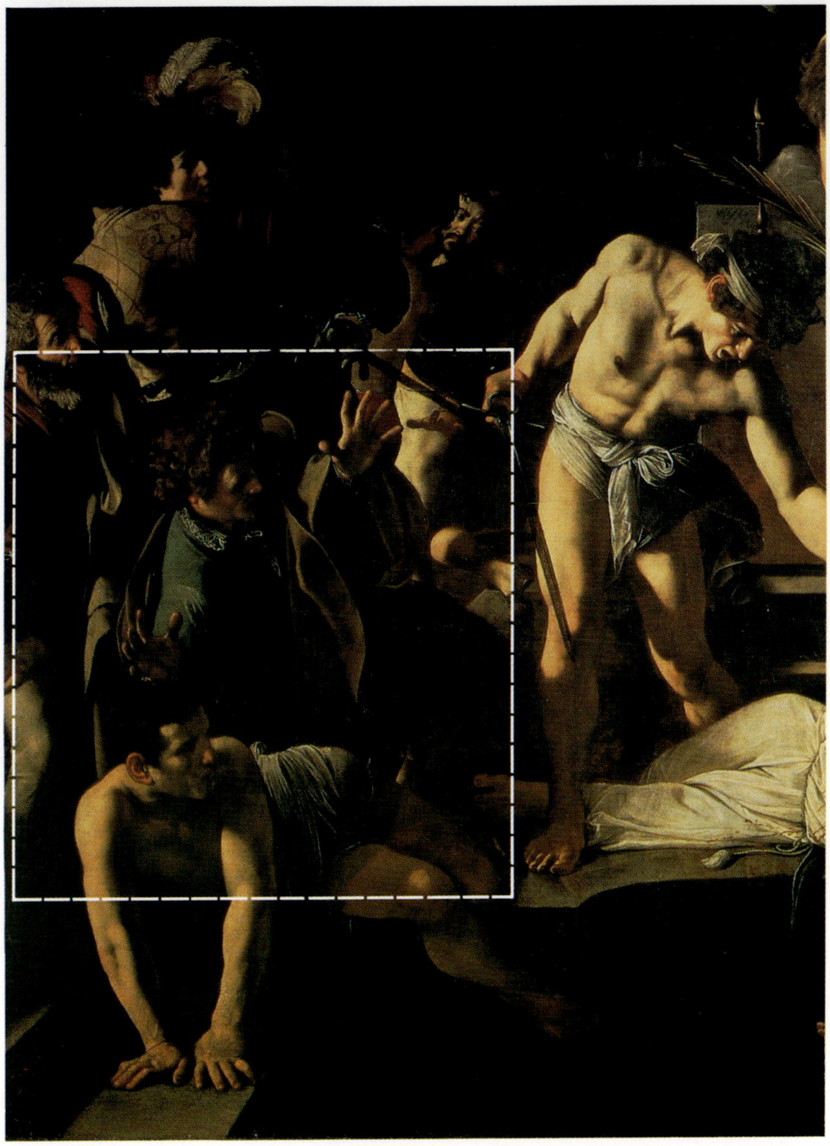
30

29. *Martyrdom of St. Matthew*
cm. 323x343
Rome, San Luigi dei Francesi

30. *Martyrdom of St. Matthew, detail with the group of figures on the left.*
Rome, San Luigi dei Francesi

31. *X-ray of the lower left part of the Martyrdom, showing three figures from the first version, later eliminated.*

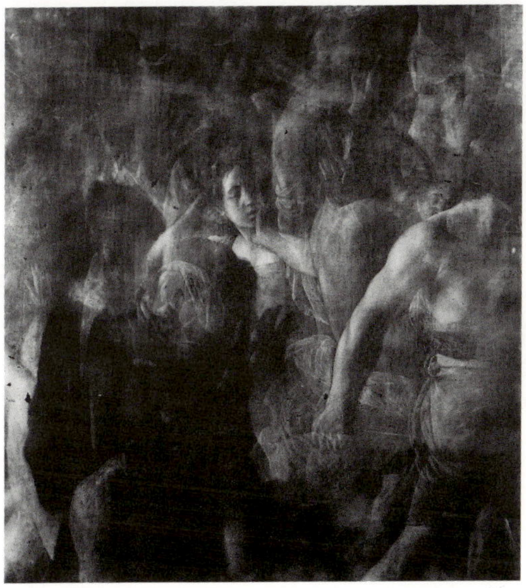
31

Capitolina). Both versions are in Rome, one in the Musei Capitolini, the other in the Galleria Doria Pamphili. The image is a masterpiece of virtuosity whose appeal lies in its soft, caressing light and velvety rendering of cloth, flesh, and plants. The figure is identifiable as St. John only by virtue of the symbols of Christ displayed in the painting: the ram (sacrificial victim), and the grapeleaves (from whose red juice, akin to the blood of Christ, springs life); otherwise the iconographical subject (the simple, immediately apparent image) appears as a nude youth with an ironic, if not allusive, expression. Its cultivated content and its destination for an aristocratic patron (Mattei) are underscored by the artist's explicit use of a great figurative source of the past: Michelangelo's Ignudi from the Sistine Ceiling. But whereas Michelangelo created abstract and ideal figures with cold lights and a merely theoretical plasticism, Caravaggio models his figure on the careful observation of nature, achieving an image of perfect realism. It releases a sort of charge of attraction, drawing in the viewer, in much the same way that the Amor Victorious in Berlin would do a few years later: through the single figure turned toward the observer.

The artist's works that we have looked at so far were all intended for private patrons, even though many of them were religious paintings. Caravaggio's achievements were not so widely acclaimed, in the beginning, that they could be set above the altars of Roman churches, before the eyes of a general public accustomed to images of a very different kind. Nevertheless, when he was called on to furnish large religious paintings for important churches in the city, he realized them without compromise, without making the slightest attempt to simplify or soften the virulence of his message. His first church commission arose just at the turn of the century. Never has another coincidence of this kind been so justifiably pregnant with meaning.

In 1565 the French monsignor Matteo Contarelli acquired a chapel in San Luigi dei Francesi, but when he died twenty years later it had not yet been decorated. The executor of his will, Virgilio Crescenzi, and later his

32. X-ray of the right part of the Martyrdom. At the top center is one of the figures still present in the painting. The classical figure in the foreground is part of the first version.

33. Martyrdom of St. Matthew, detail of the right part of the painting. Rome, San Luigi dei Francesi

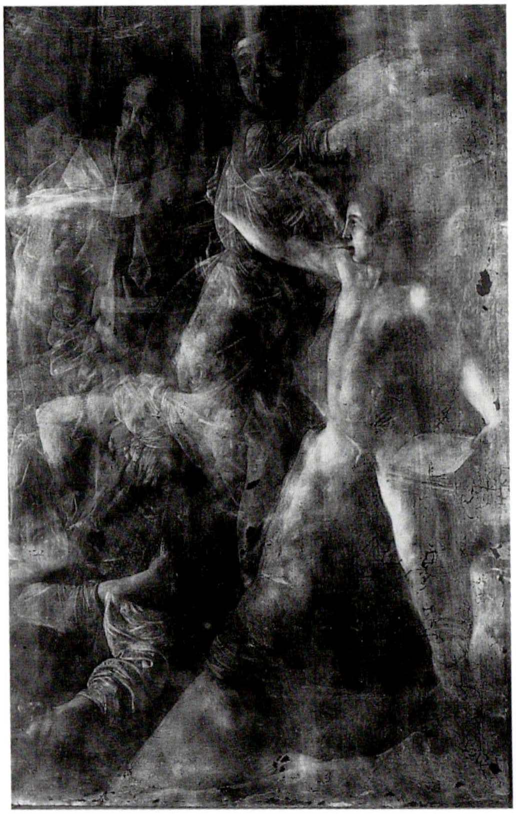

32

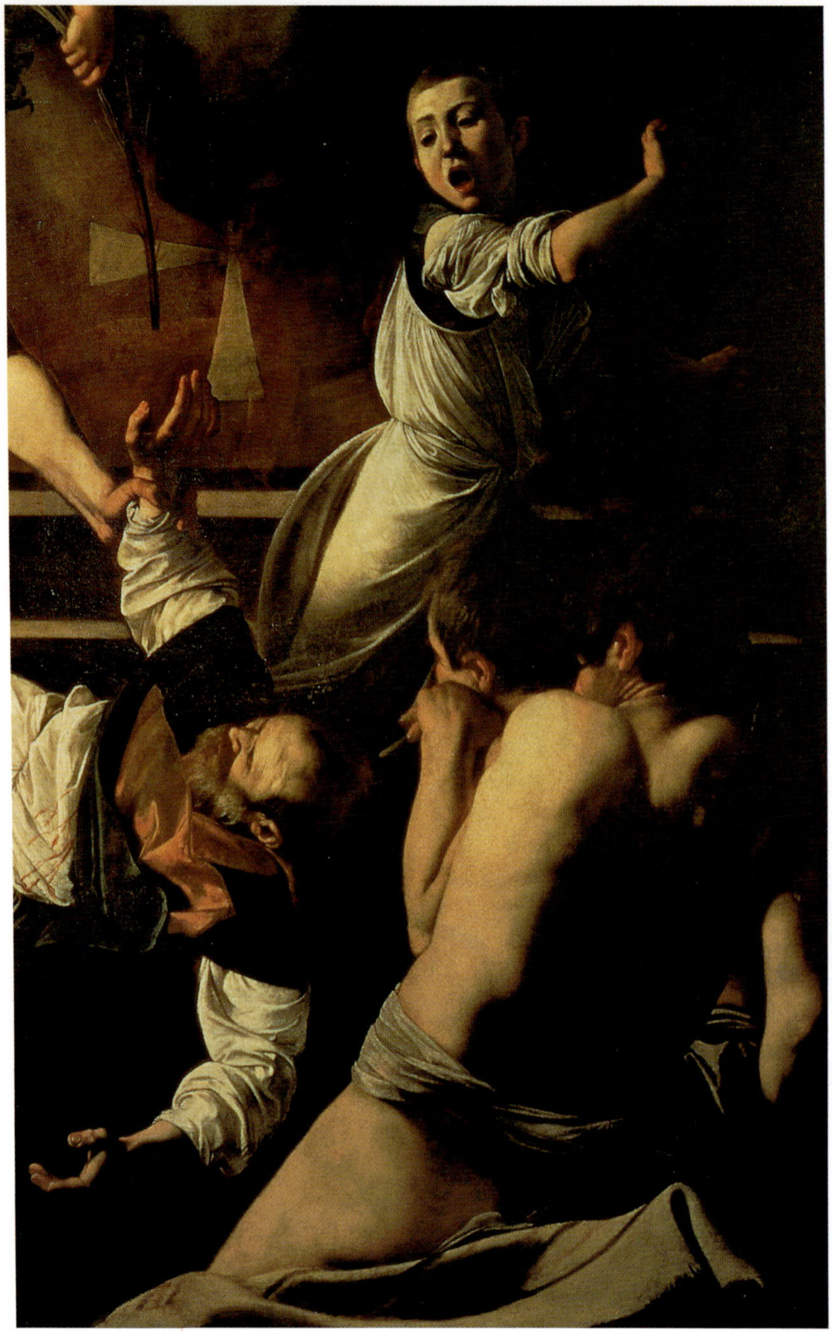

33

son, Giacomo, undertook the task. The decorative scheme called for a statue of St. Matthew and the Angel, commissioned first to Gerolamo Muziano, and then to the Flemish sculptor Cobaert, for the high altar; and for a fresco cycle for the walls and ceiling by Cavalier d'Arpino. The latter decorated the vault in 1591-93, but the walls were left bare (this may reflect at least in part the Crescenzis' intentions to speculate on the interest on the Contarelli estate). At any rate, on 13 June 1599 a contract was stipulated before a notary by which Caravaggio undertook to execute two paintings for the lateral walls, for which he was paid the following year (1600), after the paintings had been set in place. Later, on 7 February 1602, after Cobaert's statue had been judged unsatisfactory, an altarpiece was entrusted to Caravaggio in a separate contract that called for delivery of the work by 23 May, the Feast of the Pentecost. This painting, as we shall see, was rejected; the artist made another one (which was accepted) in a surprisingly brief time, receiving payment for this second work on 22 September.

The recent discovery of a series of documents that has made it possible to reconstruct the complete course of events with great accuracy, has confirmed or denied several hypotheses set forth by scholars over the past fifty years regarding the dating of the paintings for San Luigi dei Francesi. The first version of the altarpiece depicting St. Matthew and the Angel (the one that was rejected and later destroyed, unfortunately), in particular, had been given an early date which the sources showed

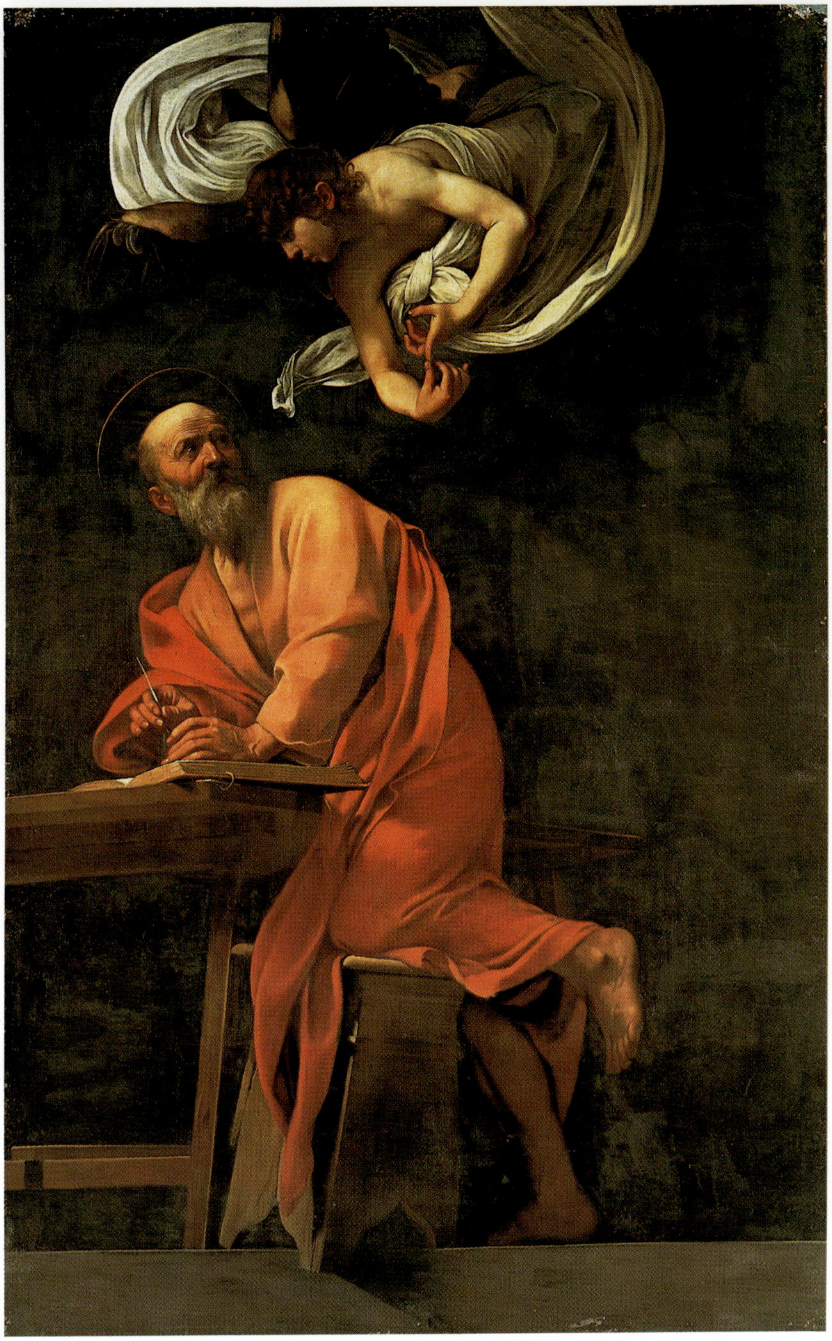

34

34. St. Matthew and the Angel
cm. 296.5x189
Rome, San Luigi dei Francesi

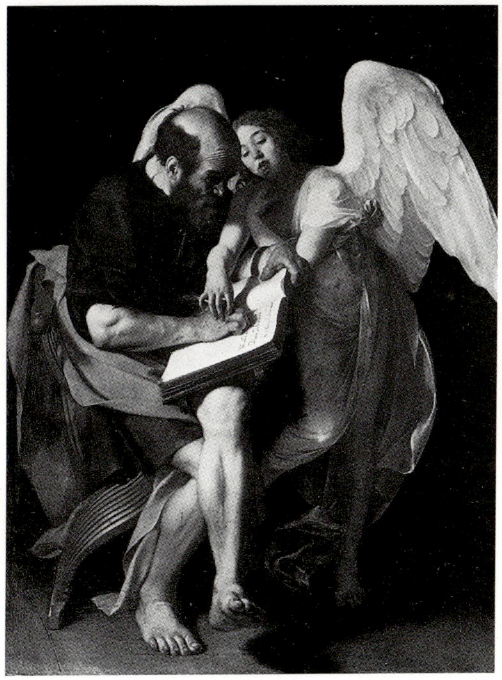

35

35. St. Matthew and the Angel
cm. 232x183
Formerly at Berlin, Kaiser Friedrich Museum, destroyed.

to be inadmissable. The discovery also casts new light on the paintings for Santa Maria del Popolo (especially the first version of the Conversion of St. Paul), which were made right after the first two paintings for San Luigi. This development should serve as a warning to those scholars who feel they know how to distinguish, with great subtlety, the smallest inflection of style, so as to obtain unquestionable relative or absolute datings, even to within a few months (despite the fact that they are dealing with events of four centuries ago). The path of an artist's career is not always straight. It is full of changes of mind, and above all, of experiments that lead in different directions but that are conducted simultaneously. Two different orders of artistic inquiry do not necessarily represent different periods in an artist's career. If the artist is open to experimentation and tends to reject normally accredited conventions, more than one line of action may appeal to him at any given time.

An examination of the two paintings of the side walls of San Luigi dei Francesi, which Matteo Contarelli
wished to show the Calling and Martyrdom of his name- 24
sake, provide us with an extraordinary panorama of 29
Caravaggio's art. We have seen that many of his compositions thus far contain a limited number of figures: normally from one to three. The subject is expressed as a rule with little interest in the depth of the painting. Even when the figures are placed before a landscape, they stand out prominently in the foreground, so that the landscape appears as little more than a backdrop. There are seven figures in the Calling of St. Matthew,

and thirteen in the Martyrdom. They diminish in size in relation to the painting's surface, leaving room for the background. In the Martyrdom, we also see an arrangement in echelons that is unprecedented in Caravaggio's art. It is even more surprising because it is achieved with very little allusion to the architecture of the setting, deriving its force from the arrangement of the figures in space.

Caravaggio did not arrive at the final version right away, and it is important to remember that even compositions that appear to have been born in an instant are the fruit of a long preparatory study. X-ray analysis has proven absolutely indispensable in revealing to our later vision forms and figures that the artist, after sketching them on the canvas, believed would remain concealed from all eyes, including his own, beneath the final version. Thus, in an early version of the Calling of
26 St. Matthew, the figure of Christ stood alone and was
25 not covered, as in the final version, by that of St. Peter. The latter's presence involved the accentuation, in the final version, of his role as mediator (he would be the first pope) between man and God. Indeed, we see a sort of division of Christ into two parts, as though two persons have germinated and branched off from the same trunk. This already emphasized Christ's human and divine nature. Peter laboriously and almost stiffly repeats the gesture of Christ, which in comparison is handled with the greatest eloquence. In addition, we immediately notice the painting's total independence from the designs of earlier religious painting. From this we may conclude that the artist is not interested in instructing, admonishing, or stirring his audience to religious feeling, as the Counter Reformation expected art to do. He felt it was not his task. He seems to say, this is what happened. Christ and Peter suddenly came in and made it clear that they wanted to talk to Matthew, while the two
28 youths, taken by surprise, prepared to face an intrusion whose nature they were unsure of; and indeed two other figures, unaware of what was going on, continued
27 counting the money. Matthew brought his hand to his chest, as though to ask if it were he that they wanted. An instant before, the scene had been different; an instant later, it would no longer be the same. If a scene is to be instructive, it must be prepared, planned, and arranged. If it is devoid of this kind of orientation toward a specific end, then the artist is virtually free to shape it as he likes and to change it from one moment to the next, not preparing it, but taking note of it.

Here, for the first time, the viewer no longer synthetically embraces all the painting's content. A more complicated scene is played out before his eyes. This calls for a diachronous reading more than a synchronous one. The eye must follow the event, running along the entire network of relations set up by the figures' gestures and gazes. Caravaggio would make extensive use of these internal references, obliging his viewers to run through the entire genetic process of the painting, to follow the artist along the path that he proposes or actually imposes on the observer. Thus guided by the artist, the viewer cannot escape his intentions. The painter is therefore able to charge the picture with meanings, knowing that his audience will have to pause and reflect on them; hence the claim to an absolutely global consideration of the work, and the particular eloquence of Caravaggio's paintings from this moment onward — an eloquence that does not proceed by classical, universal truths as in the Carracci and their current, but by contingent details whose exemplary value the artist succeeds in identifying and pointing out to the observer. This is why these paintings cannot leave one indifferent, and why the viewer who begins to look at the painting cannot stop even if he wants to, until he reaches the end.

In the Martyrdom of St. Matthew the composition is 29
expanded to cover a complexity of subject that is unprecedented in Caravaggio's work, and that frankly we could not have expected on the basis only of his earlier paintings. It is quite true that all he lacked was the chance given by a specific commission: otherwise the artist was ready to contend with the greater complexity of ideas mentioned above. The Martyrdom is not only one of the most memorable creations of Western art; it is also remarkable for its innovative power, its wealth of explicit and implicit meaning, and its ingenious composition. X-ray analysis has shown that the first conception of the scene had three classical figures in the fore- 31
ground: one in the middle seen from behind, which took up the motif of the angel in the Rest During the Flight into Egypt, and two others inspired by antique sculpture 32
filtered through the late works of Raphael, an artist whose influence can also be seen clearly in the final version. Caravaggio arrived at the definitive painting, which is very different, with astonishing rapidity, reworking, discarding, or changing his first ideas. That such an exacting work was done directly on the canvas, without the usual recourse to drawings on paper, is truly unusual; but then there is not a single drawing that can be attributed to Caravaggio with certainty. This is another feature that distinguishes him from his fellow artists.

Caravaggio leaves the setting of the event unclear. The three seminude figures in the foreground, of which the two on the right contemplate the Martyrdom (the action is not contemporaneous, but relived, as we are thus given to understand) create a chronological and spatial detachment. They belong to an indefinite space. They seem to sink, before the step of the altar on which the crime is committed, into a sort of pool, the Pool of Bethesda of the Holy Scriptures from which one reemerges regenerated. The six figures on the left show dif- 30
ferent states of mind. They are grouped together in couples. The first two, reminiscent of the figures of Gior-

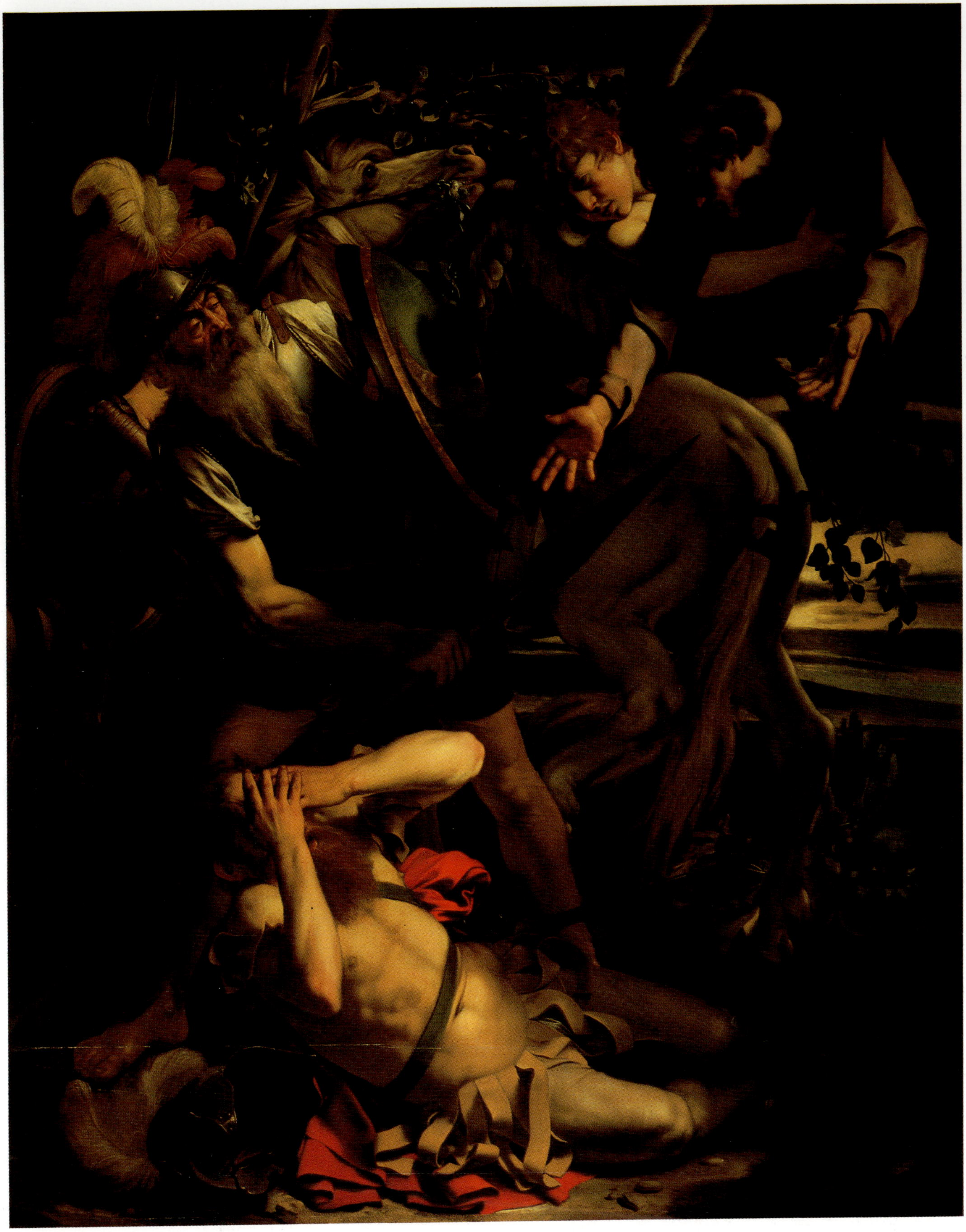

36

36. Conversion of St. Paul
cm. 237x189
Rome, Odescalchi Balbi Collection

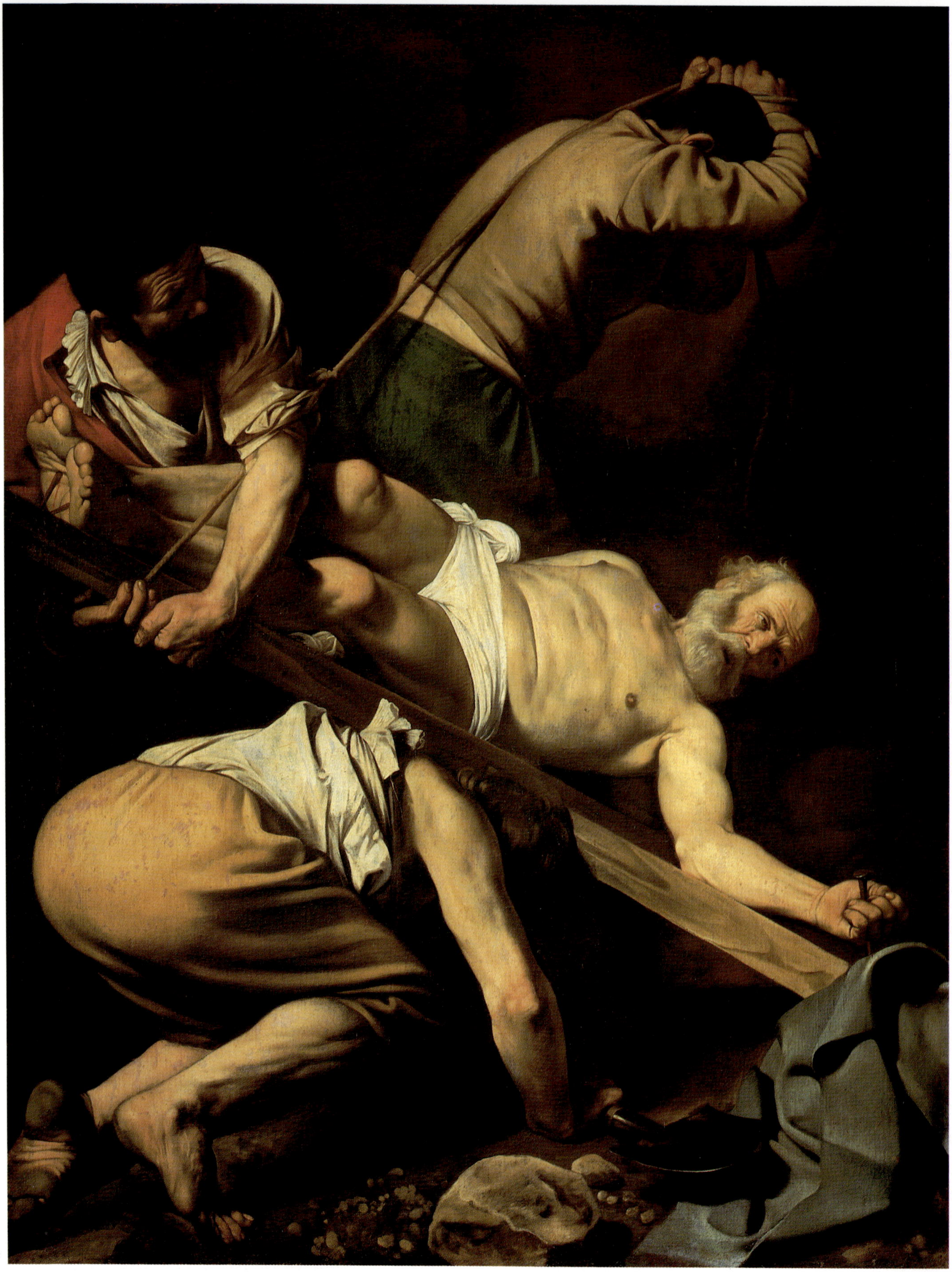

37

37. Crucifixion of St. Peter
cm. 232x201. Rome, Santa Maria del Popolo

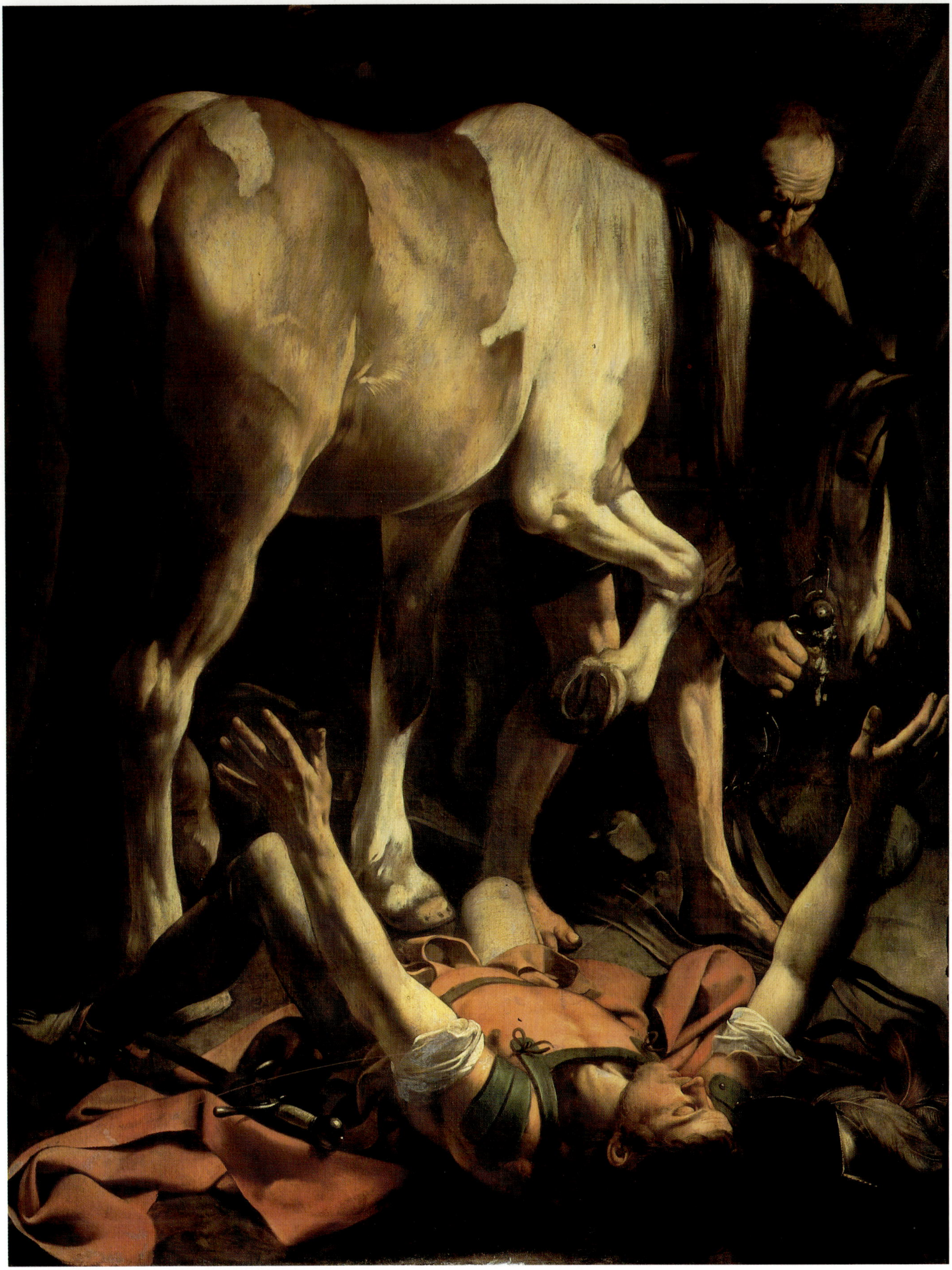

38

38. Conversion on the Way to Damascus
cm. 230x175. Rome, Santa Maria del Popolo

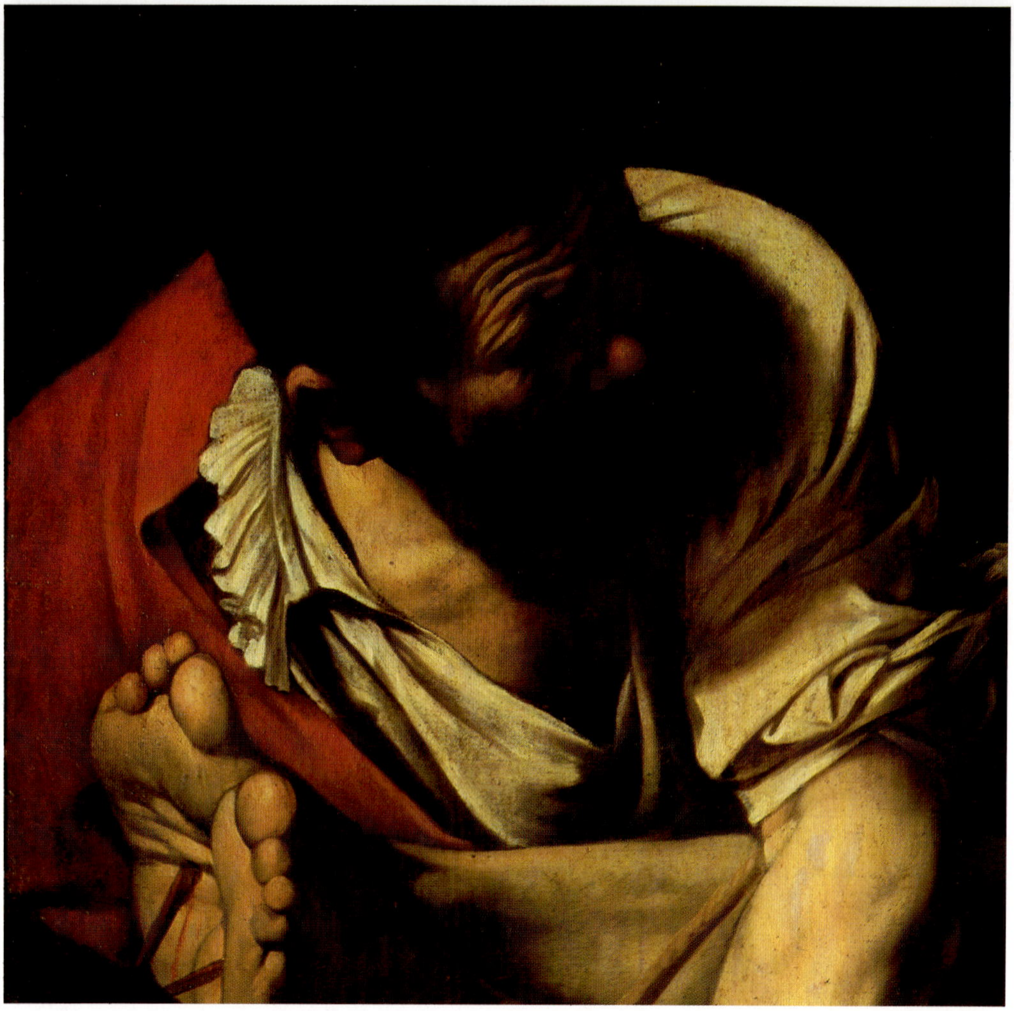

39

39. Crucifixion of St. Peter, detail of the figure at the upper left. Rome, Santa Maria del Popolo

40. Supper in Emmaus cm. 139x195 London, National Gallery

gione and Savoldo, express immense surprise and wonder — the emotions with which the one in the green gown opens his arms, offering his hands, especially his left hand, to a highly refined play of light. Two others, elegantly dressed, show their intention to call each other out of the action, in which they do not wish to become involved. One wears the usual feathered cap. The third couple moves away despite their emotional involvement, as though against their will. The figure seen frontally is Caravaggio himself, who seems to want to impress the scene well in his mind, in order to paint it later. The splendid figure of the assassin carries out a precise action that not everyone notices: he grabs the saint's outstretched arm, to keep him from receiving the palm of martyrdom from the angel who reaches dangerously downward (in a pose taken from a figure in Michelange-
33 lo's Last Judgment). The youth on the right is an explicit expression of Caravaggio's characteristic and well-known "aesthetic of exclamation." He contrasts strongly with the contemplative attitude of the figures on the right, which is the same attitude in which the classical painters represented the shepherds in the "Et in Arcadia Ego", dreamy and idyllic images that have nothing of the fierceness of this scene. The traces of setting are reduced to an absolute minimum. X-rays show that an earlier version contained classical architectural elements, which the artist removed.

Cobaert's statue for the altar of the chapel was (fortunately) rejected, and Caravaggio, as we have said, was engaged to paint a St. Matthew and the Angel. The first version of this painting was likewise refused by the patrons. The artist's desperation was appeased by Marchese Vincenzo Giustiniani's offer to acquire it, and a se-
cond, acceptable version was produced. It still stands 34
over the altar today. The first painting, which ended up 35
in Berlin, was unfortunately destroyed during the Second World War. It was another masterpiece. It contained, in the angel who with gentle indulgence guided the saint's uncertain hand as he wrote, one of the most charming figures ever painted by the artist. The first painting was criticized for Matthew's lack of decorum; the figure, which hardly appeared as a saint, was seated cross-legged, his feet turned outward toward the viewer. In the final version, likewise a splendid feat of imagination but certainly less fascinating than the first, the angel much more correctly counts on his fingers, in the traditional Scholastic fashion, the arguments than the saint should take note of and develop. A whirlwind of drapery envelops the angel. The saint balances on his bench, in precarious equilibrium, like a modern school-

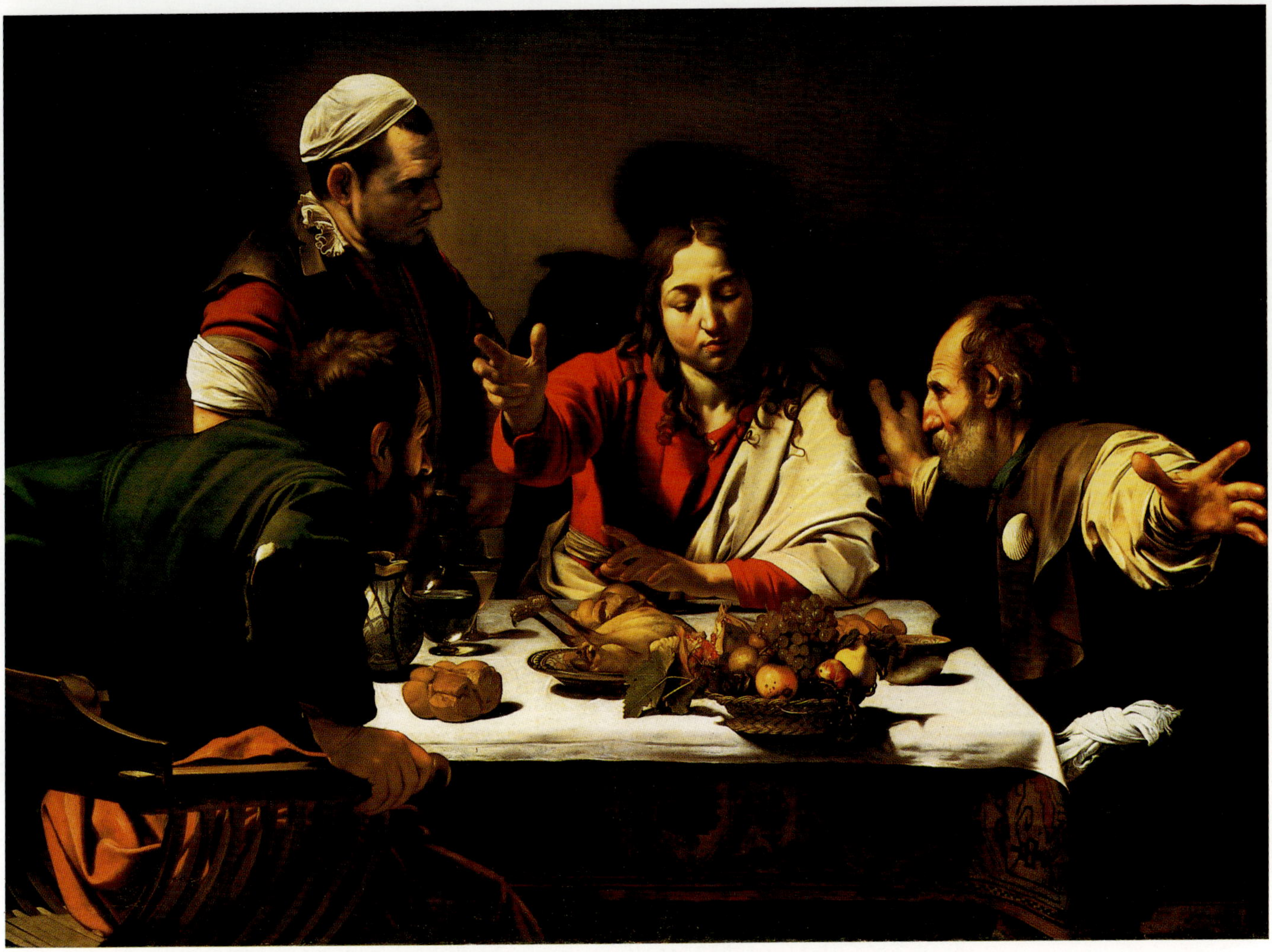

40

boy; but this time the unorthodox elements do not seem to have raised particular objections.

Caravaggio's other great ecclesiastical enterprise of these years falls between the two canvases for the side walls and the altarpiece. On 24 September 1600, immediately after finishing the wall paintings for San Luigi dei Francesi, Caravaggio received the commission for two paintings, a Crucifixion of St. Peter and a Conversion of St. Paul, from Monsignor Tiberio Cerasi, for the latter's newly acquired chapel in Santa Maria del Popolo. For the altar Monsignor Cerasi had ordered an Assumption from Annibale Carracci, certainly excited by the idea of effecting such a close comparison between the greatest (and for the time being, the only) representatives in Rome of the classical and naturalistic currents. The contract explicitly mentions two cypress panels (Caravaggio certainly did not like to work in fresco, as was more usual for commissions of this kind, because he was not able to make the corrections that, as we have seen, were so important to him). The extant paintings with the subjects indicated in the contract are on canvas; and as
36 there is another version of the Conversion of Saul in the Balbi Odescalchi Collection in Rome, painted on a cypress panel, and a Crucifixion of Peter in Leningrad, attributed to various artists, it is logical to assume that there was at one time an original by Caravaggio. The evidence seems to back up Baglione's assertion that, again, Caravaggio's first versions did not meet with the client's approval, and were acquired by others (in this case, Cardinal Sannesio) and replaced by more acceptable paintings.

The Balbi Odescalchi Conversion, after overcoming the reservations of the past regarding its attribution, has had to deal with many more concerning its date, because many scholars consider it too early to be the first version of the painting for Santa Maria del Popolo. But the considerations made above concerning the contemporaneous intersection in Caravaggio of different and even contrasting motifs and ideas, are even more valid here; and the nonstylistic evidence (subject, size, technique) is too powerful to allow for different interpretations. Certainly, the style of the painting is not nearly so exact as that of the paintings for San Luigi; and above all, the tangled and crowded composition is full of mannerist features, particularly in the figure of Saul, whose debt to Michelangelo is nevertheless superficial. But the painting contains, in the angel and in Christ, two of the best-known models for Caravaggio's figures of those years, as is readily seen; and the Lombard treatment of

41 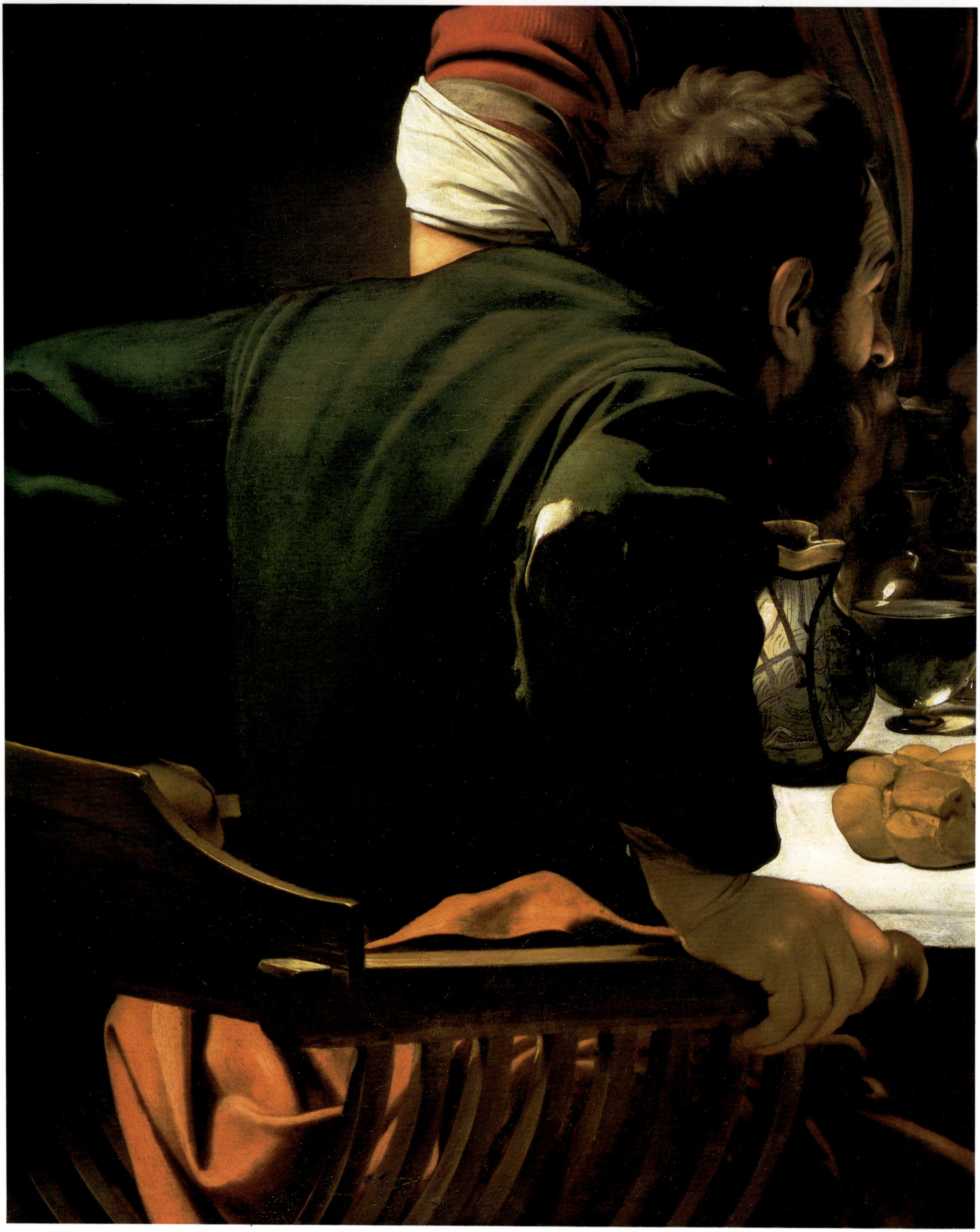

41. Supper in Emmaus, detail.
London, National Gallery

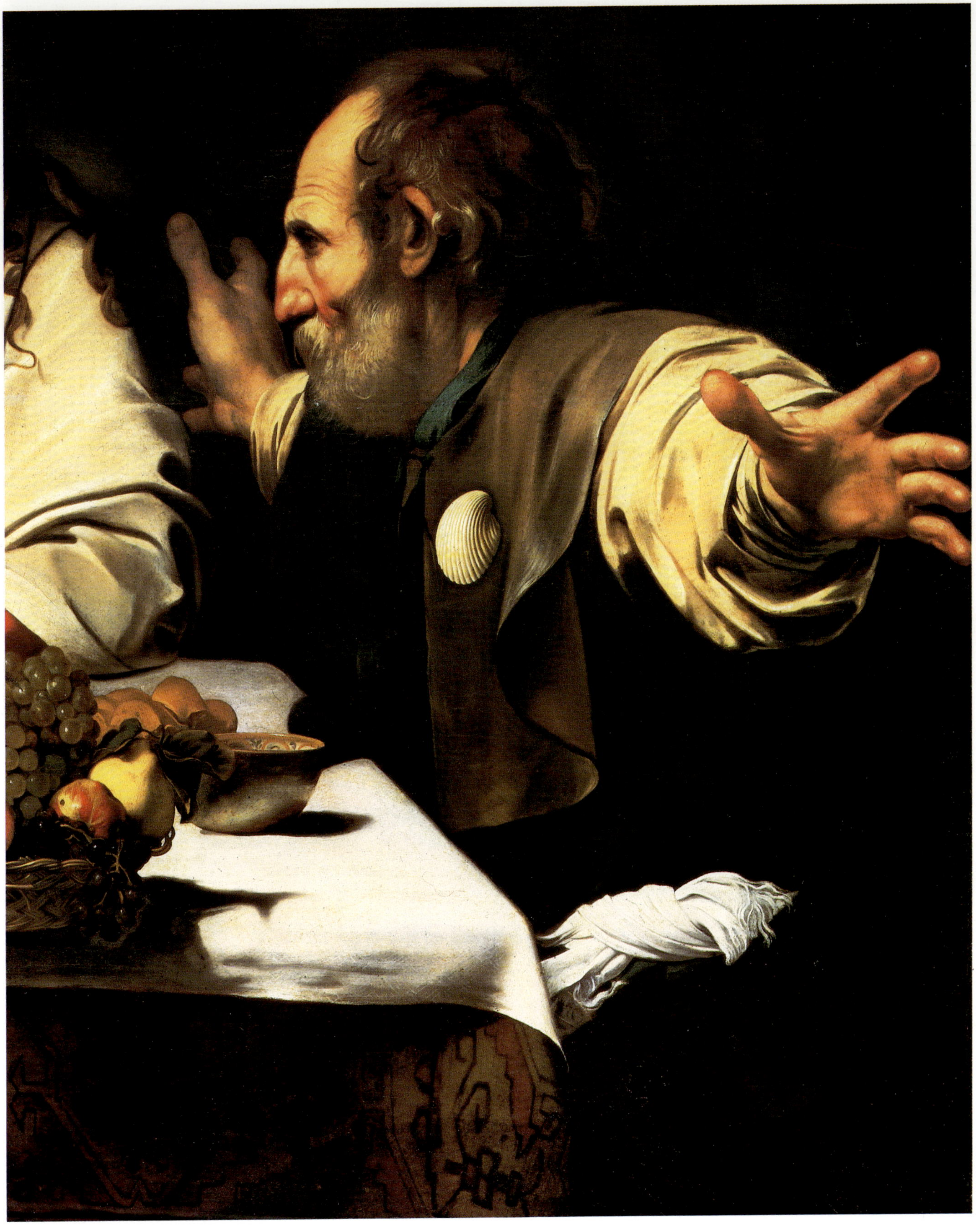

42

42. Supper in Emmaus, detail.
London, National Gallery

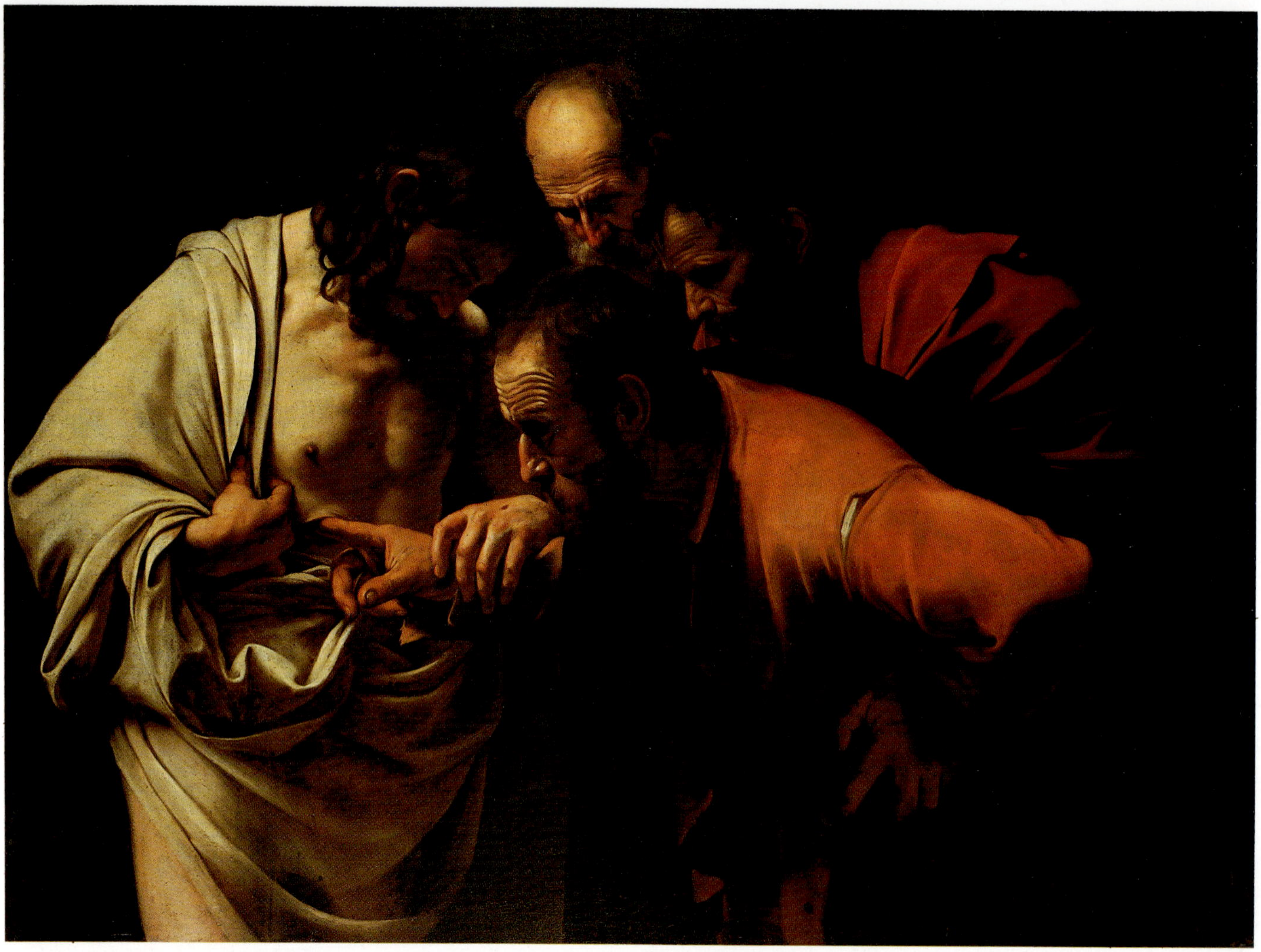

43

the landscape is a constant throughout Caravaggio's career, with the exception of his very last years.

The two later paintings for Santa Maria del Popolo compelled the artist to contend with vertical compositions, unlike those of San Luigi. Here again the scale of the figures is increased in relation to the surface. The action, instead of stretching out in a narrative, is concentrated solely on setting up the very central core of the

44

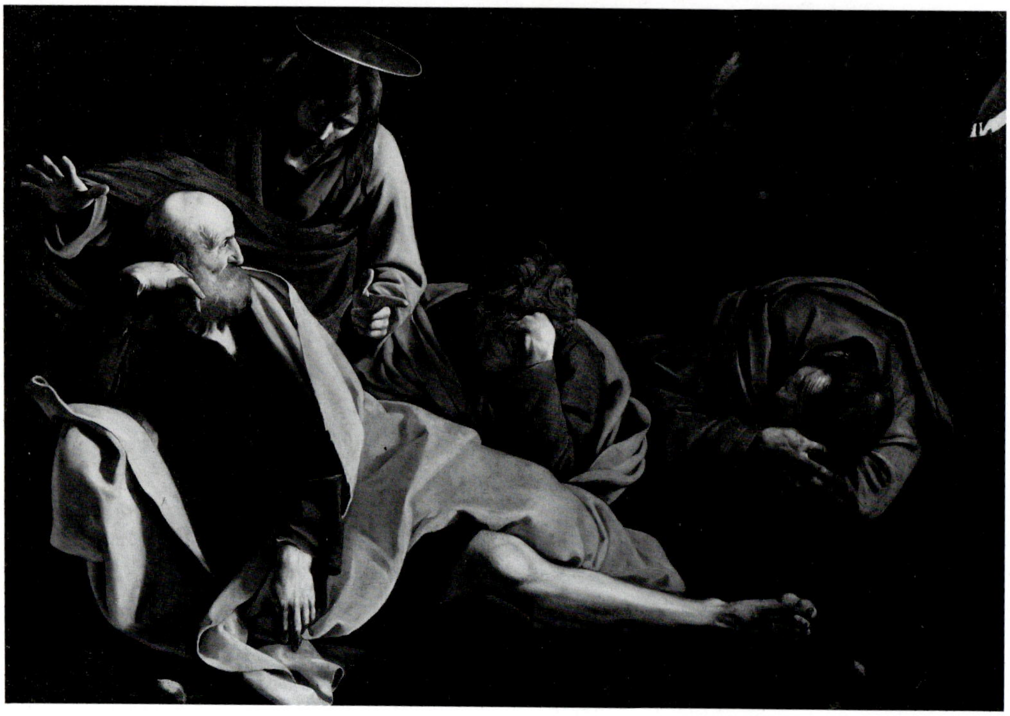

43. Doubting of St. Thomas
cm. 107x146
Potsdam, Neues Palais

44. Christ in the Garden
cm. 154x222
Formerly at Berlin, Kaiser Friedrich Museum, destroyed.

45. Capture of Christ
cm. 134x172.5
Odessa, State Museum of Eastern and Western Art

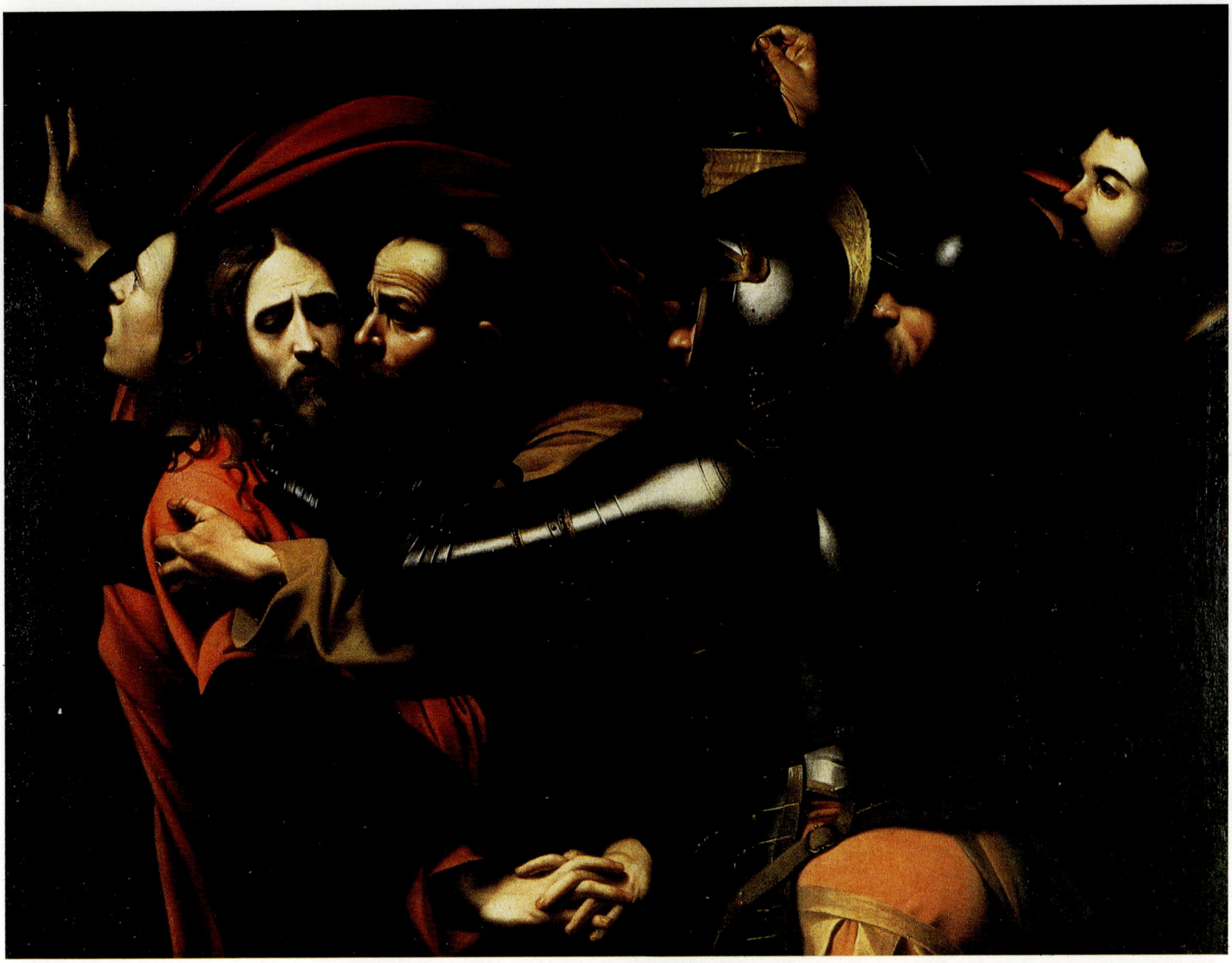

45

scene. All elements that are not absolutely necessary are
37 left out of the Crucifixion: The saint and the three executioners appear without a landscape. Caravaggio does not give up the specific definition of the gestures, to which a perfect necessity is attributed, best exemplified by the executioner who bends down, his spade still in his hand, to lift up the cross on his back. Here the artist, no doubt in deference to the severity of the setting, renounced his aesthetic of horror. The blood does not gush forth as from a fountain, but forms tiny rivulets. The expression on the saint's face is introspective, sorrowfully accepting, devoid of all expressionistic satisfaction. Even the colors are muted.

38 The same internal atmosphere pervades the Conversion on the Way to Damascus, one of the artist's finest achievements. The rendering of Saul (how different from the complacent movement of the first version!) shuns a demonstration of mere skill; his out-flung arms (whose circular rhythm is fused with the profile of the animal) express calm acceptance of the will of God, relating this figure psychologically with the greatest traditional depositary of this sentiment, the Virgin of the Annunciation. The horse does not neigh madly, but seems to return to its stall at the end of the day, tired and peaceful. The absolute rarefaction of expressive means to which Caravaggio resorts here is a new development after the extremistic superficialities of his first decade. Those who admired his skill then, find here that Caravaggio could be not only a marvellous phenomenon of cultural fashion, but one of the few very great artists who change the course of world art.

The same expressive principles are to be found in another group of paintings that appear to have been done around the same time as the Contarelli and Cerasi
cycles. The Supper in Emmaus in the National Gallery 40
in London, formerly in the collection of Ciriaco Mattei, brings the flowing gestures of the figures together in a mood of noble containment. It is the moment of the disciple's recognition of Christ. The latter is young and beardless, his left hand transfixed by the light. The still-life is rendered with the artist's characteristic naturalism, but in duller tones. Even the decorative element of the rug or tablecloth on the table lacks that masterful effect of texture and color visible elsewhere in the earlier works.

Three other paintings of episodes drawn from the life of Christ attest to the artist's interest in unprecedented treatments of themes already dealt with at length by

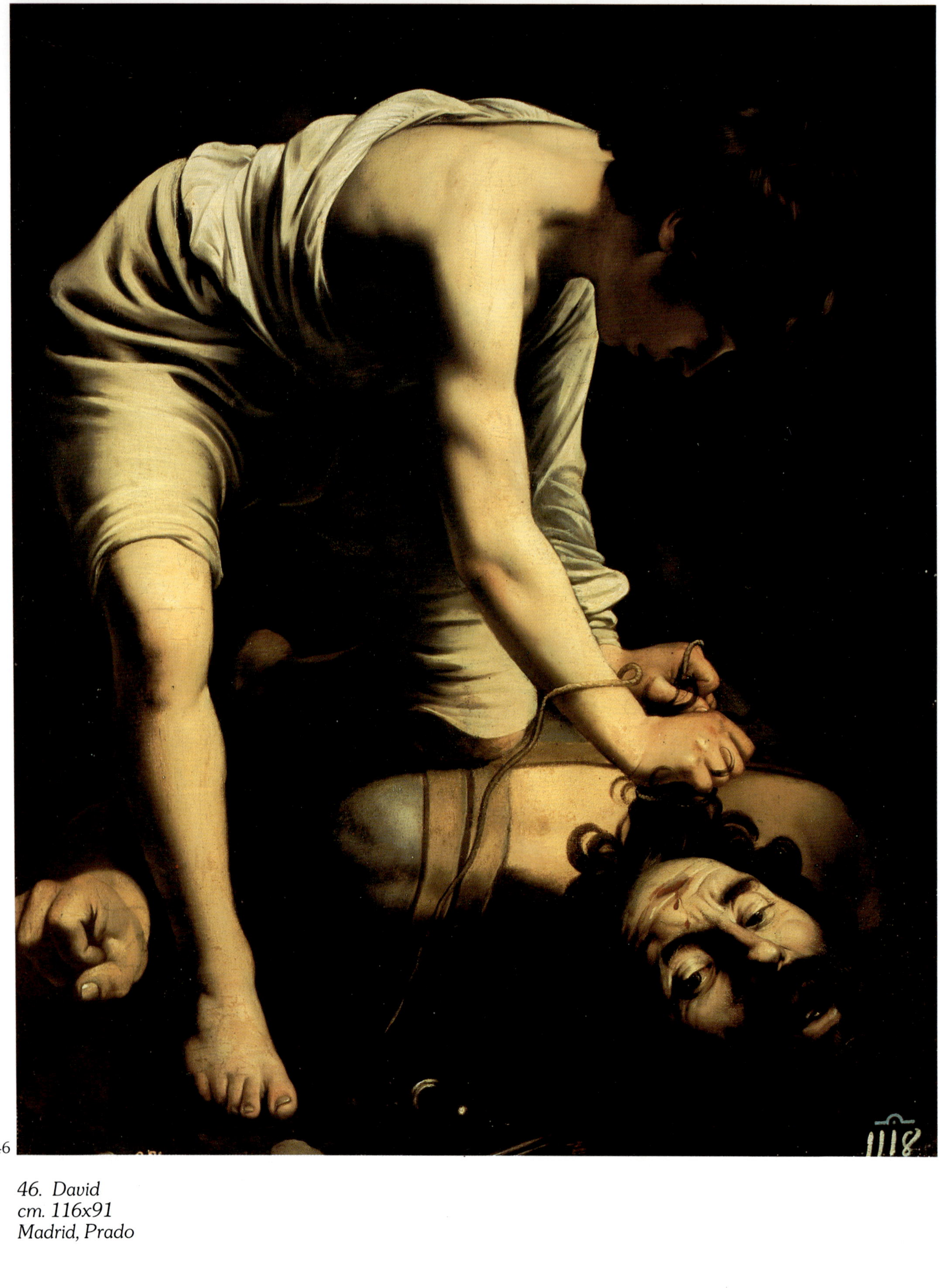

46

46. David
cm. 116x91
Madrid, Prado

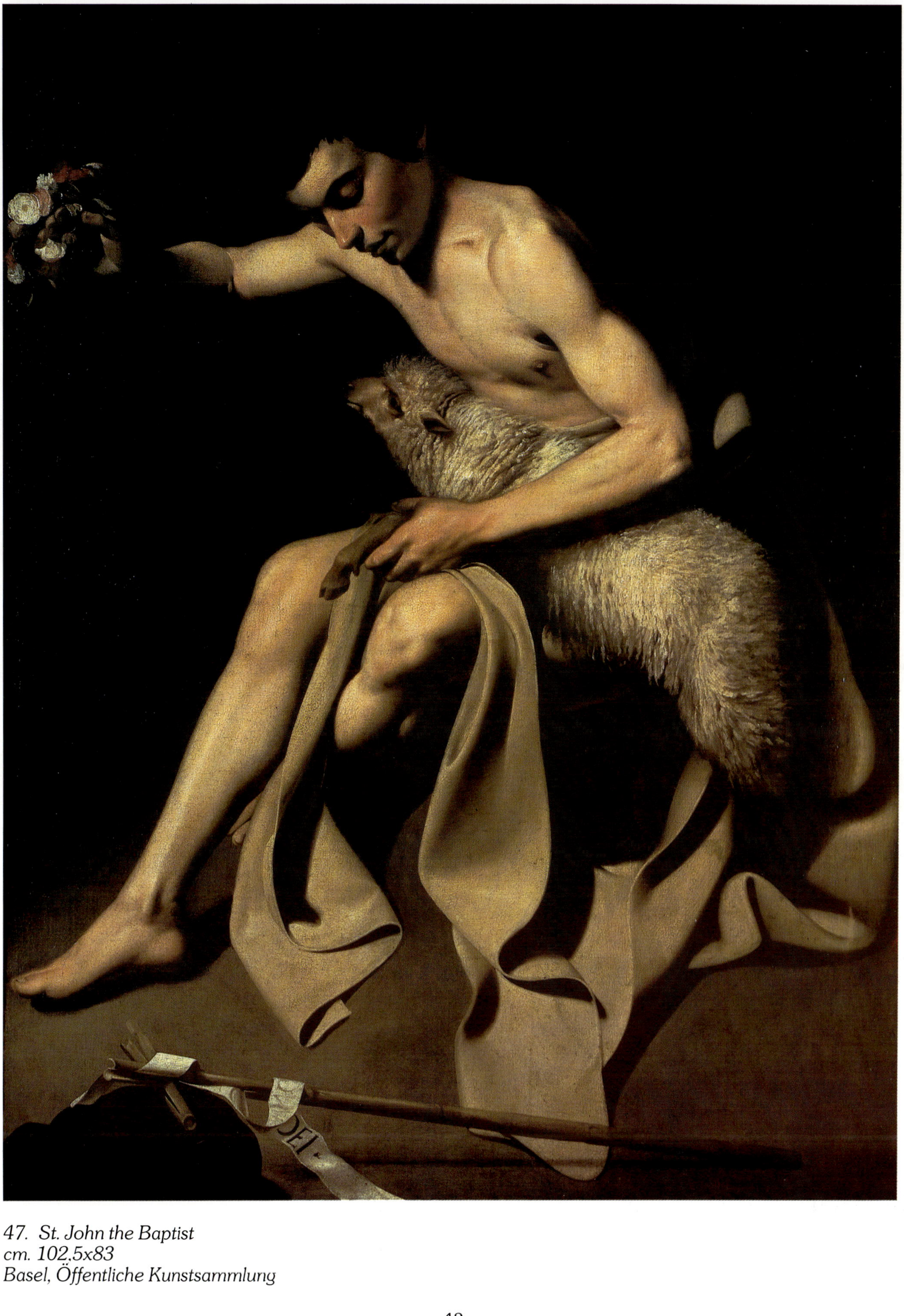

47

47. St. John the Baptist
cm. 102,5x83
Basel, Öffentliche Kunstsammlung

44 traditional iconography. A Christ in the Garden from the Giustiniani Collection, destroyed in Berlin during the war, is known to us today through extant photographs. This was a wonderful composition that caught the instant in which Christ awakes the sleeping apostles. The construction of the scene descends toward the lower right corner. St. Peter in particular is shown in a classical position (which has been called Carracci-like), with the containment that characterizes this moment in the artist's career. The palace in Potsdam known as Sans-
43 souci houses a Doubting of St. Thomas surely by Caravaggio (and also originally from the Giustiniani Collection). This is another of his major masterpieces. The tightly closed composition concentrates the viewer's attention, like that of the apostles, on the physical act of proving the identity of Christ, which is studied with objective naturalism, without a touch of the complacent realism that the theme would have allowed. Here we have one of the surest precedents for the art of Velasquez (this is not a general reference: the Spanish artist may have seen this painting during his two visits to Rome); indeed the composition is so modern that a straight line may be drawn from paintings like this one, to Manet.

45 The Capture of Christ in the Museum of Eastern and Western Art in Odessa, though still of uncertain attribution, is very probably the original known through a series of copies. In evaluating the composition we must bear in mind that the left side has been mutilated; but the tight rhythm, with which the curve that descends slightly toward the left also describes a normal rotation of the paintings, is among Caravaggio's greatest creations. The artist's followers, and especially the Frenchman Valentin, would have liked this theme very much.

Other themes of Caravaggio's reexamine the single-figure painting in a new light. A probable original in the
46 Prado in Madrid addresses the subject of David and Goliath, which the artist repeatedly dealt with later in his career, with a perfect linearity of means and intelligence of iconographic invention. As in the early Renaissance, David is shown as the adolescent who triumphs not by his strength, but by his power of character and his faith. The oblique pose of the figure (David stands partly parallel to the picture plane) is constructed with admirable skill.

Another painting that may belong to this moment of
47 Caravaggio's career is the much-debated St. John in Basel, who seems to draw the bouquet of flowers in his right hand away from the lamb to keep him from nib-
48 bling on it. The Amour Victorious in Berlin, clearly attributable to the artist, has always been considered one of his greatest masterpieces. Caravaggio painted it for Marchese Giustiniani, in competition with Baglione (a rival artist who at one point actually sued Caravaggio, even if he was later to become his biographer). Caravaggio's painting, which, as we know from the sources, Giustiniani preferred over all the other paintings in his collections, is described with singular felicity in the inventory of 1638: "A painting with a laughing Cupid, in the act of mocking the world." In effect the figure sets up a direct, special, and privileged relationship with the viewer, with an immediate appeal that is truly extraordinary. One is bewildered by this painting, by the absolute freedom that the subject obviously enjoys, detaching himself from mere mortals who must obey the laws of nature. The figure is indeed "in the act of mocking the world," with a complete impunity, a self-assurance that produce a mixture of astonishment and envy. As early as 1603 Murtola wrote: "Don't look don't look / in this canvas Love / will set fire to your heart." The painting probably shows Earthly Love (Baglione had painted Divine Love) triumphant over the Virtues and Sciences, symbolized by the musical instruments, pen and book, compass and square, scepter, laurel, and armor at his feet.

The next phase of Caravaggio's career was distinguished by intense creativity. Single figures alternate with small groups in paintings for private collectors and a few splendid altarpieces, two of which are still among his most admired works. But these are also years in which his increasing fame as an artist collided headlong with the highly censurable episodes to which a quarrelsome and trouble-making character compelled him. This was the extremist aspect of a potentially positive character, akin to his passionate nonconformism. Unfortunately his lack of self-control, coupled with his desire to crush all opponents almost physically, resulted in bloody and even fatal conflicts which, in addition to placing his life in jeopardy, obliged him to flee from Rome and to wander around for years before meeting with his solitary death on the Tuscan coast. The same excessive and irrepressible desire to make himself known that led him, as soon as he had a little money, to parade around town expensively dressed and accompanied by a page who held his sword, caused him to suspect offences and enemies where in all likelihood there were neither. In any event the acts of blood and violence with which he was associated became increasingly numerous after 1600. They also became more and more

48. Amor Victorious
cm. 154x110
Berlin, Staatliche Museen

49. Deposition
cm. 300x203
Vatican, Pinacoteca

50. Madonna dei Pellegrini
cm. 260x150
Rome, Sant'Agostino

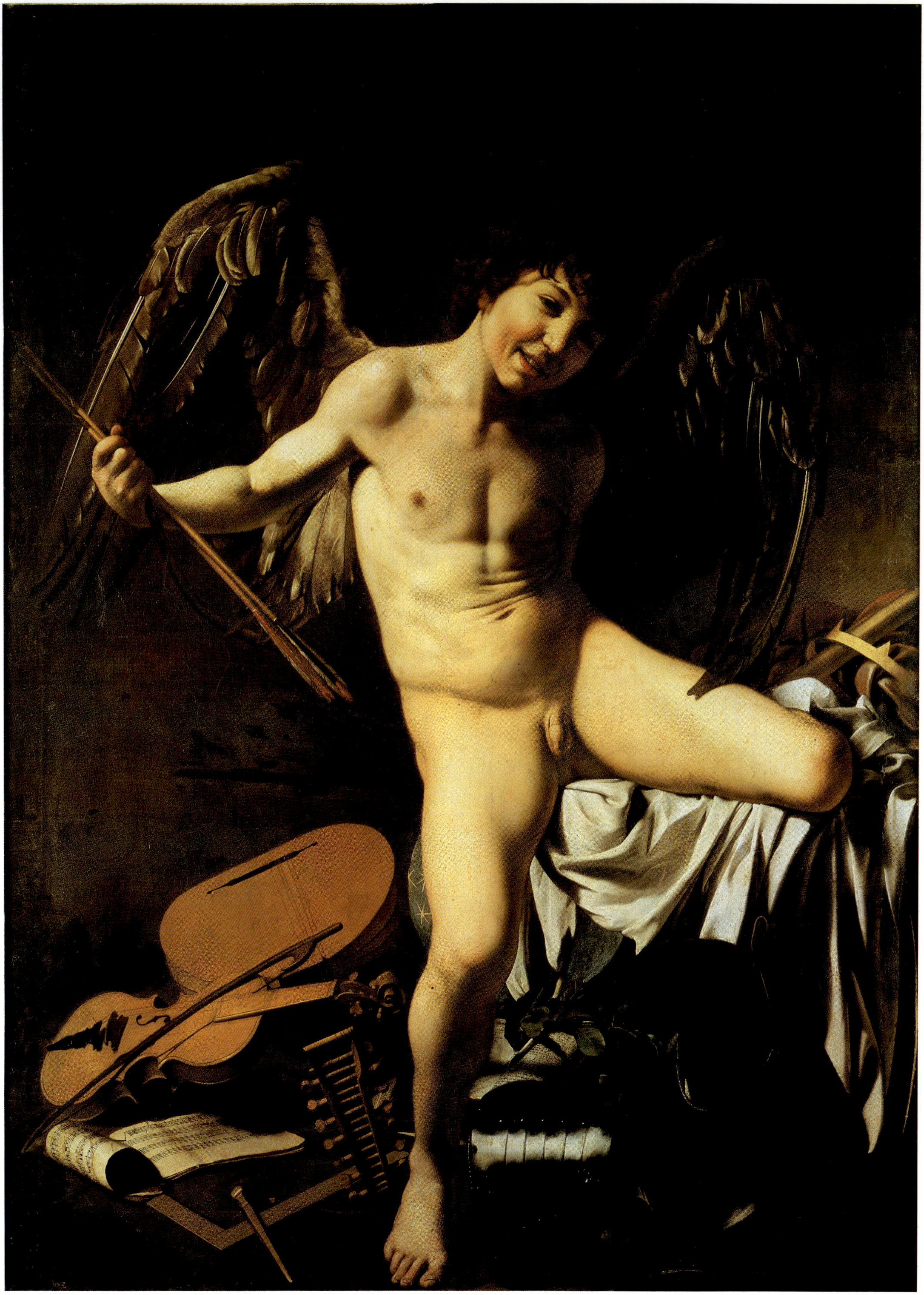

48

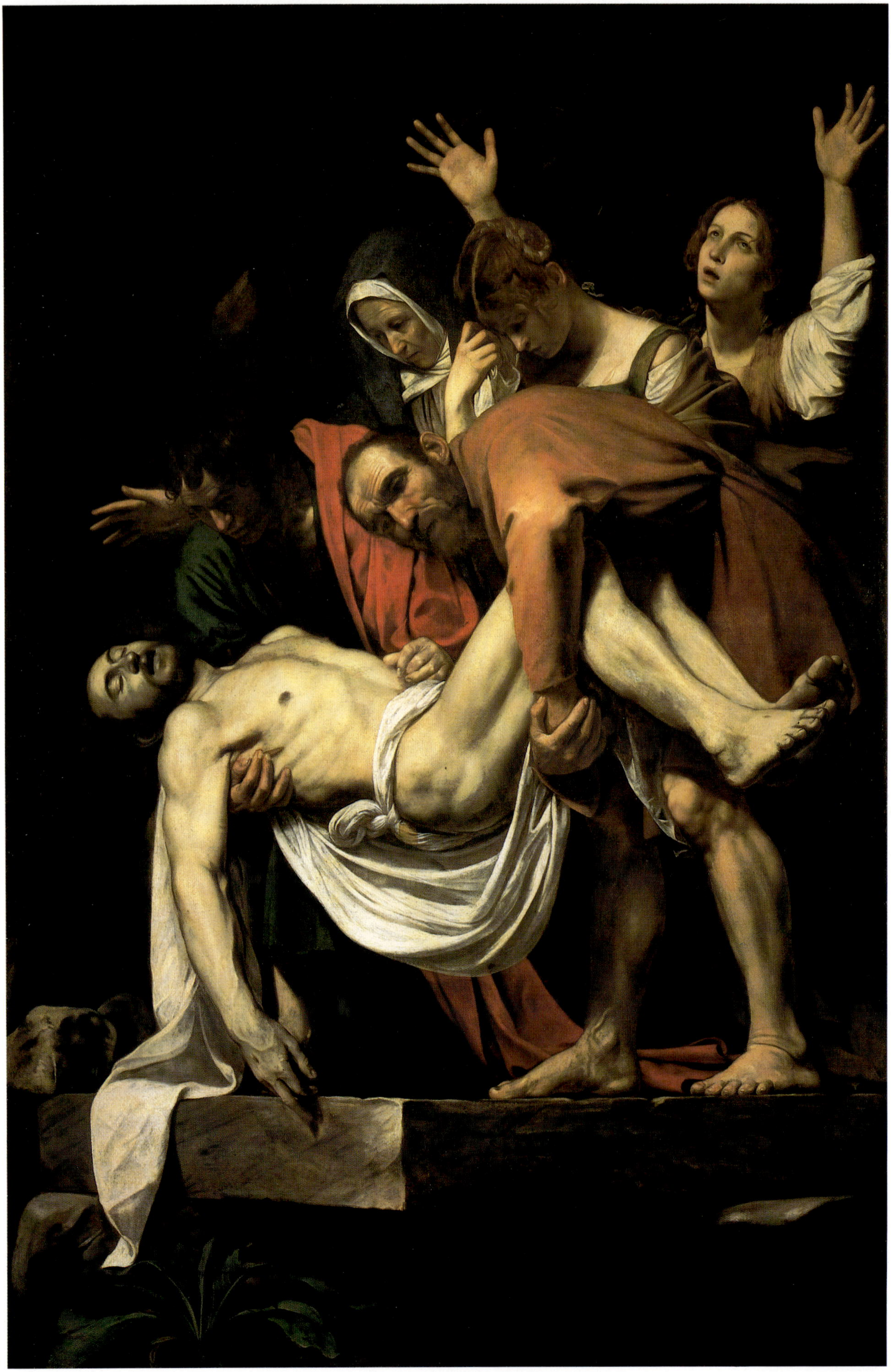

49

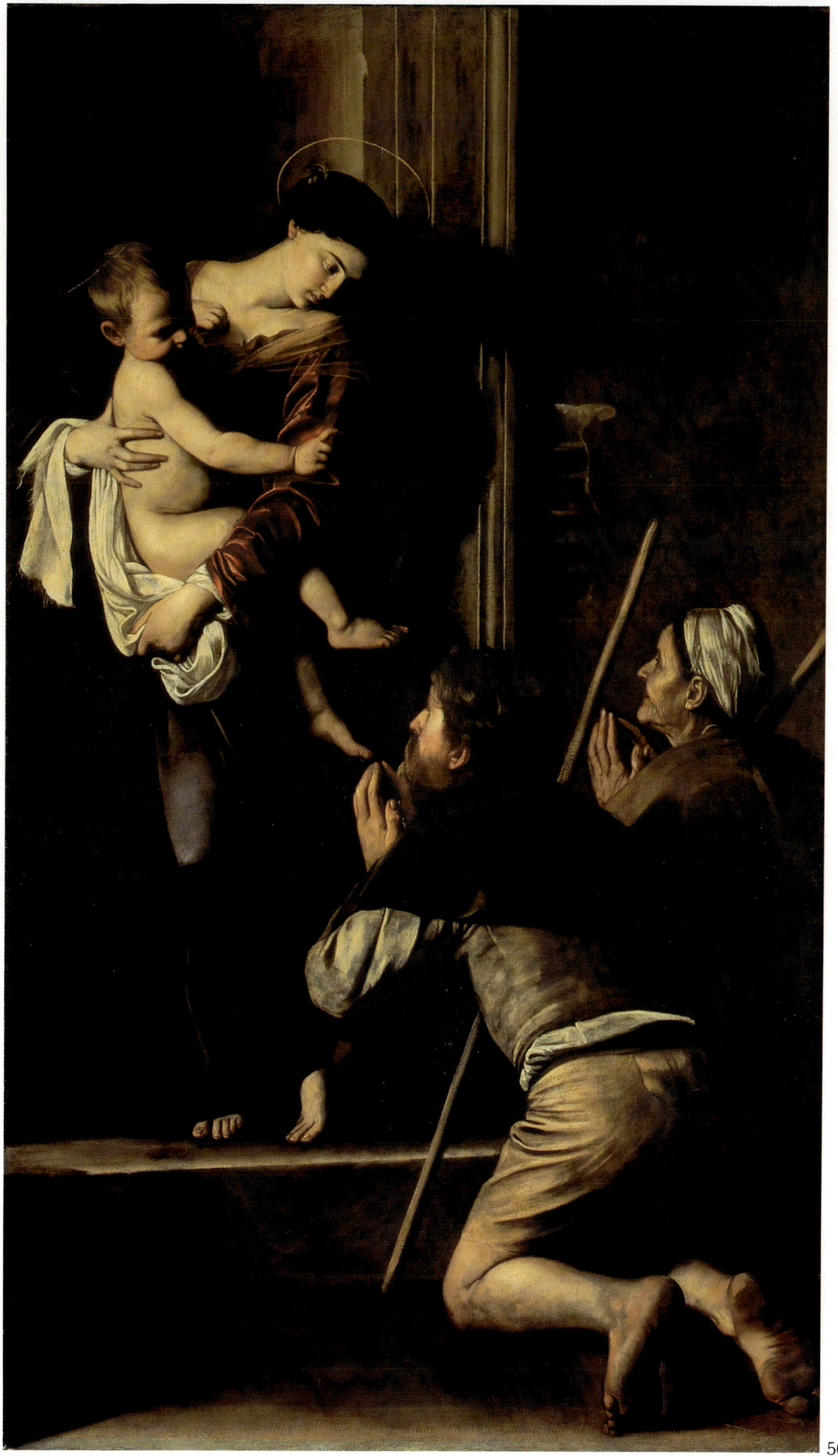

50

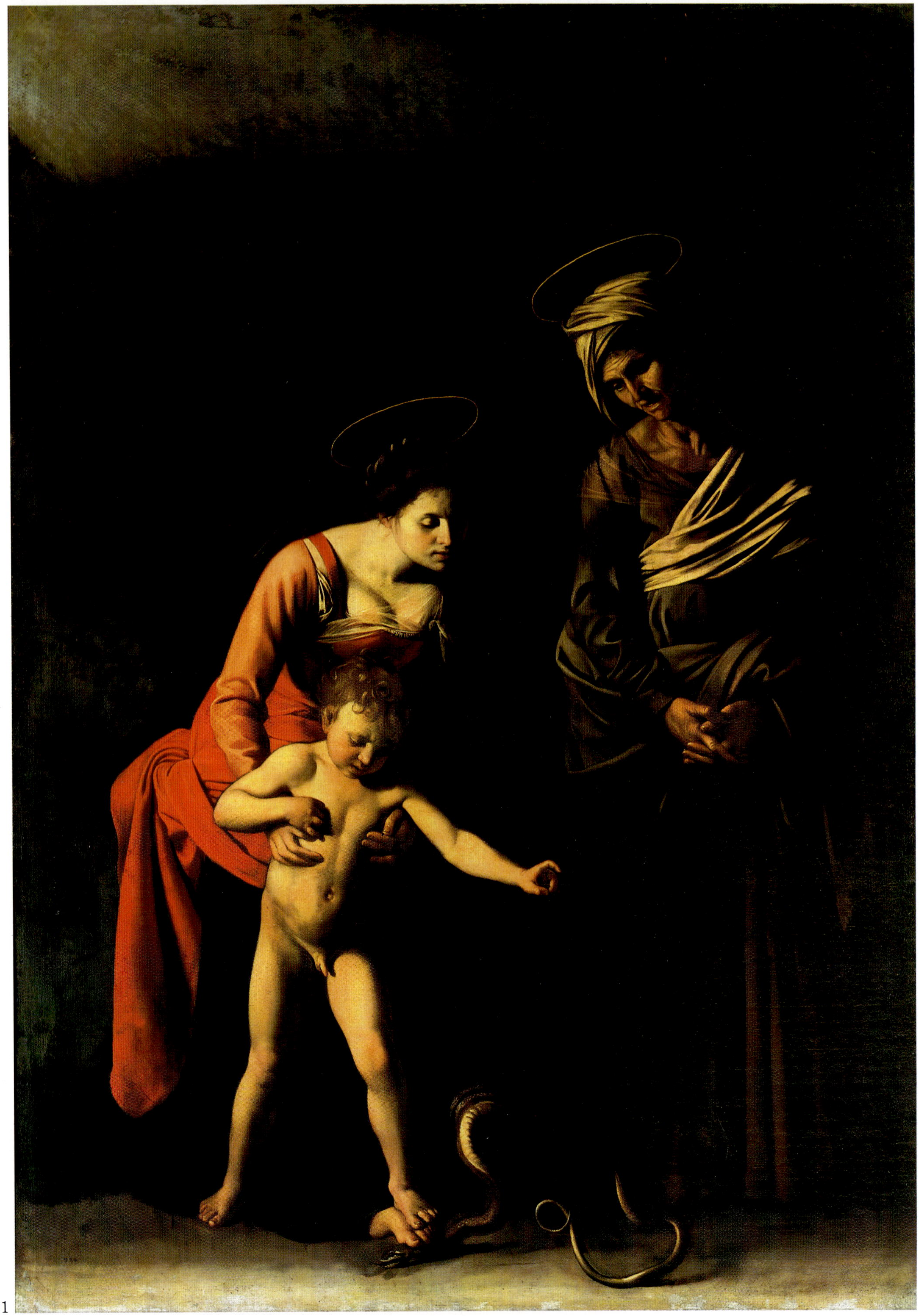

51

51. Madonna dei Palafrenieri
cm. 292x211
Rome, Galleria Borghese

52. St. John the Baptist
cm. 172.5x104.5
Kansas City, Nelson Gallery

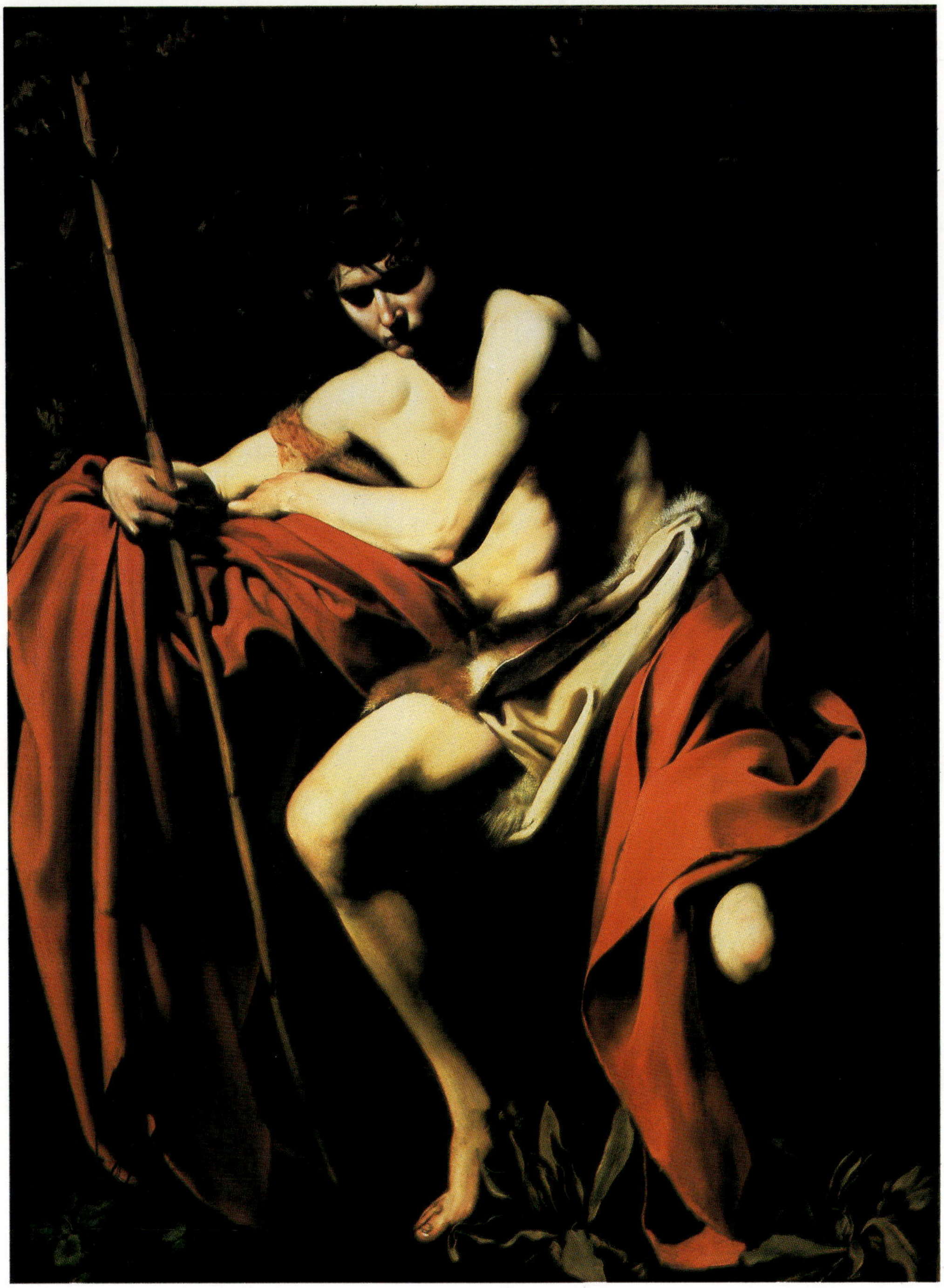

52

serious, culminating in murder in 1606. On 19 November 1600, he was sued for assaulting a certain Girolamo Stampa with a club and sword. On 7 February 1601 he reconciled himself with a sergeant at arms of Castel Sant'Angelo whom he had wounded with his sword. The year 1603 witnessed the lengthy episode of the suit for defamation brought against him by Baglione, of which there are numerous reports, and which got Merisi a brief prison term. On 24 and 25 April 1604 a waiter in a tavern denounced him for having thrown a tray of artichokes in his face (when Caravaggio had asked which were cooked in butter and which in oil, and had been told to stick his nose in them and he'd figure it out by himself, he reacted as mentioned), and possibly for having threatened him with his sword. In October and November 1604 he was brought in twice by the police for having insulted them with cries of "up my ass," apparently without provocation. On 28 May 1605 a dagger and sword were confiscated from him. On 20 July he was back in prison for slander against a certain Laura and her daughter. On 29 July the notary Pasqualone reported him for the blows on the head received from Caravaggio's sword over a certain Lena, the painter's girlfriend. On 1 November he was denounced for throwing stones through his former landlady's windows. On 24 October, when questioned after being injured, he replied in typical mafia style: "I cut myself [on the throat and on the left ear!] with my own sword. I fell down on

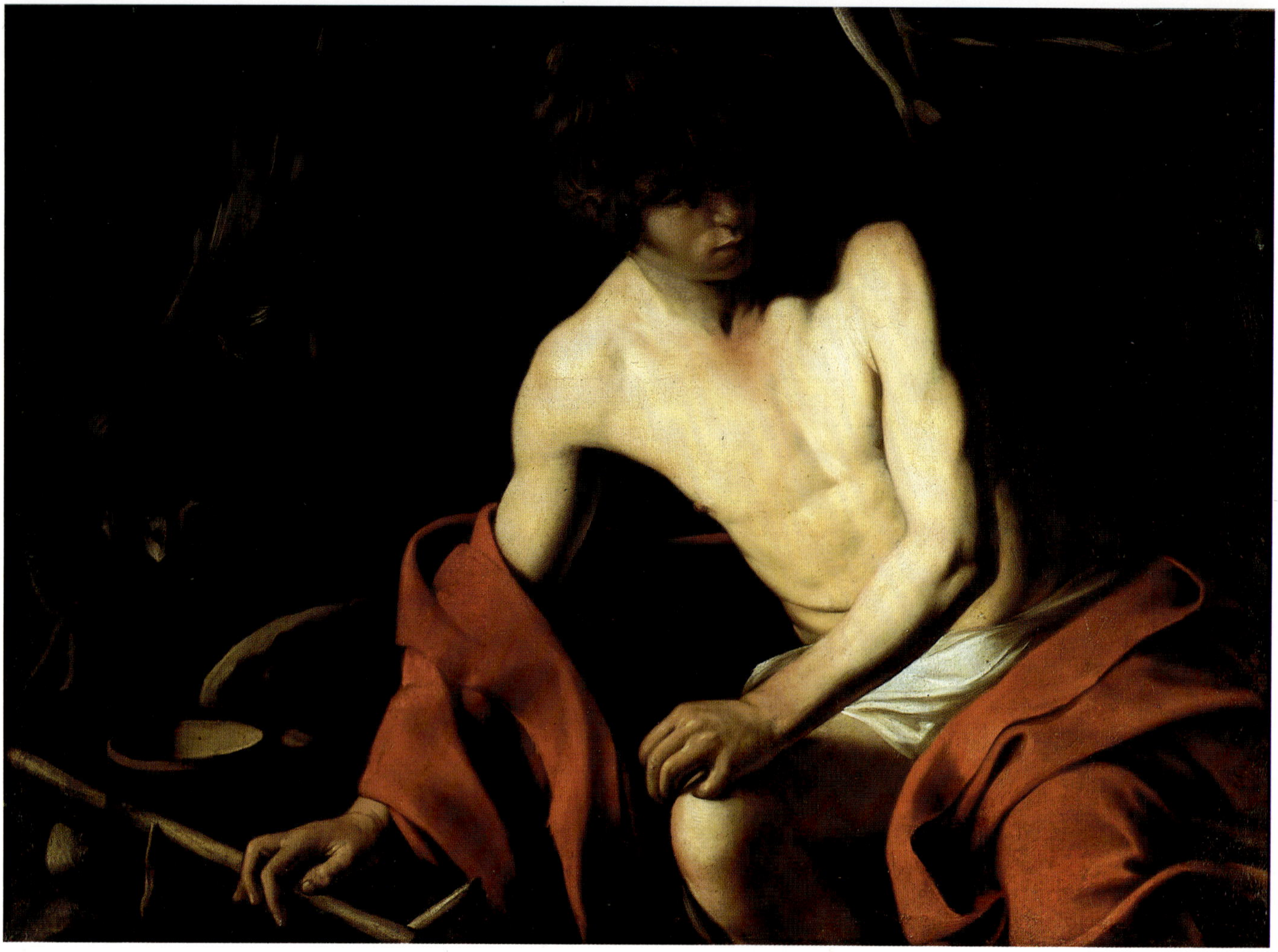

53

the street, I don't remember where, and there wasn't anybody around". He wound up with a 500-scudo fine and confinement to his own home. This unbelievable crescendo led to the quarrel of 31 May 1606, which broke out on the sidelines of a tennis court and involved Caravaggio and seven others. Caravaggio killed Ranuccio Tommasoni of Terni, and, himself injured, was compelled to take refuge in the fiefs of his friends, the Colonna. Some writers have taken great pleasure in Caravaggio's "criminality," particularly in the positivist period. It seemed all too easy to link the artist's tenebrous aesthetics, the use of dark tones as a general policy (Bellori writes, "he always used a black background," and says of Caravaggio himself, "he was of a dark countenance"), with a similarly colored soul. Certainly, of our three great innovators of painting, Caravaggio makes an abysmally bad impression, as opposed to Giotto, who may be taken as an "average" figure (Giotto was well immersed in his century, intent on building himself a name and fortune), and to Masaccio, as "positive" (Masaccio is the fair and unselfish person par excellence).

Nevertheless Caravaggio produced the supremely
49 "classical" Vatican Deposition during these troubled years. Executed between 1602 and 1604 for the so-called Chiesa Nuova, Santa Maria in Vallicella in Rome, this was one of the more widely admired and closely studied paintings of its age, as the free copies by Rubens, Fragonard, Géricault, and Cézanne, its extreme popularization through immense series of prints, and the numerous contemporary copies attest. The interpretation of the event is, as in the second St. Paul for Santa Maria del Popolo, restrained and limited in its effects; even Mary Cleophas, with her arms outstretched, expresses a gesture of universal execration that leads the viewer to pious meditation, rather than to a piercing cry as in his earlier aesthetics. A precise equilibrium governs the composition. The physical weight of the body becomes the moral weight of the world's grief. The figure on the right, Nicodemus, turns toward the observer to establish a psychological bond that is also a specific reference: the scene is viewed as from the tomb; the impression is almost as if the figures are about to surrender the body of Christ, if not to the observer, at least to someone standing in the same place. The identification is therefore complete, the involvement inescapable. The way the painting affected nineteenth-century artists is understandable. It combines a structural classicism that is timeless (Cézanne) with an extremely strong sense of drama (Géricault).

There are two other altarpieces that do not aspire to

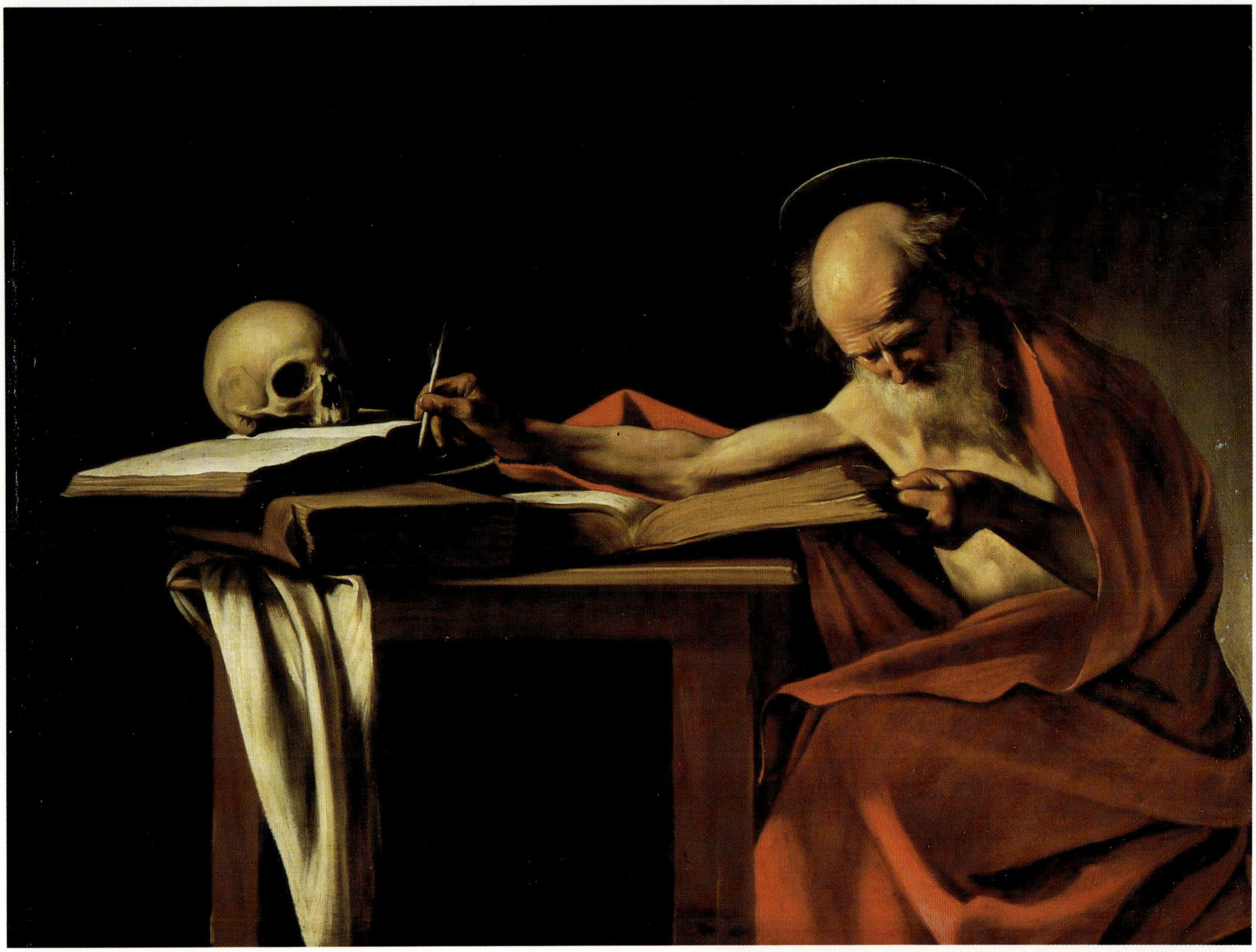

54

53. St. John the Baptist
cm. 99x134
Rome, Galleria Nazionale di Arte Antica

54. St. Jerome
cm. 112x157
Rome, Galleria Borghese

55. St. Jerome
cm. 110x81
Montserrat, Monastery

55

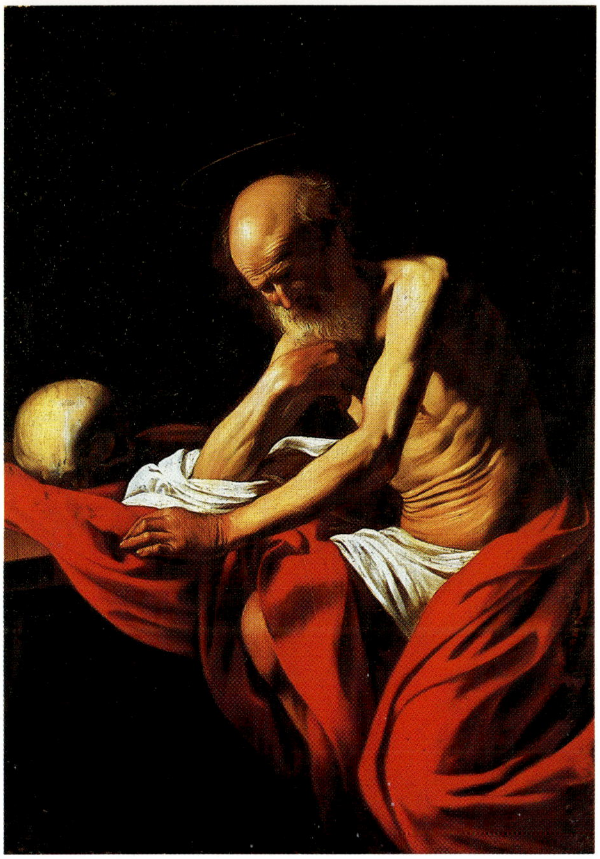

56

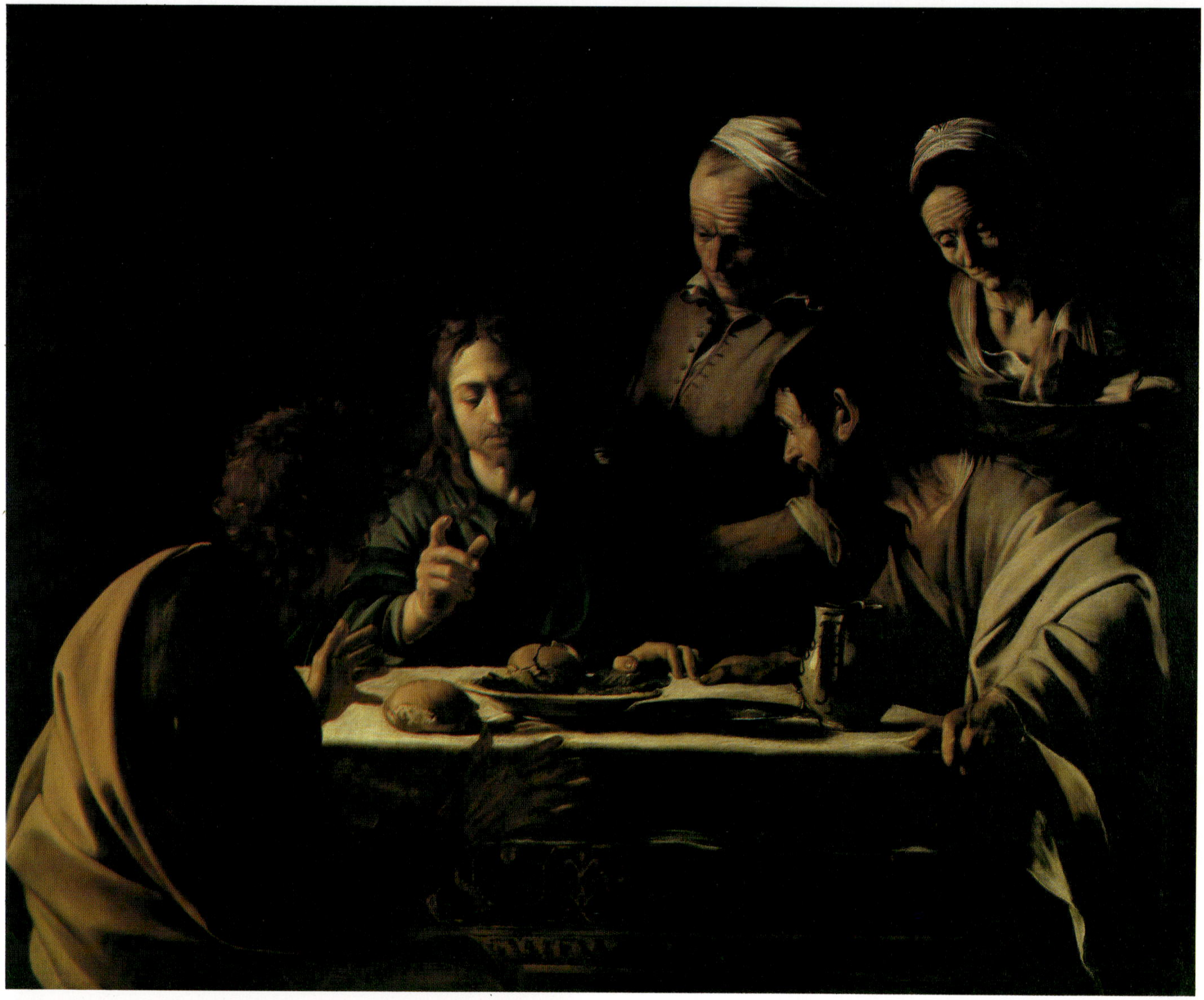

57

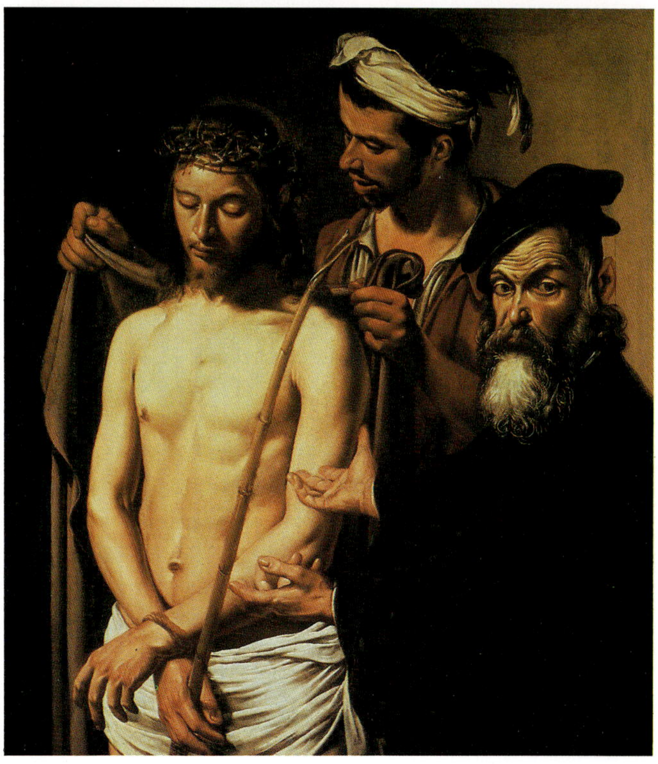

56. Supper in Emmaus
cm. 141x175
Milan, Pinacoteca di Brera

57. Ecce Homo
cm. 128x103
Genoa, Palazzo Rosso

58. Supper in Emmaus, detail.
Milan, Pinacoteca di Brera

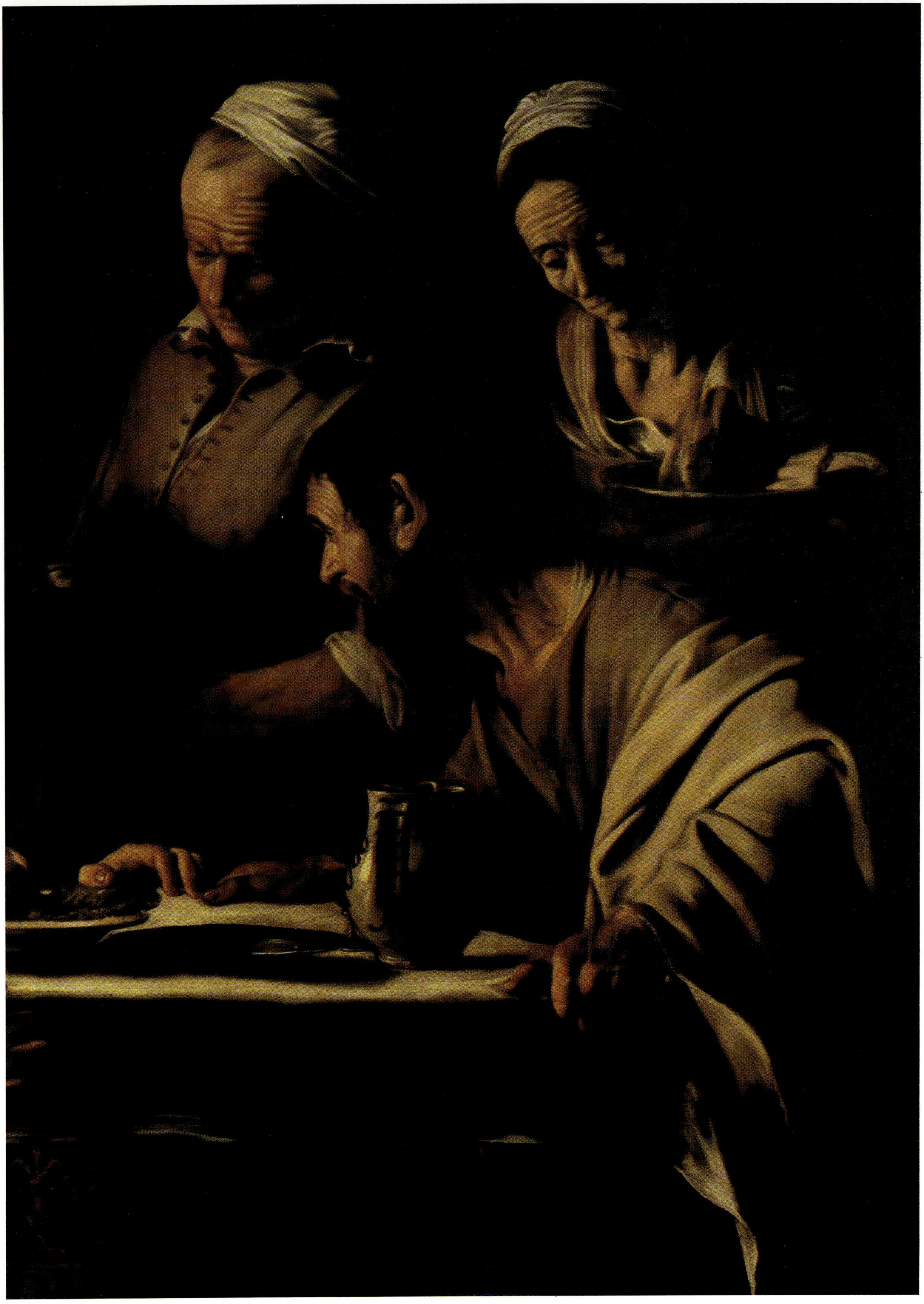

58

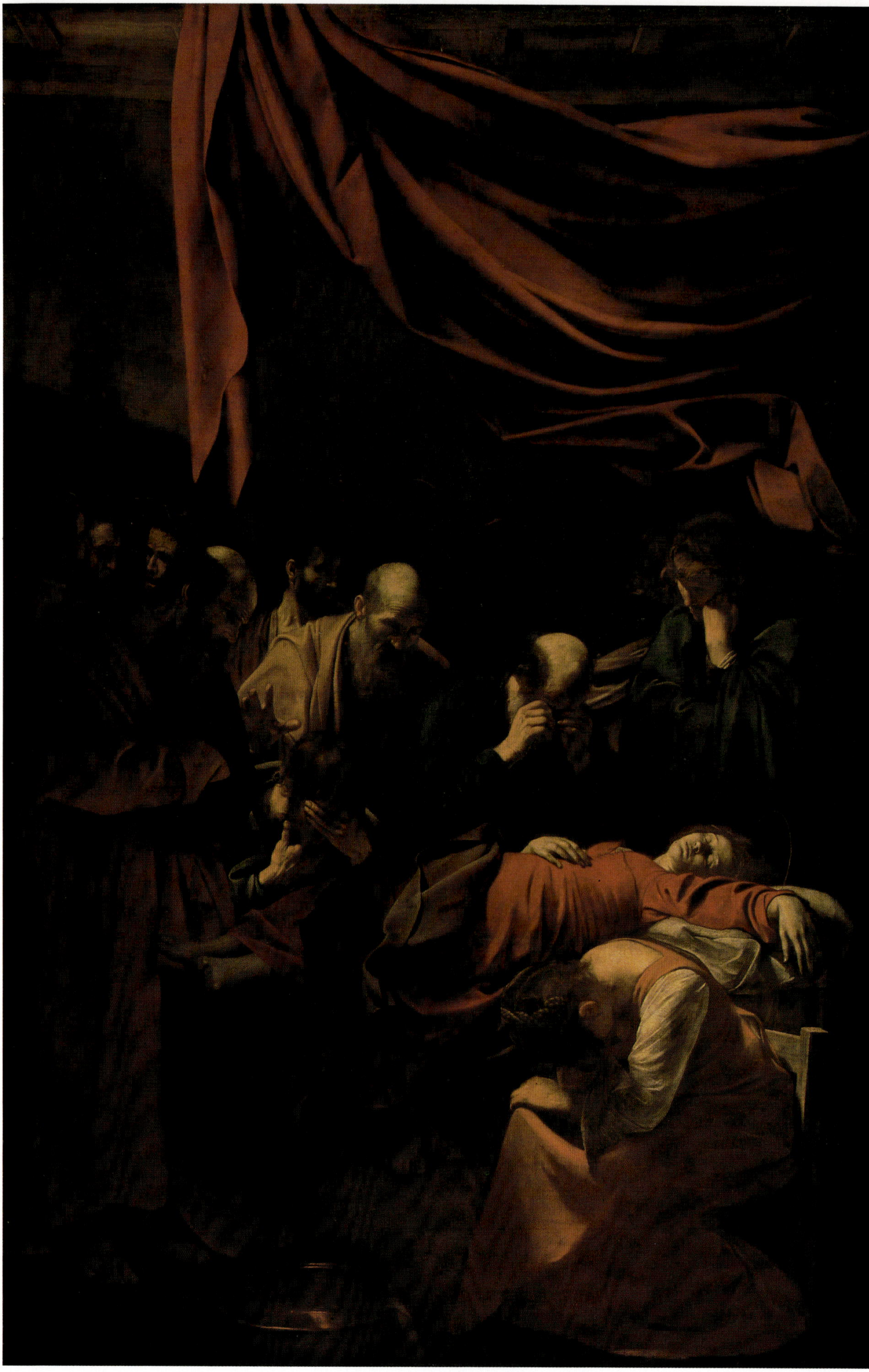

59

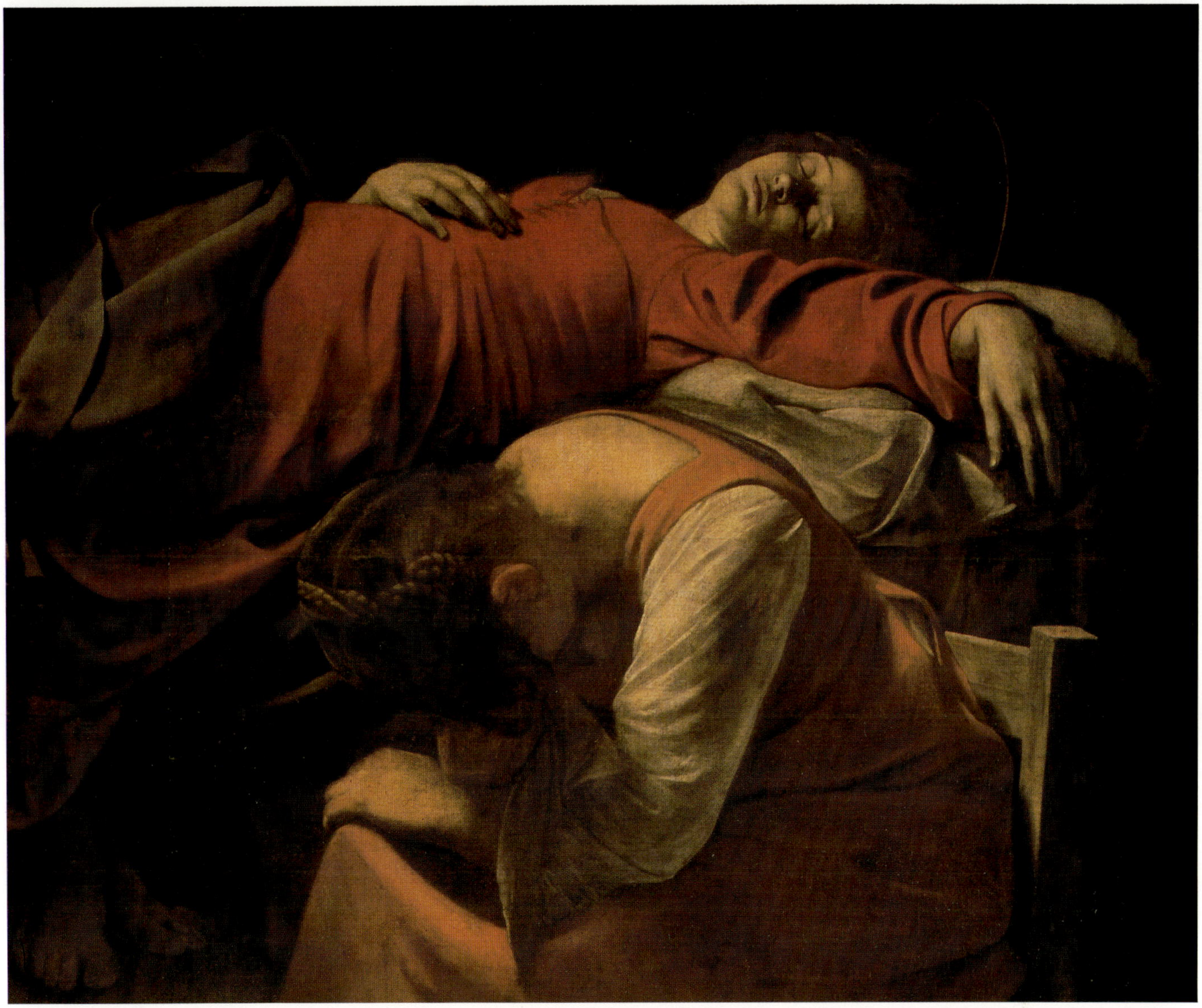

60

59. *Death of the Virgin*
cm. 369x245
Paris, Louvre

60. *Death of the Virgin, detail.*
Paris, Louvre

61. *The Seven Acts of Mercy*
cm. 390x260
Naples, Church of Pio Monte della Misericordia

62. *Madonna del Rosario*
cm. 364x249
Vienna, Kunsthistorisches Museum

the majesty of the Vatican Deposition. The Madonna di Loreto, or Madonna dei Pellegrini, which may still be seen on the altar for which it was painted, in Sant'Agostino in Rome, was criticized, according to Baglione (1642), for the indelicacy of the pilgrims' muddy feet and ragged bonnets. But it has been rightly observed that the criticisms that were levied in academic circles must have regarded instead the absolute iconographic novelty of the painting, which consisted in making no reference to the Sacred House of Loreto, but in showing the pilgrimage itself — and as usual, devoid of hagiographic references. The portrayal of the Madonna as a woman who appears at the door to show the pilgrims the blessing Child, the goal of their journey, is achieved less through the barely noticeable halos, than through the true majesty of her splendid person (for whom the model was that Lena on whose behalf Caravaggio fought with the notary Pasqualone, the girl's disillusioned suitor). Portrayed in a precocious nineteenth-century manner that foreshadows Courbet, the woman appears in the statuary pose of classical art, as further proof of

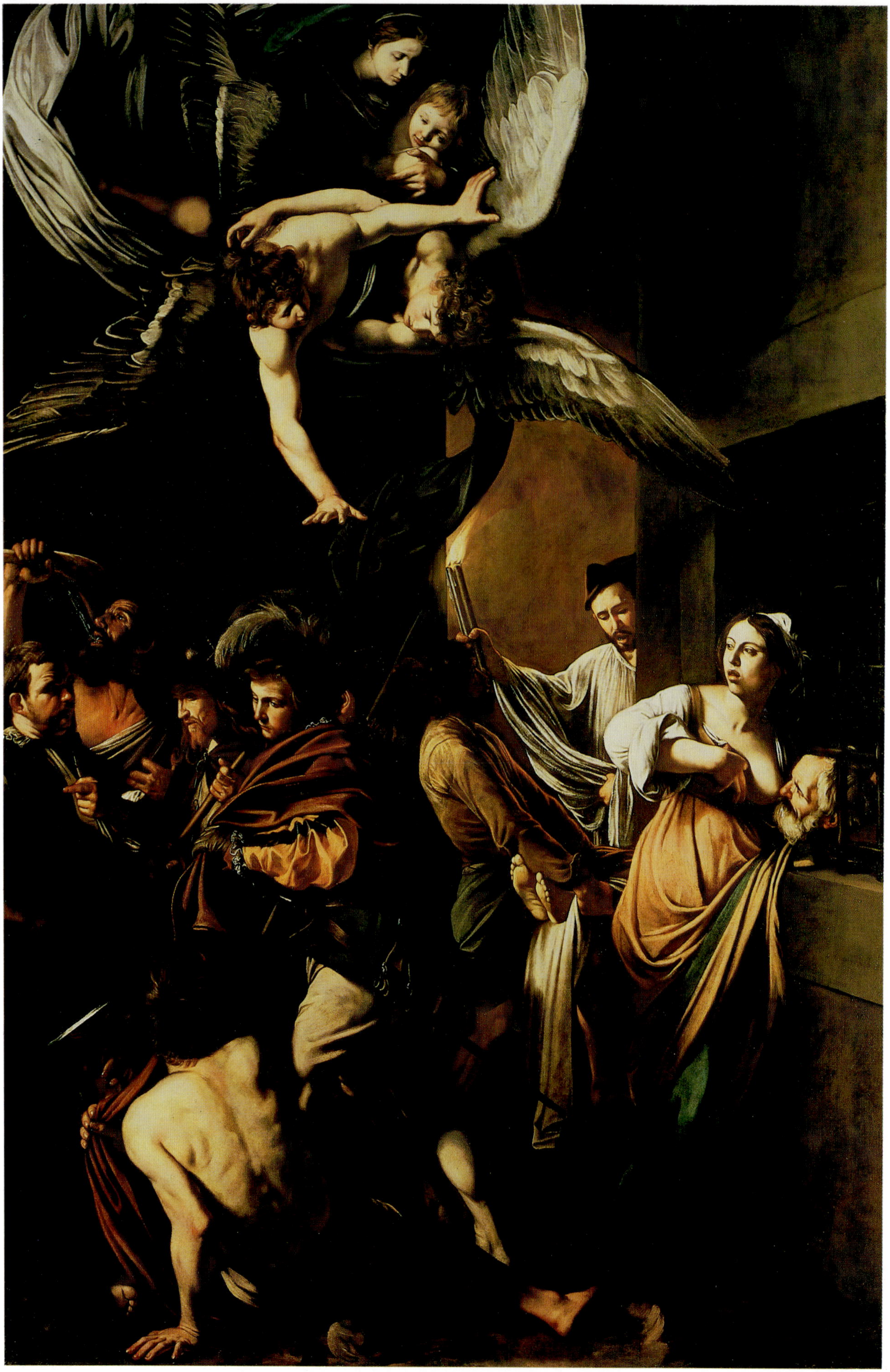

61

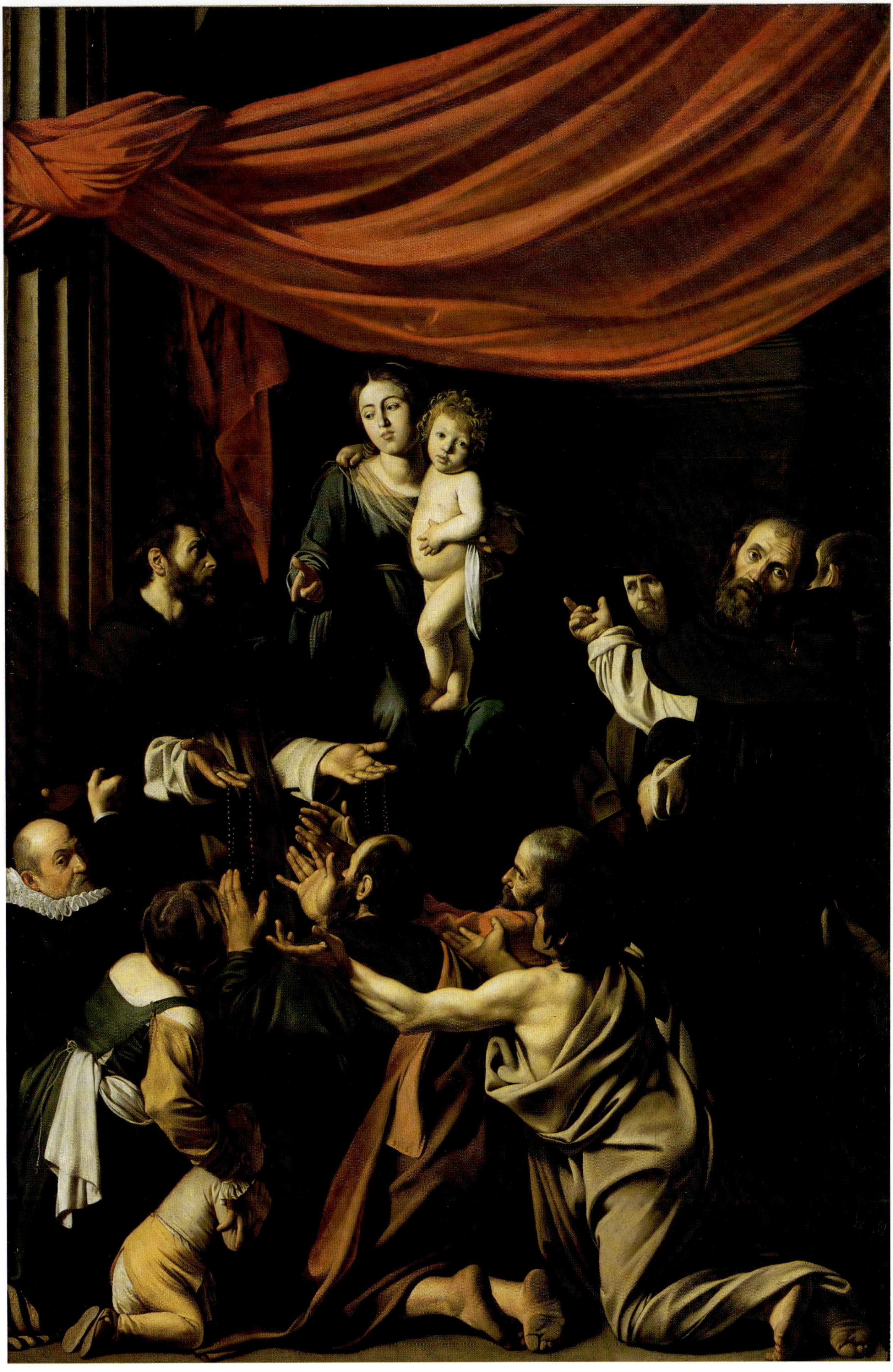

62

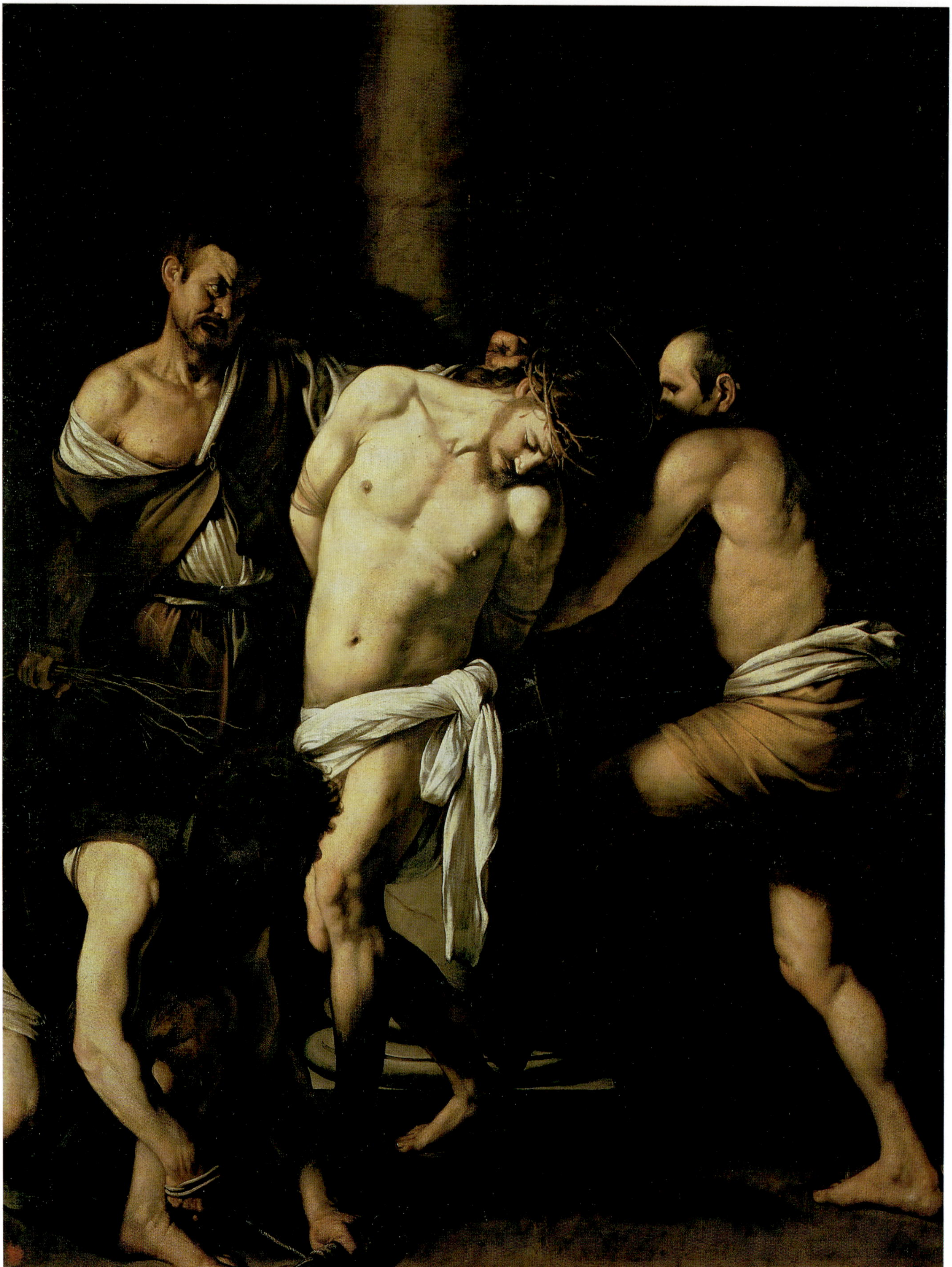

63

63. Flagellation of Christ
cm. 286x213
Naples, Pinacoteca di Capodimonte

64. Crucifixion of St. Andrew
cm. 202,5x152,7
Cleveland, Museum of Art

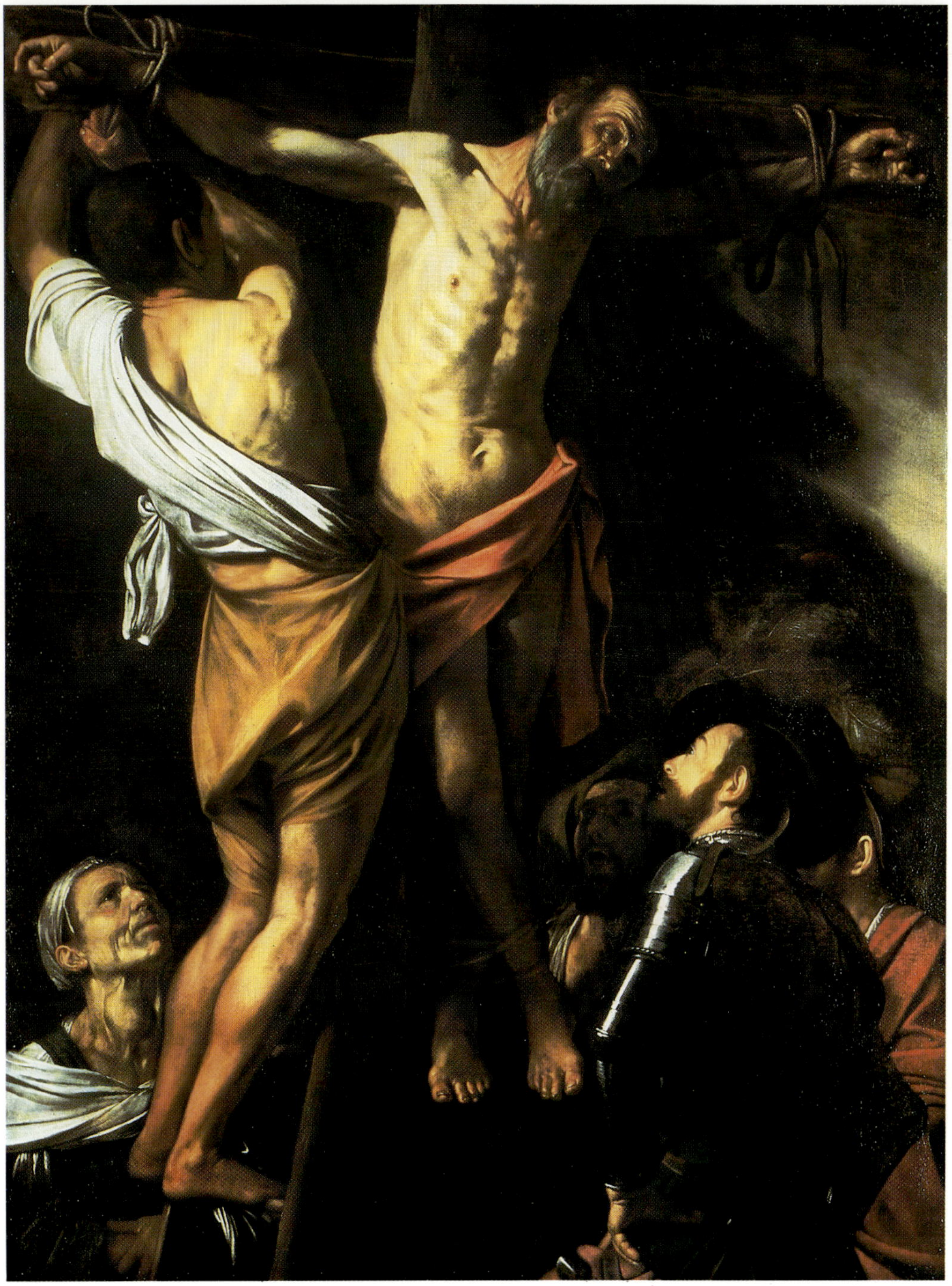

64

Caravaggio's ability to see ordinary events as history.

51 The so-called Madonna dei Palafrenieri was painted for an altar in St. Peter's, but was removed after only two days. Today it is in the Galleria Borghese. In this allegory of the Immaculate Conception, the Madonna and Child crush the serpent in the presence of St. Anne, patron saint of the Palafrenieri. St. Anne's pose (her head is tilted and her hands are joined) takes up the conventional iconography of one of the witnesses of the Crucifixion (the Virgin and St. John), as though to introduce the purpose of the Conception, Redemption. At the same time St. Anne, over whom the light plays forcefully, drawing her out of the shadows just far enough, is painted in the same style that would predominate in Caravaggio's last years. Once again the artist alludes skillfully, almost tacitly, to a room of which he gives no description. The parts that the artist has chosen to model in the light emerge from the darkness. Certainly we cannot help remembering Bellori's observation that Caravaggio's paintings could not be viewed to advantage in dark chapels.

These two paintings bring us to the years 1505-06. In this period Caravaggio did not put aside his private commissions; indeed, they became ever more numerous (he was actually well enough off to turn down a commission from the duke of Modena). At this point in his career, as earlier, this kind of commission called for paintings containing one or more figures. Two figures of

65 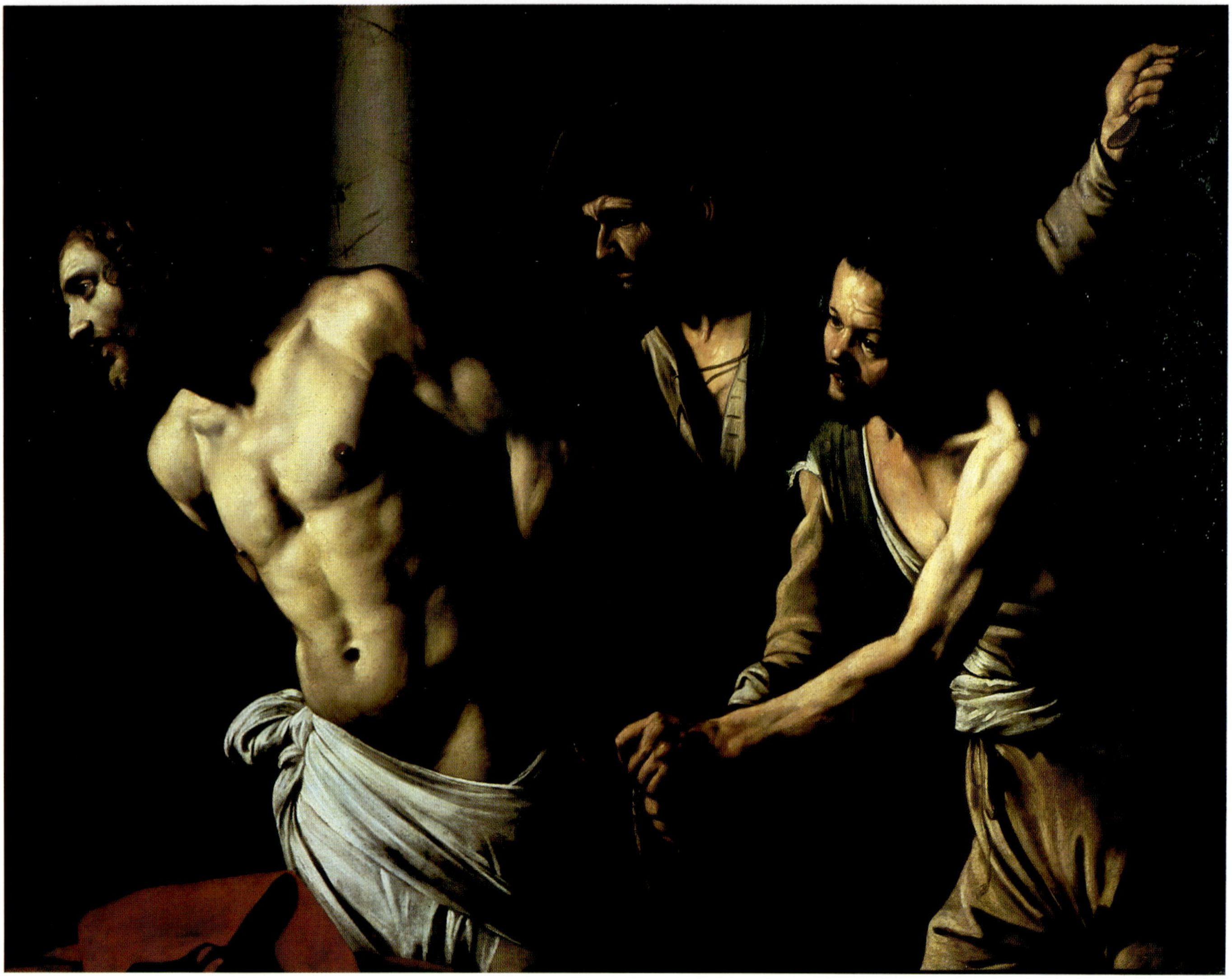

saints appear in more than one version. The artist dealt with St. John the Baptist in two splendid compositions,
52 one in the Kansas City gallery, the other in the Galleria
53 Nazionale di Arte Antica in Rome. The former is laid out vertically, the latter horizontally. Both lend themselves to a modernistic reading aimed at pointing out a certain air between contempt and arrogance. In effect what we are dealing with here are splendid exercises in modeling the body through the play of light and shadow. In the version now in America, the figure is set before a dense curtain of plants; in that in Rome, there is only the trunk of a cypress tree, on the left. Both are admirable feats of painting, and it is understandable that collectors competed with each other for the artist's works. Caravaggio in turn knew how to make apparently uninteresting religious themes into paintings desirable even for his aristocratic patrons.

54 The St. Jerome is another of these. In both the horizontal version in the Galleria Borghese, and the vertical
55 one in the Spanish monastery of Montserrat (the latter painting was in a private collection in Rome until the beginning of our century), Caravaggio redeems the apparently dry theme by his brilliant handling of the color of

65. Christ at the Column
cm. 134.5x174.5
Rouen, Musée des Beaux-Arts

66. Salome with the Head of the Baptist
cm. 90.5x107
London, National Gallery

67. David with the Head of Goliath
cm. 90.5x116.5
Vienna, Kunsthistorisches Museum

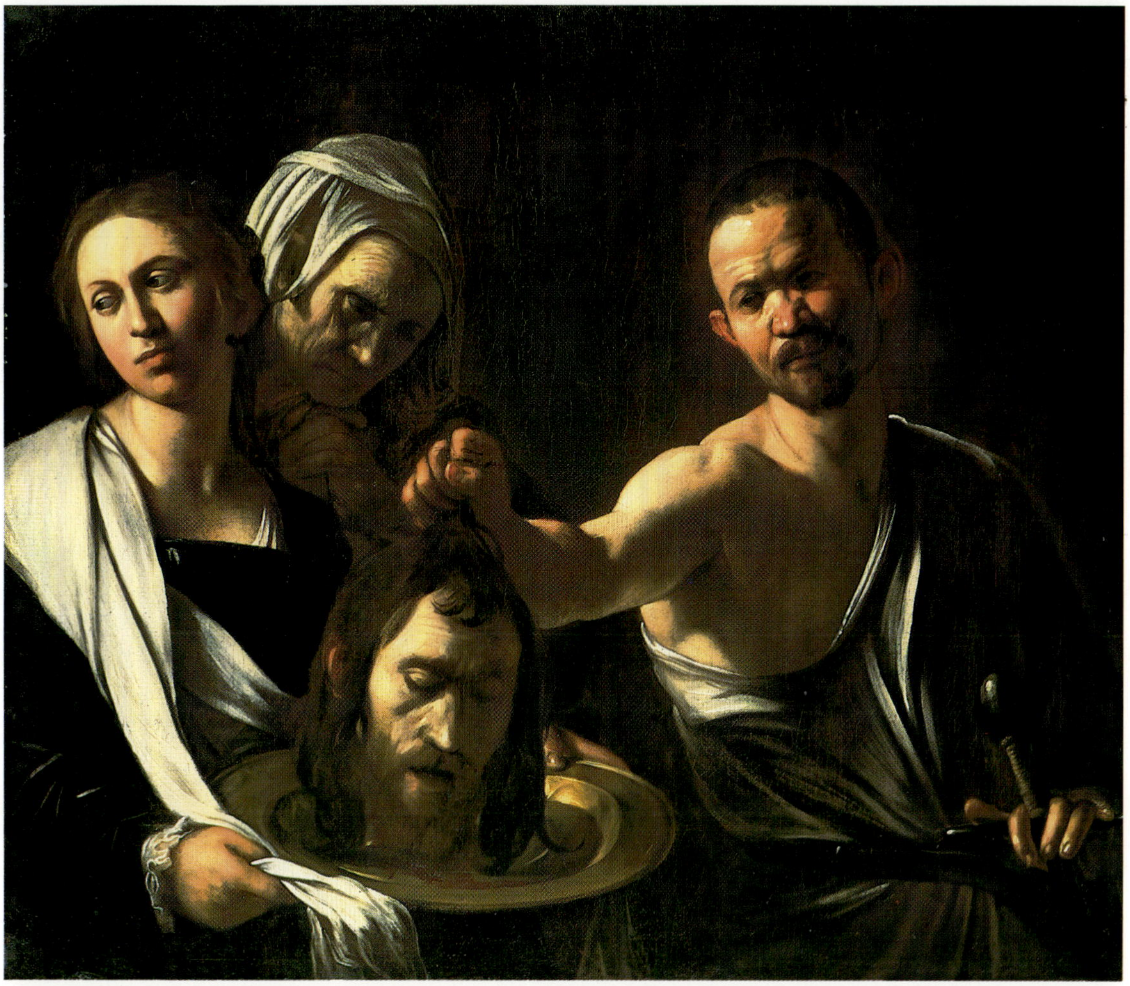

66

67

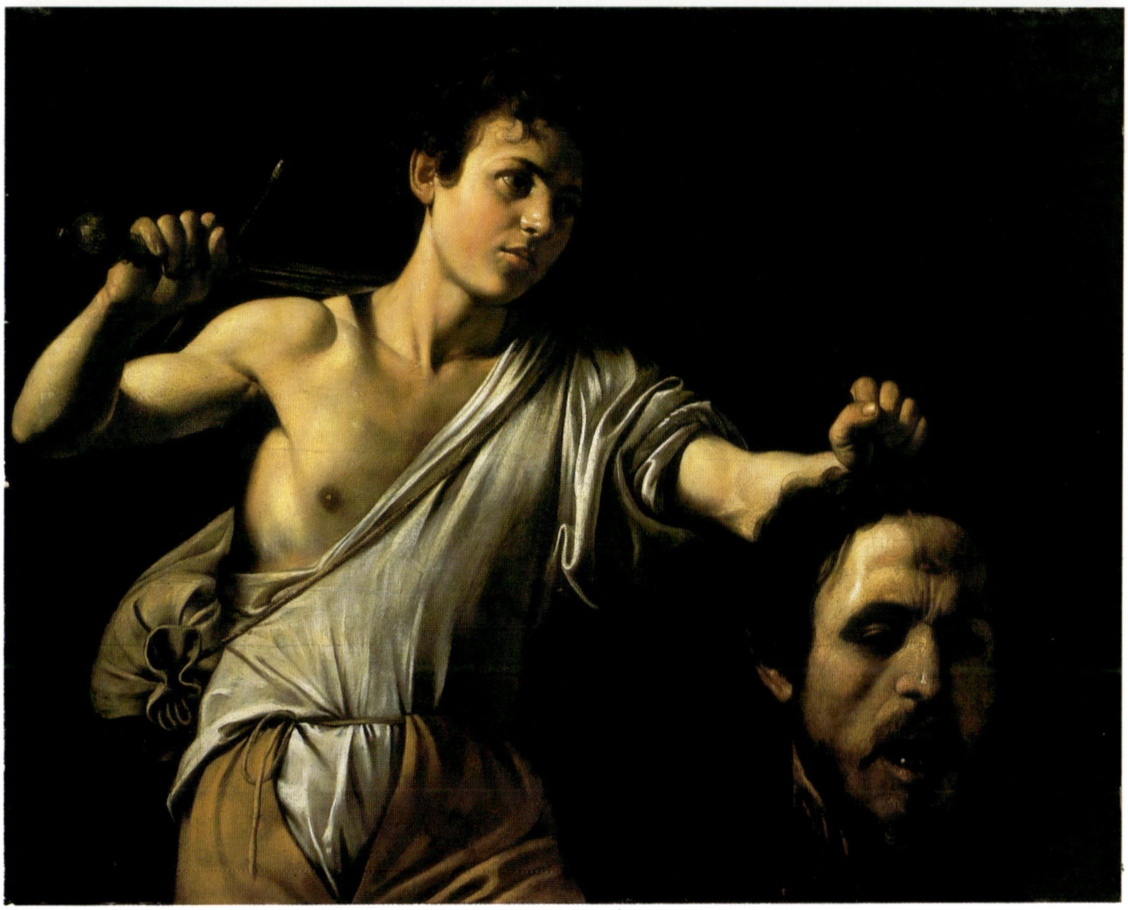

68. *Portrait of Alof de Wignacourt*
cm. 195x134
Paris, Louvre

69. *Portrait of Alof de Wignacourt*
cm. 144x95
Florence, Palazzo Pitti

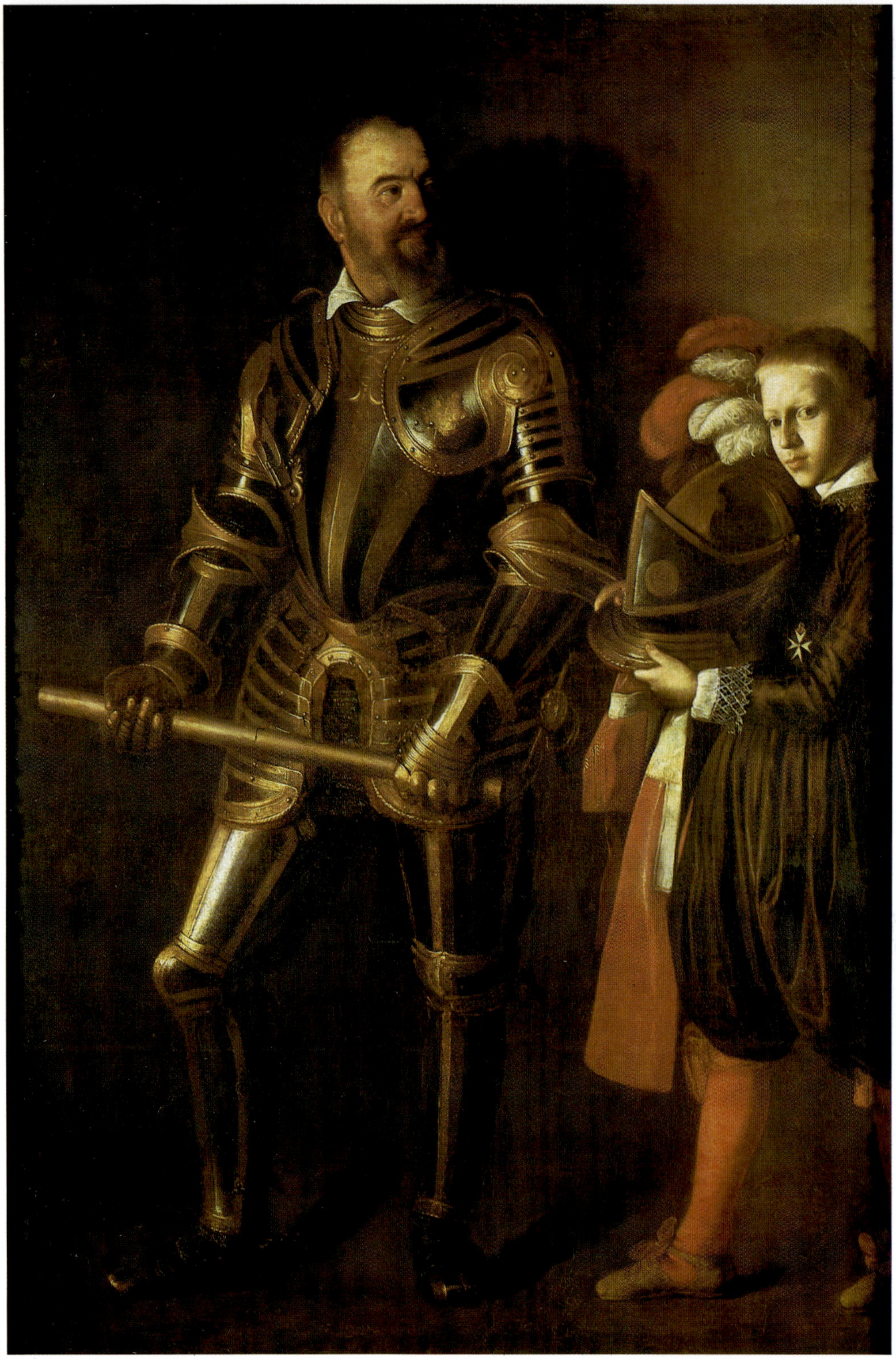

68

the mantle, which seems to flow briskly through the painting. Finally, a St. Francis in Meditation removed from the church of Carpineto Romano to Palazzo Venezia in Rome (which appears to be better than another version in the Chiesa dei Cappuccini, also in Rome) proposes again an intimate, self-absorbed figure. Caravaggio's attention to the texture of the drapery reaches extraordinary heights of refinement, recalling the intense works of Velasquez. A copy in the Pinacoteca in Cremona shows another way in which Caravaggio approached the same subject.

Among the compositions with more than one figure, a Supper in Emmaus painted for Marchese Patrizi and 56
documented by Bellori, today in the Pinacoteca di Brera in Milan, appears to have been painted some years after the other version, in London. The atmosphere in which the figures are immersed is barely perceptible, as is the psychological feeling; and the painting style,

which by now has become that of Caravaggio's last years (relatively speaking: the artist was thirty-five), is frayed and tenuous, devoid of the boldness that characterizes the London painting. This is a singular qualitative achievement. It corresponds to a substantial and definitive ripening of the painter's artistic thought. It is exactly because of this quality that I cannot imagine that
67 the Christ with Pilate in the Pinacoteca at Palazzo Rosso in Genoa is by Caravaggio's hand. It is distinguished by a hard and schematic sign that seems to do little credit to a painter who, at more or less the same time, was making paintings like the Brera Supper.

Just before leaving Rome as a result of the murder of Tommasoni (he had already had to go briefly to Genoa because of the Pasqualone affair) Caravaggio executed his most complex painting thus far (with the possible exception of the Martyrdom of St. Matthew). The
69 Death of the Virgin for Santa Maria della Scala in Trastevere was, like many of Caravaggio's paintings, rejected by the religious community of the church for which it was intended. But in this case, in addition to the testimonies of the artist's contemporaries, it is quite clear why the painting must have provoked the patrons' outrage. Fortunately the work was acquired by the duke of Mantua, to whose attention it had been brought by his vigilant emissary, Rubens. From Mantua the painting reached the collection of Charles I of England, and following later vicissitudes, ended up in the Louvre.

In this immense canvas, the apostles speak in groups or contemplate their sorrow in silence. Mary,
70 "swollen, her legs uncovered" (Baglione), lies as though suspended on the coffin. It has rightly been observed that this painting, rejected on the grounds that it lacked religious emotions, is the most deeply religious painting of the entire seventeenth century. It has also been pointed out that the artist has not made a representation of death, but has shown a real death. Thus the painting offends the sensibility not only of its own time, but of all times, because of what it suggests about the obscure, fearful meaning of the end of life. The legends that accuse Caravaggio of having used a woman drowned in the Tiber as his model, appear posterior. But the painting expresses a sense of tragically imminent death, and communicates a deep anguish even to those who know nothing of the external circumstances. The large, red drape is one of the chromatic devices to which the artist turned, as we know, to enliven a surface too heavily laden with dull colors. But it is also used to close the background and to concentrate attention on the central figure of the Virgin, whose short axis, from her hands to her face, is the real expressive center of the painting. It is no coincidence that the baroque painter par excellence, Rubens, immediately understood a painting so different from his own principles. His great intelligence led him straightaway to admire and respect Caravaggio's unquestionable dramatic force.

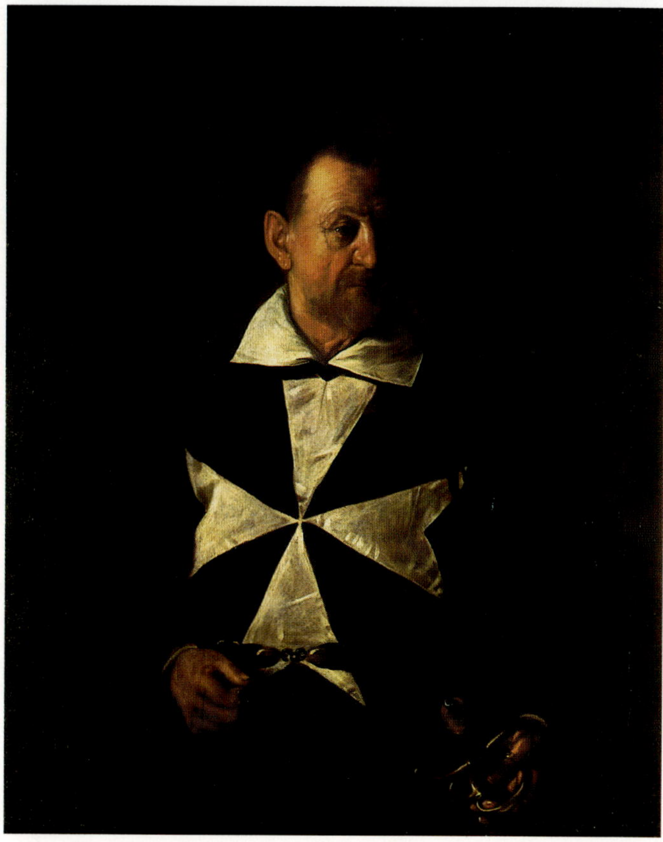

69

Real-life drama and drama relived came together in the artist's flight from Rome, which took place at this time. On one of the Colonna estates, probably at Zagarolo, he executed a half-figure painting of the Madonna in Ecstasy known through numerous copies, the original of which is in all likelihood a painting in a private collection in Rome, recently brought to light by Marini (1974). The Saint Francis in Cremona may also be from this period, if it is by Caravaggio.

From the fiefs of the Colonna family Caravaggio took refuge in Naples, in 1606. There he began to work again with his usual, astounding speed. Early in January 1607 he was paid for the immense altarpiece commissioned to him by the Pio Monte di Misericordia (where it
may still be seen today). The painting shows the Seven 61
Acts of Mercy. It is as complicated in its organization as the Death of the Virgin. Caravaggio actually had to add a series of figures (two angels and the Madonna and Child, the latter painted later) in the upper part of the painting, which make the composition of the picture the most complex, perhaps, in any of his works. Caravaggio did not paint exemplary episodes intended to stir the viewer to religious piety through the illustrative emphasis of gestures and feelings. Rather, he entrusted the educational effectiveness of his works to the evidence of things in themselves, in the conviction that nothing should be added above and beyond what is already contained in the intrinsic eloquence of the various poses. On the right appear the burial of the dead and the epi-

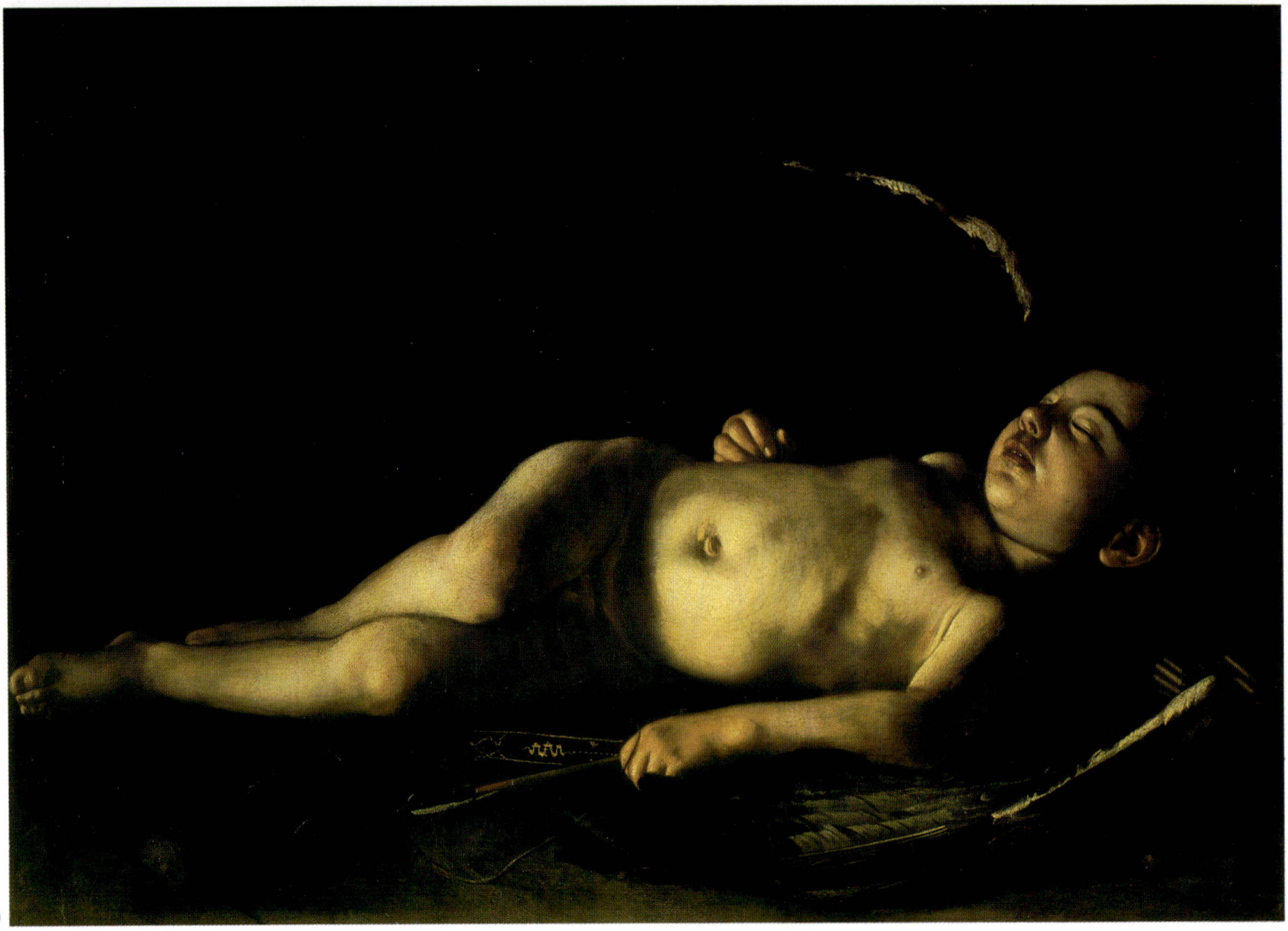

70

sode of the so-called Carita Romana (Cimon's daughter giving her father suck in prison), which contains at once the two charitable acts of visiting prisoners and feeding the hungry. Dressing the naked appears in the foreground, symbolized by St. Martin and the beggar. Next to this scene, the host and St. James of Compostela allude to the offering of hospitality to pilgrims. Relieving the thirsty is represented by Samson drinking from the ox jaw. The youth on the ground behind the beggar of St. Martin may also represent the merciful gesture of caring for the sick. We readily apprehend the artist's power of synthesis, which concentrates a conceptual content that is potentially quite dispersive, in the model behavior of a few figures. The large painting was widely copied and studied by seventeenth-century Neapolitan painters, who drew ideas and formal devices from it. Caravaggio's presence in Naples, limited to a few months divided between two stays, was of decisive importance to the development of the Neapolitan school of painting. From Giovan Battista Caracciolo, called Battistello, to the Spaniard Juseppe de Ribera and Mattia Preti, painters working in Naples received a fundamental impulse from Caravaggio. The major exhibition of seventeenth-century Neapolitan painting that originated in London toward the close of 1982 and traveled to Washington and other cities, testifies to this influence.

Caravaggio painted another great ecclesiastical work immediately after the Seven Acts of Mercy. This is the so-called Madonna del Rosario, which after various turns of fortune (at the end of the seventeenth century it reached Anversa through the successive attentions of Frans Pourbus, Louis Finson, and Rubens) is now in Vienna's Kunsthistorisches Museum. Three different levels of participation are visible in the picture's pyramidal structure. At the bottom is the host of the faithful, the people of humble birth. Among these is the patron of the painting, turned toward the viewer. On the middle level appear the Dominicans (the painting was undoubtably made for a Dominican church, possibly even San Domenico in Naples), mediators between the faithful and the Virgin. The latter is shown at the top with the Christ Child. The painting further demonstrates the artist's ability to transfer the themes and techniques of his usual manner to a grand and noble painting. One who knew the Caravaggio of the first ten years might well have asked how and if it would have been possible to reconcile the novelty and nonconformist attitude implicit in his style with the unavoidable rules of large church altarpieces. Here the familiar pyramidal scheme, used by Leonardo and Raphael in their easel paintings, is extended to unprecedented dimensions, although it is balanced by the addition of the Dominican group on the

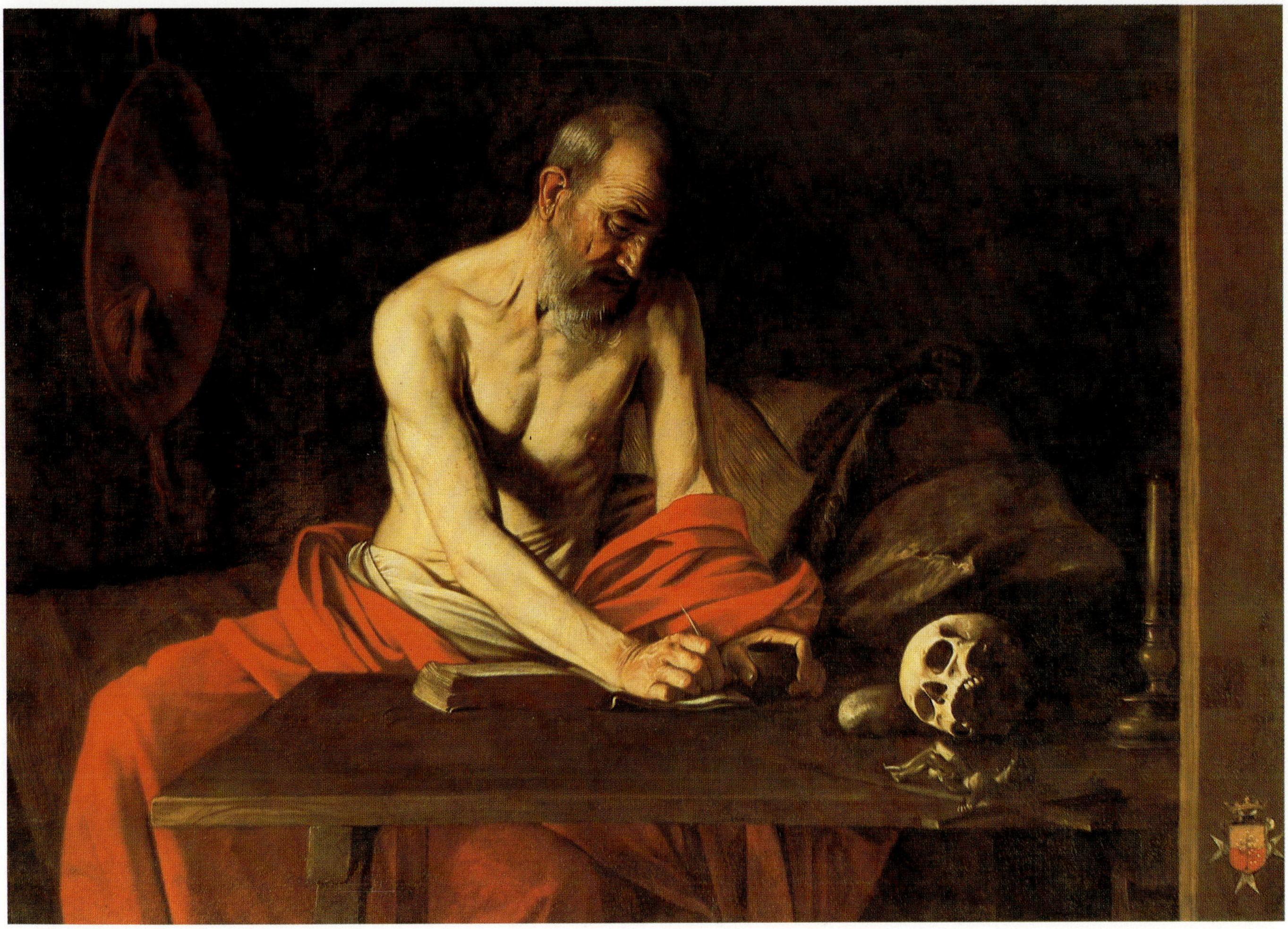

71

70. *Sleeping Cupid*
cm. 71x105
Florence, Palazzo Pitti

71. *St. Jerome*
cm. 117x157
La Valletta, St. John Museum

right. Between the latter and the central pyramid is a diagonal up-grade that ends in the drape, which is more schematically rendered than in the artist's other works. The viewer is left with a feeling of admiration for the nobility of this extraordinary work, which is eloquent without being emphatic or rhetorical.

It is still a matter of opinion among scholars whether the Flagellation of Christ (located in San Domenico in 63
Naples until a few years ago, when it was transferred for safer keeping to the Pinacoteca di Capodimonte) was also painted during Caravaggio's first stay in Naples, or if it was made during the few months that he spent in the city just before his death. We prefer to keep it in this realm of ideas, but not without pointing out that the doubts as to the date are entirely justified, as Caravaggio's style is essentially uniform during the later part of his career. The shadows are denser, the contours are frayed, the colors are softened, and the light takes on an increasingly important role in modeling, defining, and building up forms. The only reality that exists is the one we see, not the one we expect, guess at, or imagine. This extraordinary painting lost half of its meaning when it was removed (for apparently irrefutable reasons) from the church and placed in the museum. It stood out on the distant altar of its chapel as soon as the visitor entered the church, magically capturing his eye with

magnetic force. Stylistically, the painting returns (through its patent reference to a famous prototype by Sebastiano del Piombo in San Pietro in Montorio, in Rome) to manneristic conventions. It owes much to Michelangelo in the twisting of Christ's body, in his contorted step, and in the positions of his tormentors, which seem to make reference to Michelangelo's late work in the Pauline Chapel in the Vatican.

Another important painting, already mentioned by Bellori (according to whom it was taken to Spain by the viceroy, Benavente), has come to light fairly recently and has been acquired by the Cleveland Museum. This
64 is a Crucifixion of St. Andrew, in which four variously characterized onlookers witness an unusual event narrated in the Golden Legend of Jacopo da Varazze. It seems that an order was given to take the dying saint down off the cross after two days of agony; but his will to die as his Savior had died struck the ruffian charged with the task and paralyzed him in the act. The painting is executed in a fast and summary manner. Changes of mind are not lacking (as the restoration of the painting showed), but this is usual for Caravaggio. In the head of the old woman Caravaggio indulges in a grotesque allusion of a kind that would be developed by his followers to the point of exaggeration.

Another work probably done by the artist at this
65 time is a Christ at the Column in the Museum of Rouen, which Longhi recognized as autograph. This is a splendid composition, full of life and movement, carried out in grand style (the copies are all more contracted, unable to reproduce the ease of the original). The outstanding rendering of the anatomy of Christ's torso is the fruit of a truly admirable observation and understanding of nature.

66 The three figures of the Salome in the National Gallery of London are larger in scale. This painting was also recognized by Longhi, who was undoubtedly the greatest modern connoisseur of Caravaggio. Much more than in the artist's other canvases, attention is concentrated on the psychological differentiation of the faces. Caravaggio would take up the same composition in a later painting.

Finally, mention should be made of a fine painting in the Kunsthistorisches Museum in Vienna, representing
67 David with the Head of Goliath. Although the attribution to Caravaggio is still uncertain, the painting is very probably an original from the artist's first period in Naples, carried out in a style that Battistello would have liked particularly.

From Naples, for no apparent reason except his own personal choice and a nomadic inclination that reflects a deeply restless character, Caravaggio went to Malta. Here the Grand Master of the Order named him "Cavaliere di Grazia" on 14 July 1608. The artist's stay in Malta could have been an oasis of calm, a moment of rest, a reflective pause. Instead it marked the point of no return after which Caravaggio's misshapen life raced toward an all too appropriate end. Just three months after receiving his knighthood, on 6 October, documents show that Caravaggio escaped (in the most classical way, by climbing down the walls on a rope) from the prison and then from the island of Malta. Why he was imprisoned is not known. There is reason to believe he had an argument with a higher-ranking knight, a "Cavaliere della Giustizia." It must have been serious, if Caravaggio chose to escape. The order expelled him "tamquam membrum putridum et foetidum," and relentlessly persecuted him.

In Malta the artist made at least five paintings that are still extant today. Two are portraits of the Grand Master of the Order, Alof de Wignacourt: one full-
figure, showing the master in armor and accompanied 68
by a page, now in the Louvre; and the other, more of a
sketch than a finished painting, individuated a few years 69
ago by Mina Gregori in the Florentine collections of Palazzo Pitti. The former is an uneven painting that leaves a lot of questions unanswered; but the opinion that Caravaggio executed only some of the "noble" parts, such as the grand master's head, seems correct. The latter is a fine painting, but it must be seen through its incompleteness and its poor state of conservation.

Another of the Maltese paintings, a Sleeping Cupid, 70
is in the Galleria Palatina in Florence. It came to the Medici Collections at a very early date: In 1620 it had already been copied in a fresco by Giovanni da Sangiovanni. An inscription on the back not only helps in attributing the painting to Caravaggio, but tells that it was done in Malta in 1608. This is an anguished, irreverent reworking of a theme that had enjoyed great success and had been painted in many different ways since classical antiquity. What counts is that Caravaggio transformed an idyllic motif into a darkly dramatic one, eliminating all trace of pleasure and bathing the putto in restless sleep and deep shadow. This abandonment takes on a sick quality, giving the image an extraordinary psychological modernity.

Another excellent work is the St. Jerome in the Mu- 71
seum of La Valletta in Malta. The saint, it has been shown, is a portrait of Grand Master de Wignacourt. The half-figure, executed with the ascetic precision that characterizes Caravaggio's late nudes, stands out against the dark shadow of the background. The still-life of few objects — the stone for beating his breast, the candlestick, the crucifix, and the skull, which make up an unusual "memento mortis" — is equally severe and restrained. A St. John Drinking, in a private collection in Malta, may also be by his hand. But without a close examination it is difficult to hazard an attribution.

The most important painting that Caravaggio made
in Malta is the Beheading of the Baptist, which is still in 72
the Oratorio di San Giovanni (now St. John Museum) in La Valletta. This is one of Caravaggio's most extraor-

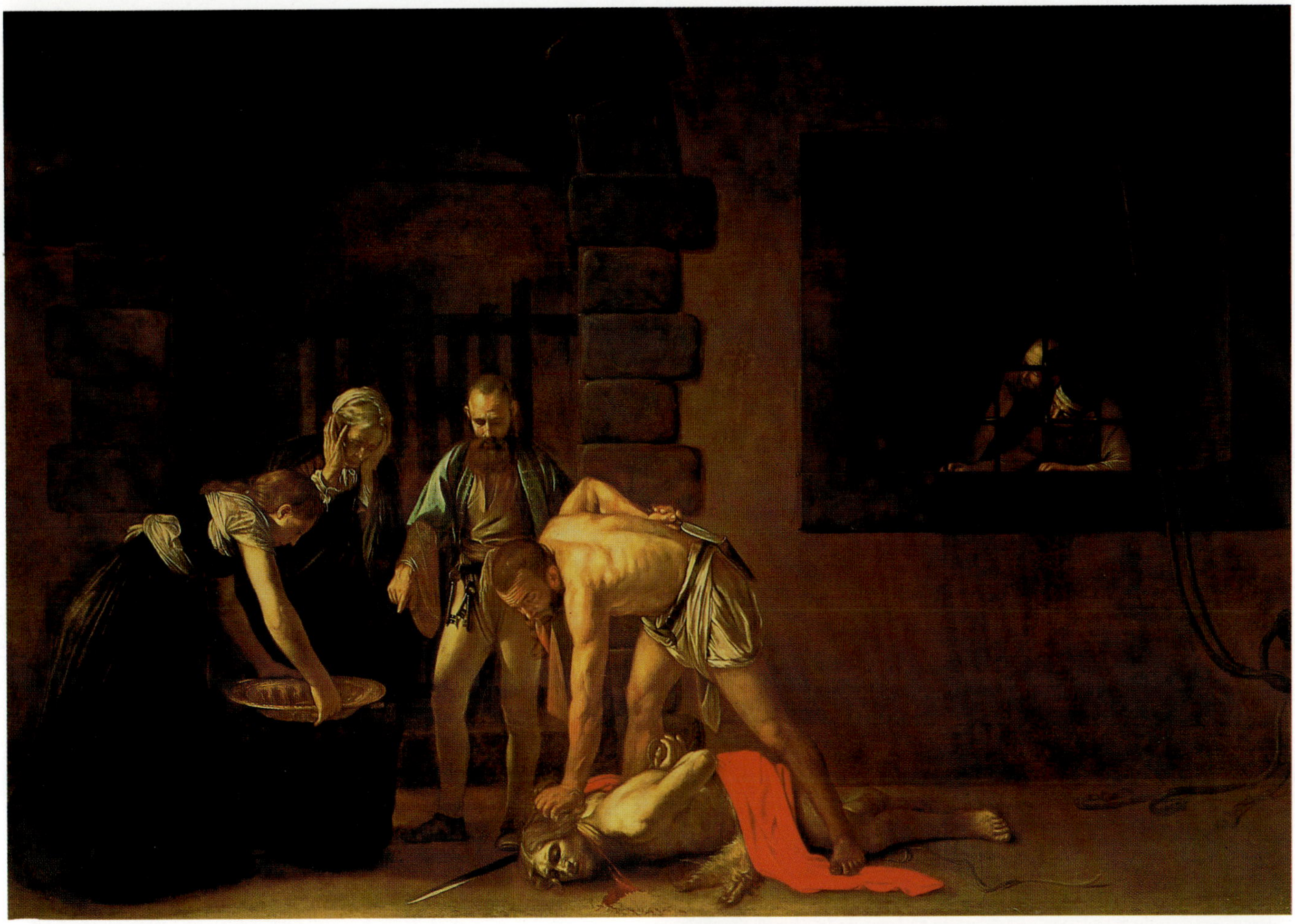

72

73

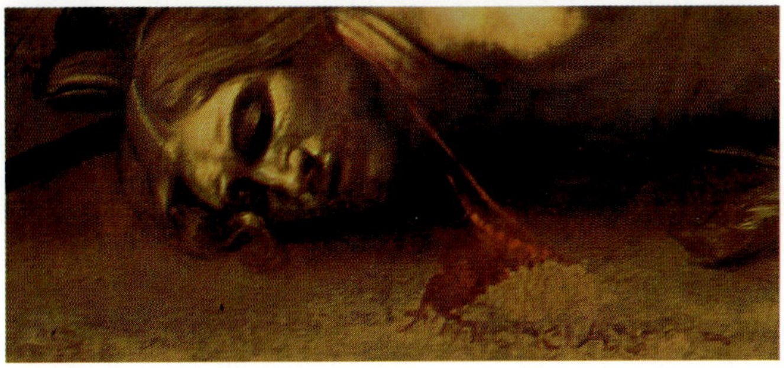

72. Beheading of the Baptist
cm. 361x520
La Valletta, St. John Museum

73. Beheading of the Baptist, detail of the artist's signature.
La Valletta, St. John Museum

dinary creations. For many it is his greatest masterpiece, as meaningless as such a choice may be. It is characterized by a magical balance of all the parts. It is no accident that the artist brings back into the painting a precise reference to the setting, placing behind the figures, as a backdrop, the severe, sixteenth-century architecture of the prison building, at the window of which, in a stroke of genius, two figures silently witness the scene (the commentators are thus drawn into the painting, and no longer projected, as in the Martyrdom of St. Matthew, toward the outside). This is a final compendium of Caravaggio's art. Well-known figures return (the old woman, the youth, the nude ruffian, the bearded nobleman), as do Lombard elements. The technical means adhere to the deliberate, programmatic limitation to which Caravaggio adapts them; but amid these soft tones, these dark colors, is an impressive sense of drawing that the artist does not give up, and that is visible even through the synoptic glints of light of his late works. This eminently classical balance, which projects the event beyond contingency, unleashes a harsh drama that is even more effective to the extent that, having given up the "aesthetic of exclamation" forever, Caravaggio limits every external, excessive sign of emotional emphasis. The painter signed in the Baptist's blood: "*f* 73
[perhaps to be understood as *fecit*, rather than *frater*] michela...": This is the seal he placed on what may well be his greatest masterpiece.

Caravaggio fled from Malta to Sicily, and the extraordinary reputation that accompanied him immediately brought him a series of ecclesiastical commissions. Four of these paintings are still extant. They were executed with the same dizzying speed, as though the painter felt a disturbing impatience that compelled him to complete a task as quickly as he could, as soon as he had solved the artistic problems it posed. Like other artists in their later works — Titian, Michelangelo, and Rembrandt, for instance — he attained a rarefaction of form, a severity in the use of decorative artifices, that ruthlessly seem to correspond to a sort of inner moral dialogue, more than to a commission addressed to the public. But Caravaggio's case is unique, because he had begun to paint in this way before he was forty — an age that he would never reach. One cannot help thinking that it foreshadowed his demise.

The first of the Sicilian paintings to be completed
74 was the Burial of St. Lucy. It was recently restored at the Istituto Centrale per il Restauro in Rome (all the Sicilian paintings have come down to us in a poor state of preservation). An immense empty space hovers above the crowd of onlookers, in one of the most potentially hazardous, but successful designs in the history of painting. The figures are rendered in a cursory manner, with glints of light. The viewer is struck by the enormity of the figures in the foreground with respect to the others. Such variations of size are unusual in the artist's works.

75 In the Resurrection of Lazarus, painted at the end of 1608 or the beginning of 1609 for a Genoese merchant named Lazzari (and today in the Museo Nazionale in Messina), Caravaggio makes vague references to an antique sarcophagus with the death of Patroclus. However he abandons all trace of classicism in the livid body, caught at the instant it begins to return to life, stirring the onlookers to a series of wonderfully varied expressions and poses. The ancient gesture of predilection that we encountered in the Calling of Matthew and (limited to the wrist and hand) in the angel of the Abraham and Isaac in the Uffizi, returns in the painting in Messina in the pose of Christ who indicates the beautiful group of the two sisters who lovingly bend over Lazarus restored to life. Here, too, we find a large empty area in the upper portion of the canvas, not unlike that which existed
76 in the Adoration of the Shepherds (where the top of the stable is summarily traced out), before it was cut down to its present size, to fit the space available in the church of Santa Maria degli Angeli (the painting is now in the Museum of Messina).

Here again Caravaggio appears as a powerful innovator, owing not to an eccentric abstract intention, but to a personal, unprecedented meditation on themes that would appear not to have anything to disclose. The Adoration, which contains in the group of shepherds one of the more beautiful examples of paintings of the century, is by no means idyllic and peaceful. The joy for the birth of the Savior is overshadowed by the melancholy for the destiny of suffering and death that awaits him. A deep sadness pervades the entire composition, a sense of imminent death.

A similar painting represents the Nativity with St. 77
Lawrence and St. Francis, unfortunately stolen in October 1969 from the church of San Lorenzo in Palermo, where it had been since it was made. There is no question that the composition is less successful than in other cases: the contained and pensive atmosphere, howerer again shows that at this stage Caravaggio associated the idea of the advent of Christ not with the joy of Redemption but with a future that was at best uncertain.

In Sicily Caravaggio did at least one other work, a Christ Bearing the Cross that has disappeared altogether. But soon afterward, in the same year (1609) he returned to the continent and set out for Rome, the city to which he felt most closely tied, but where he would never again set foot. In October 1609 he was wounded ("they say he was disfigured"), probably by emissaries of the Knights of Malta, who had not forgotten him, in a tavern near the harbor of Naples. In the months before and after the event he painted, in Naples, his last works. The final phase of his career has been reconstructed only recently, and many of the particular assertions regarding this period, made in the last few years, have yet to be confirmed. We wish to take account of them here, because taken as a whole these attributions faithfully reflect a period whose very identification (scholars have only lately begun to speak of a second Neapolitan period) is no simple matter.

None of the paintings from this period is documented, but there are likely hypotheses. Bellori (1672) tells us
that Caravaggio had executed a Salome to send to the 78
Grand Master of Malta to appease him. And it is natural to identifiy this work with the painting in the Casita of the Prince in the Escorial in Madrid, which essentially follows the Roman version, today in London. The only, slight change is in the pose of the executioner. And yet the two works are very obviously different. The later version rises out of an abyss of shadow. The executioner thoughtfully observes the result of his work, instead of lifting up the Baptist's head with certainty.

Another comparison can be made between the

74. Burial of St. Lucy, detail.
cm. 408x300
Syracuse, Santa Lucia

75. Resurrection of Lazarus, detail.
cm. 380x275
Messina, Museo Nazionale

76. Adoration of the Shepherds
cm. 314x211
Messina, Museo Nazionale

77. Nativity with St. Francis and St. Lawrence
cm. 268x197
Formerly at Palermo, San Lorenzo

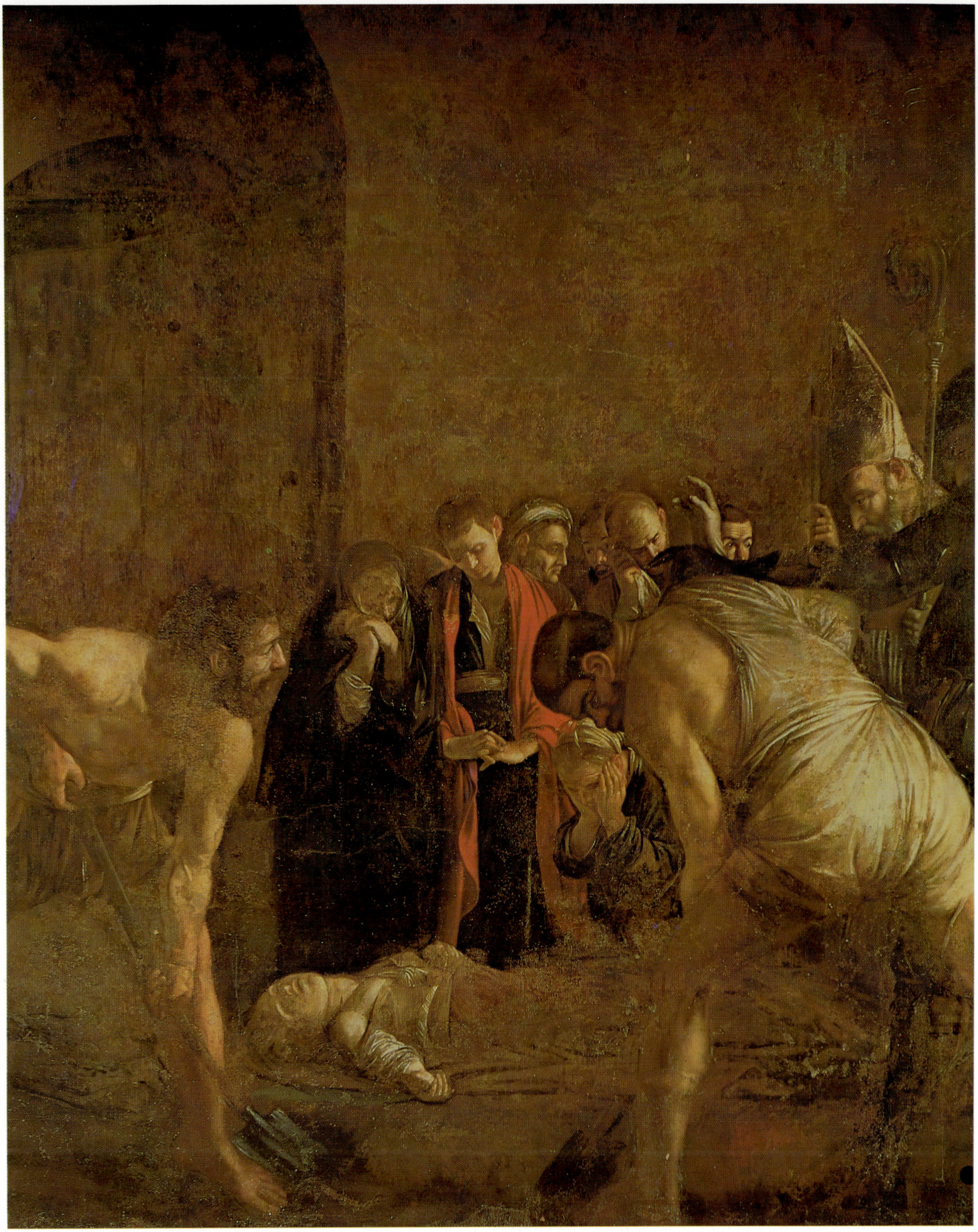

74

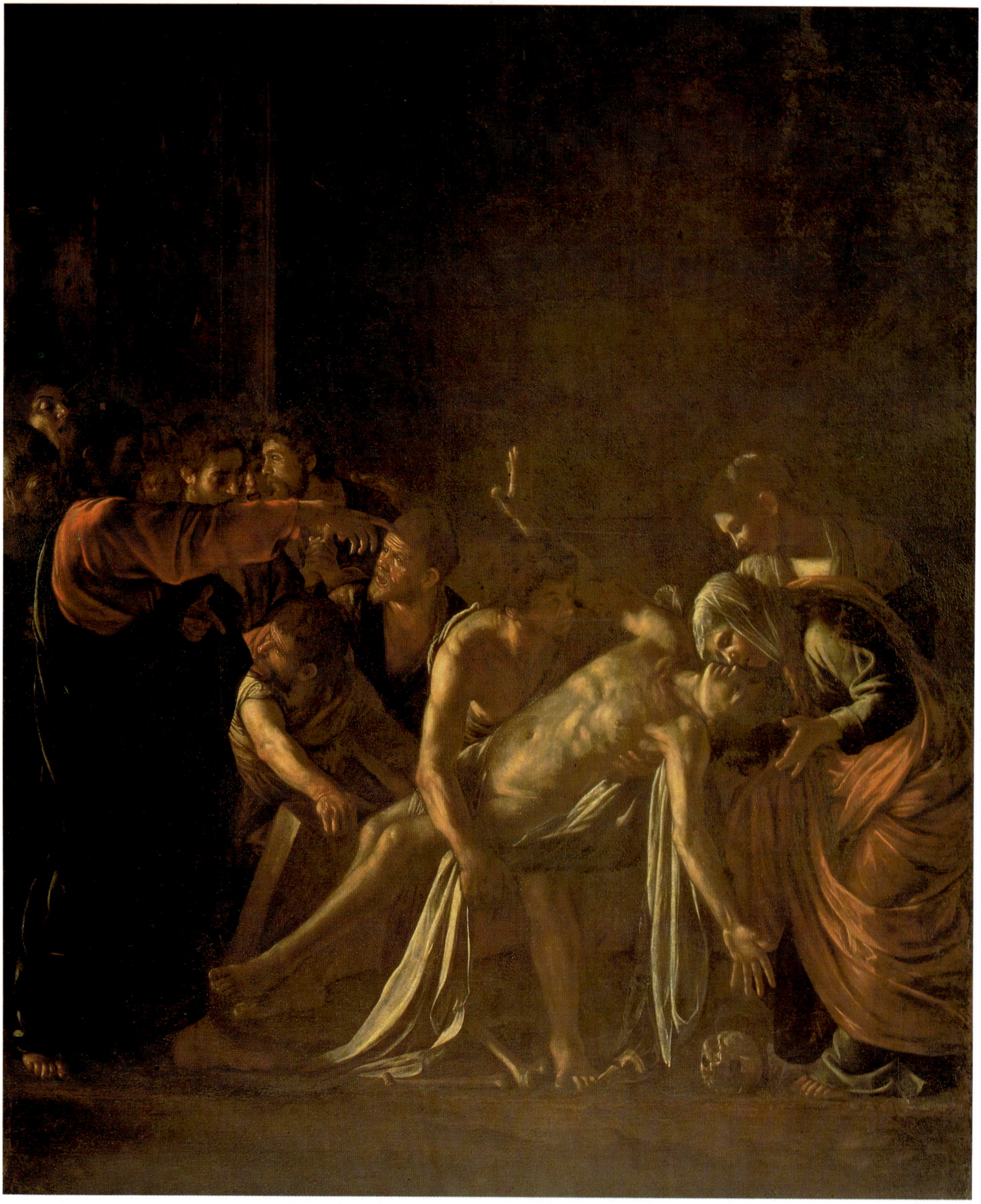

75

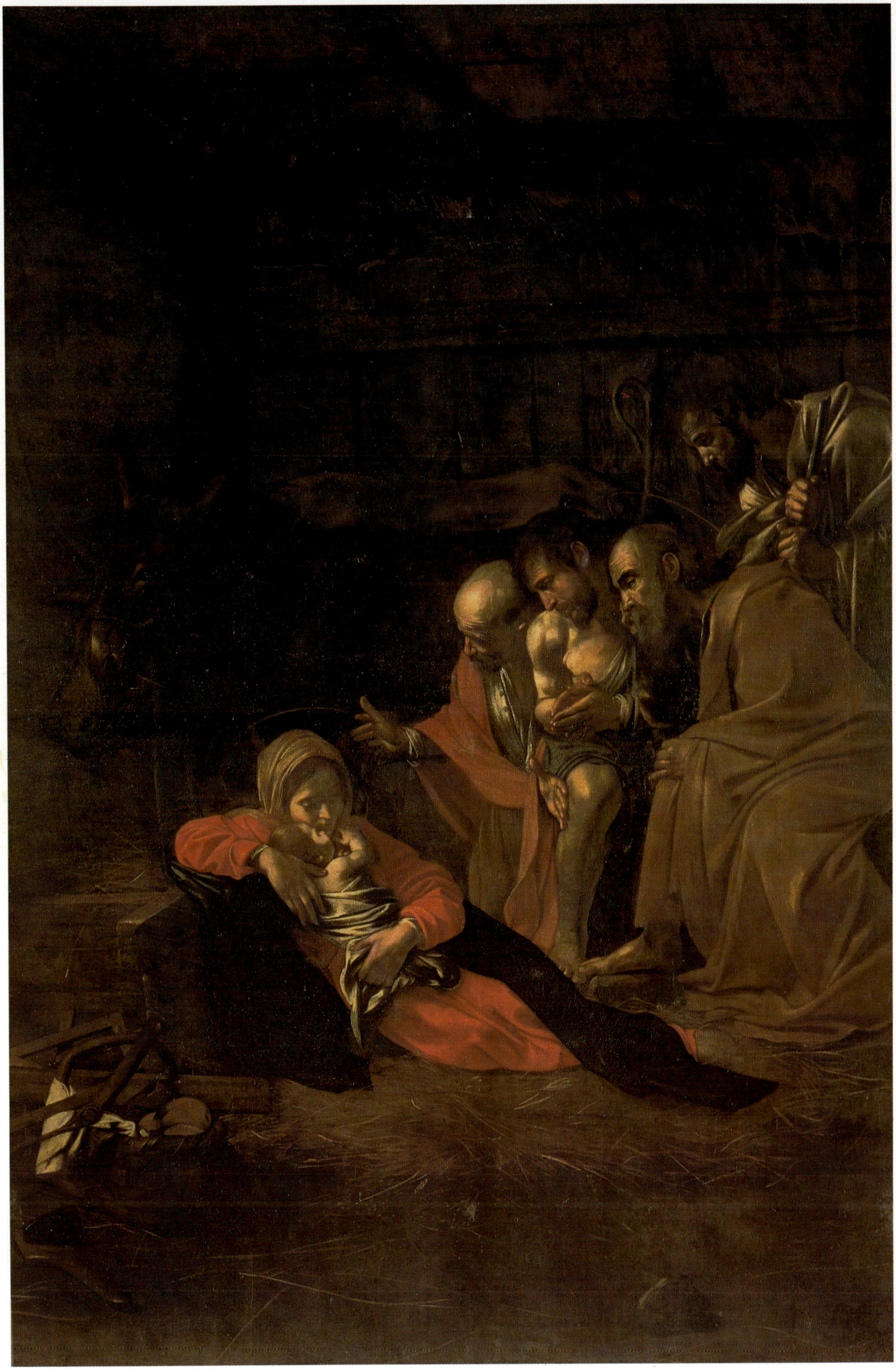

76

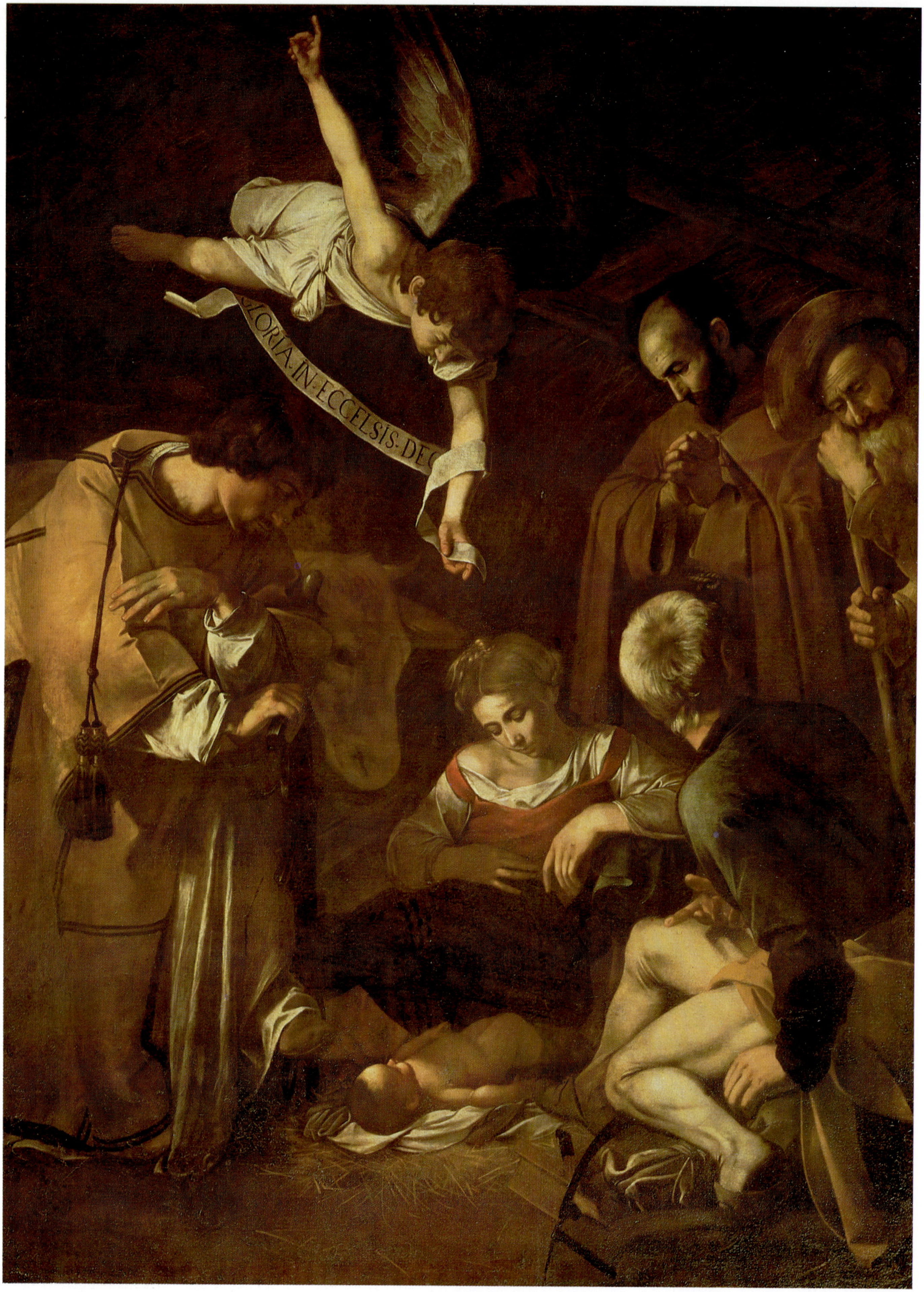

77

78. Salome with the Head of the Baptist
cm. 116x140
Madrid, Escorial

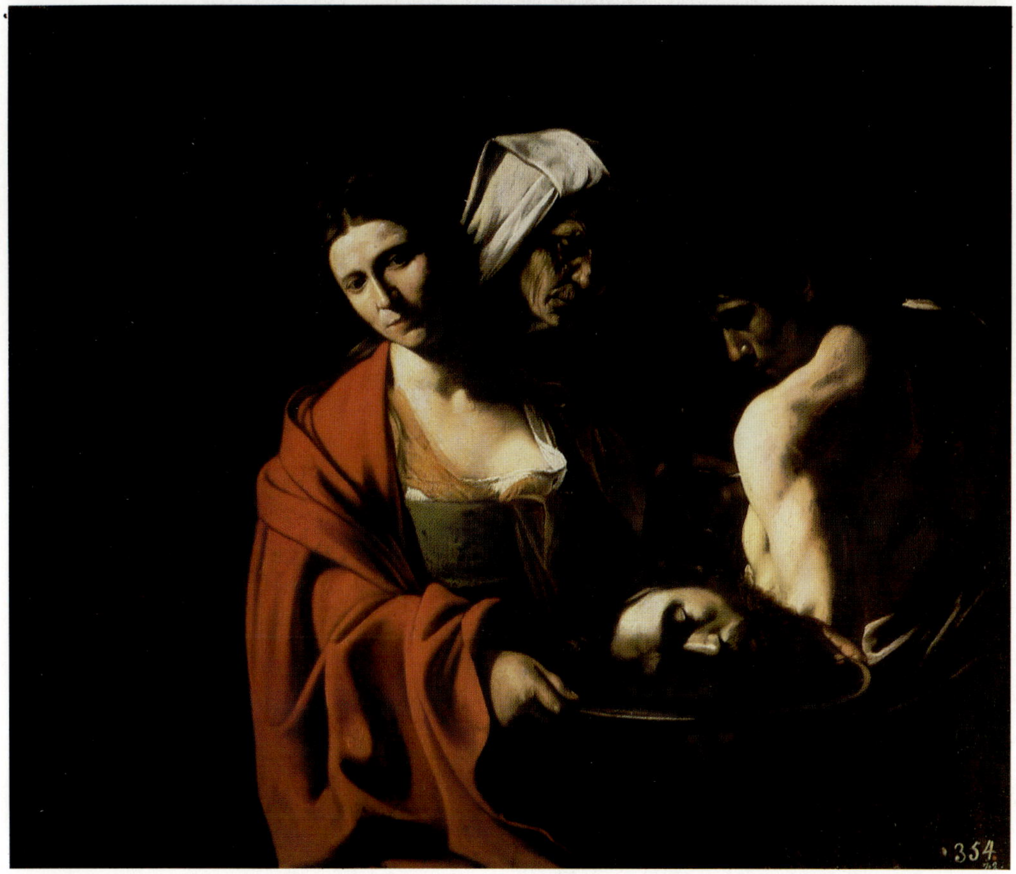

78

79 Young St. John in the Galleria Borghese in Rome and the paintings of the same subject in Kansas City and in Palazzo Barberini in Rome, which we have already mentioned. The Borghese St. John is also the most soberly thoughtful. The body is delicate and the expression is dreamy, so much so as to suggest a considerable distance in time from the other two.

The David with the Head of Goliath, also in the Galleria Borghese in Rome, is considered by some scholars to be the artist's last work. Much has been written about the overpowering invasion of real space that results from David's gesture, the meager painting style, the artist's identification with the head of Goliath (undoubtedly a self-portrait). The expression on David's face is devoid of boldness, the clothing he wears is light, little more than a veil, by no means a pretext for painting folds cleverly given relief. The youth's head is also a kind of idealized self-portrait that gazes with sadness on the giant's severed head.

The three paintings we have discussed so far are attributed to Caravaggio by general consensus. Other attributions are more "open". In the case of the Martyrdom of St. Ursula now in the Banca Commerciale in Naples, documents that were discovered and published five years after the attribution had been made by Mina Gregori on purely stylistic bases, confirmed Caravaggio as the author of this painting. It was executed for Marcantonio Doria of Genoa in May 1610, just two months before the artist's death. The painting was shown in the exhibition in London and other cities, mentioned above, and on this occasion it was possible to evaluate its absolute originality. For the first time Caravaggio painted not only an action as it was taking place, but its results as well, giving the painting an allusive aspect (rather than an immediately real one) that corresponds to the "baroque" propensities that have been acknowledged in his late works. It is clear that in the close space of the painting the King of the Huns would not have been able to shoot the arrow that has struck St. Ursula, right next to him. Until now Caravaggio had never painted an event on a level that was not that of direct reality, without reproducing it as it actually would have appeared.

Also included in the exhibition was a Denial of St. 80
Peter from an unnamed private collection, known to the specialists for some years and considered by many to be a very late, autograph Caravaggio. The attribution appears justified by the quality of the stylistic features (the painting's relation to a similar subject cited by Bellori in Naples has yet to be determined). Here we see only the three figures, from the waist up. In the total absence of references to objects, the meaning is conveyed entirely by the obvious evidence of the poses. The direct specification of the light source is so precise that it completely excludes the entire profile of the ruffian's face from our field of view, in a solution of unprecedented boldness. The rendering becomes extremely synoptic: the face of the woman servant is little more than a pure volume. Peter's wrinkled forehead is a series of tightly con-

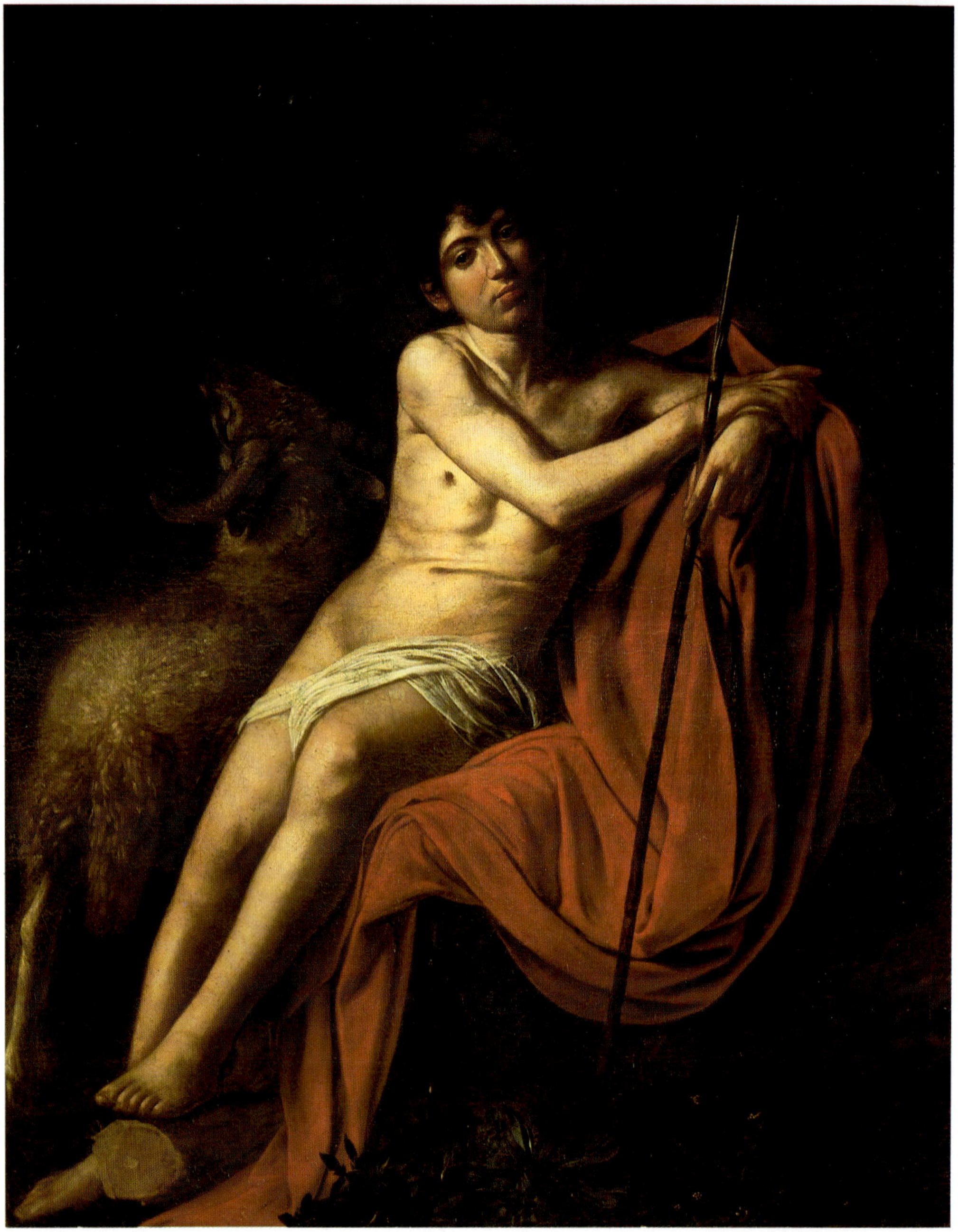

79

79. Young St. John
cm. 159x124
Rome, Galleria Borghese

80. Denial of St. Peter
cm. 94x125
New York, Shickman Gallery

81. The Tooth-Drawer
cm. 101x150
Florence, Galleria degli Uffizi

densed brushstrokes (with reference to the Martyrdom of St. Ursula, a Neapolitan correspondent of the Doria family wrote them that Caravaggio laid his paint on the canvas thickly, as a rule).

82 The Crowning with Thorns, which recently came into the collections of the Cassa di Risparmio of Prato is extraordinarily modern in style. The scene is viewed as through a telephoto lens, with the figures pressed against each other. The attribution, proposed by Mina Gregori, is undoubtedly appropriate to the end of Caravaggio's career. Another attribution by this scholar is the
81 so-called Tooth-Drawer (*Cavadenti*) belonging to the Gallerie Fiorentine and deposited at Montecitorio (where it was restored in an incompetent and harmful way, making it more difficult to study). It is easy to understand why such a proposal, which presents a plebeian and vulgar aspect of Caravaggio that we encounter in his life but not in his works, met with much opposition. It must be pointed out, however, that even in the painting's unsatisfactory state of preservation an original quality of execution transpires that corresponds to the epitomized achievements of the late Caravaggio. It is also to be thought that there must have been a prototype, as so many of the works of Caravaggio's followers deal with this type of genre scene. The presence of the prototype in Naples would help explain some of the returns to this theme, including the late and striking works of the eighteenth-century Neapolitan painter, Gaspare Traversi.

Caravaggio also painted church paintings during his last period in Naples: in particular, a Resurrection of Christ in the Certosa di San Marino, which unfortunate-

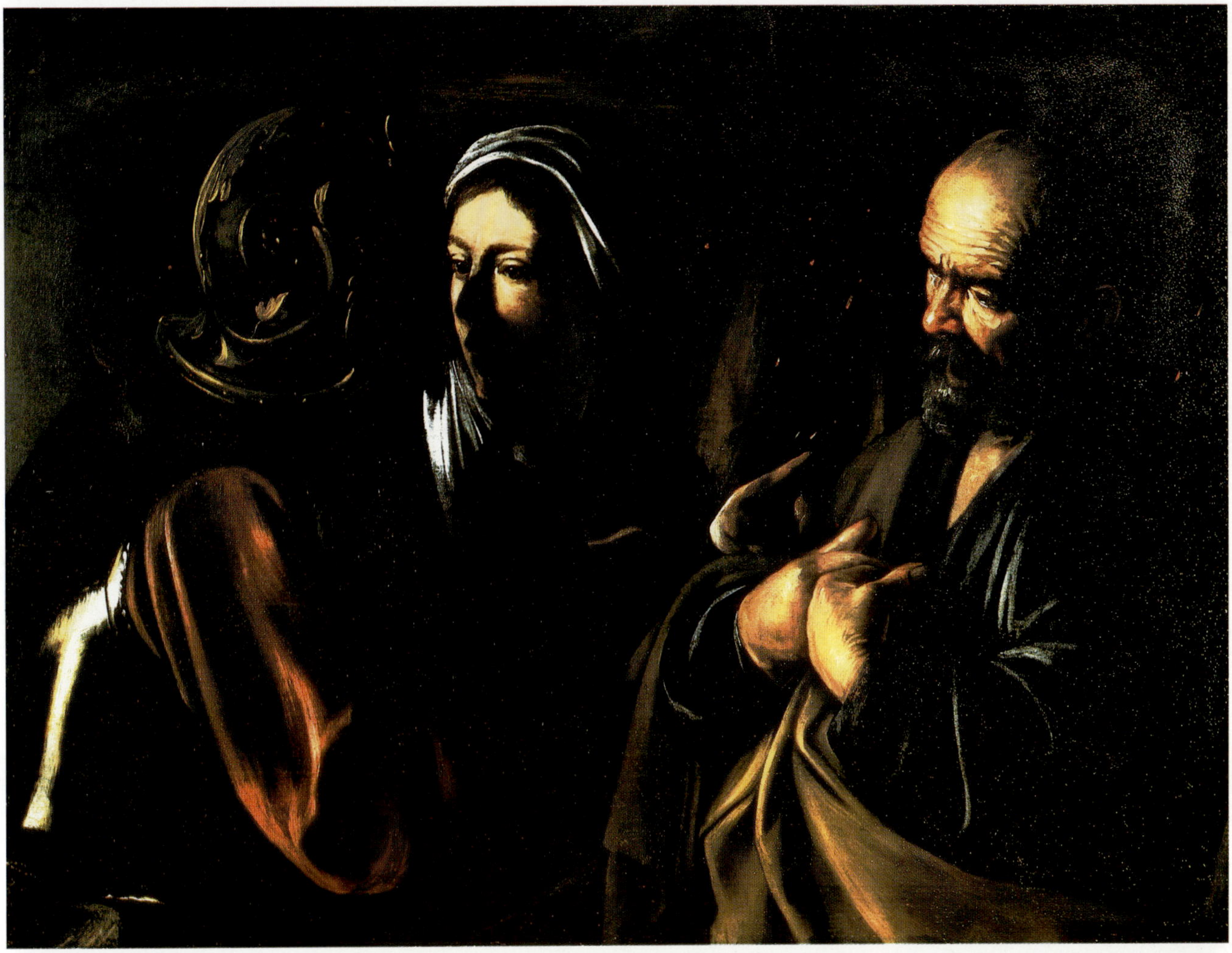

80

81

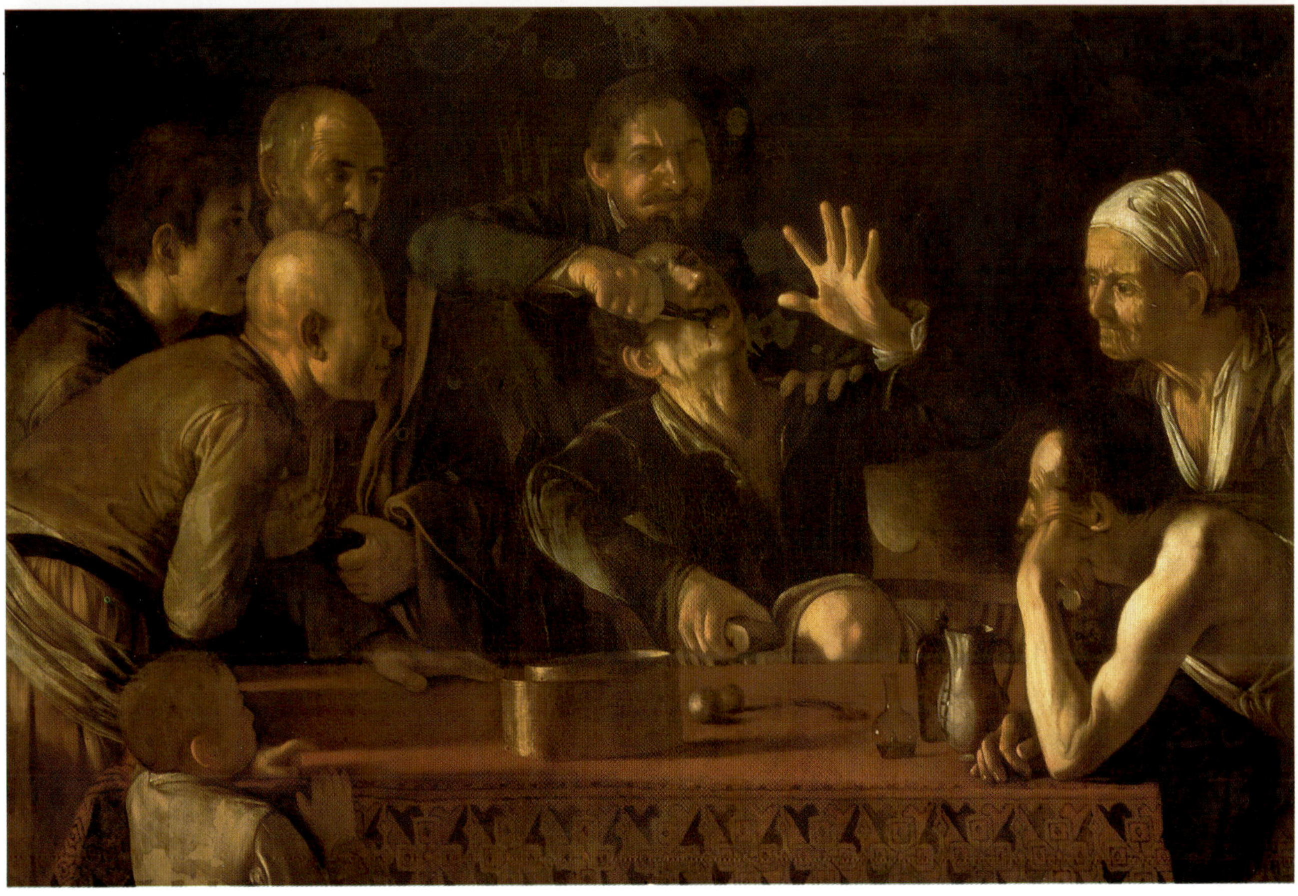

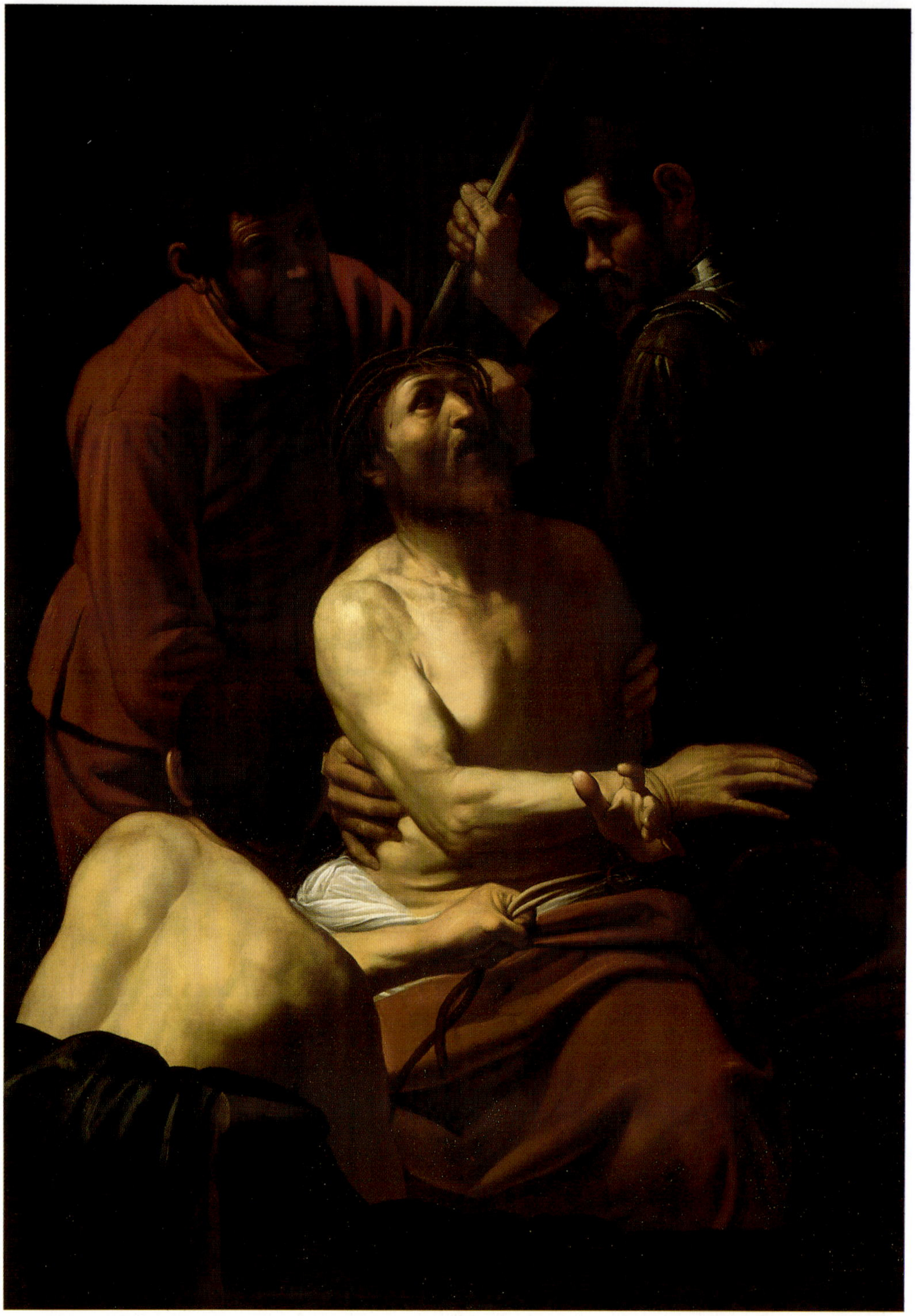

82

82. Crowning with Thorns
cm. 178x125
Prato, Cassa di Risparmio

83. Annunciation
cm. 285x205
Nancy, Musée des Beaux-Arts

ly has been lost but which, judging from the descriptions, contained the usual iconographic innovations. There is reason to believe that the artist's last altarpiece
83 is the Annunciation that reached the high altar of the
cathedral of Nancy in Lorraine just after the church was founded (1609). Today it is in the museum of that city. Whether the painting was made in Sicily or during the second period in Naples is not known. Its style would seem to exclude earlier datings, for it is clearly a very late work. It has been pointed out that the angel comes into the painting from real space, cancelling the separation between the picture and the viewer in a way typical of the baroque aesthetic (as we also saw in the Borghese David). Here, too, the angel's face is practically invisible. Nor does the Virgin look at him: She is completely self-absorbed, her pose is devoid of joyous acceptance. She seems instead crushed by the expectation of an unbearable future. The spiritual testament that Caravaggio left us with this large, two-figural painting, where once again the Virgin is not distinguished by deifying attributes, is an infinite existential sadness, which seems to contain no hope of redemption.

Few artists have had as great an influence, directly or indirectly, as Caravaggio. When he died on 18 July

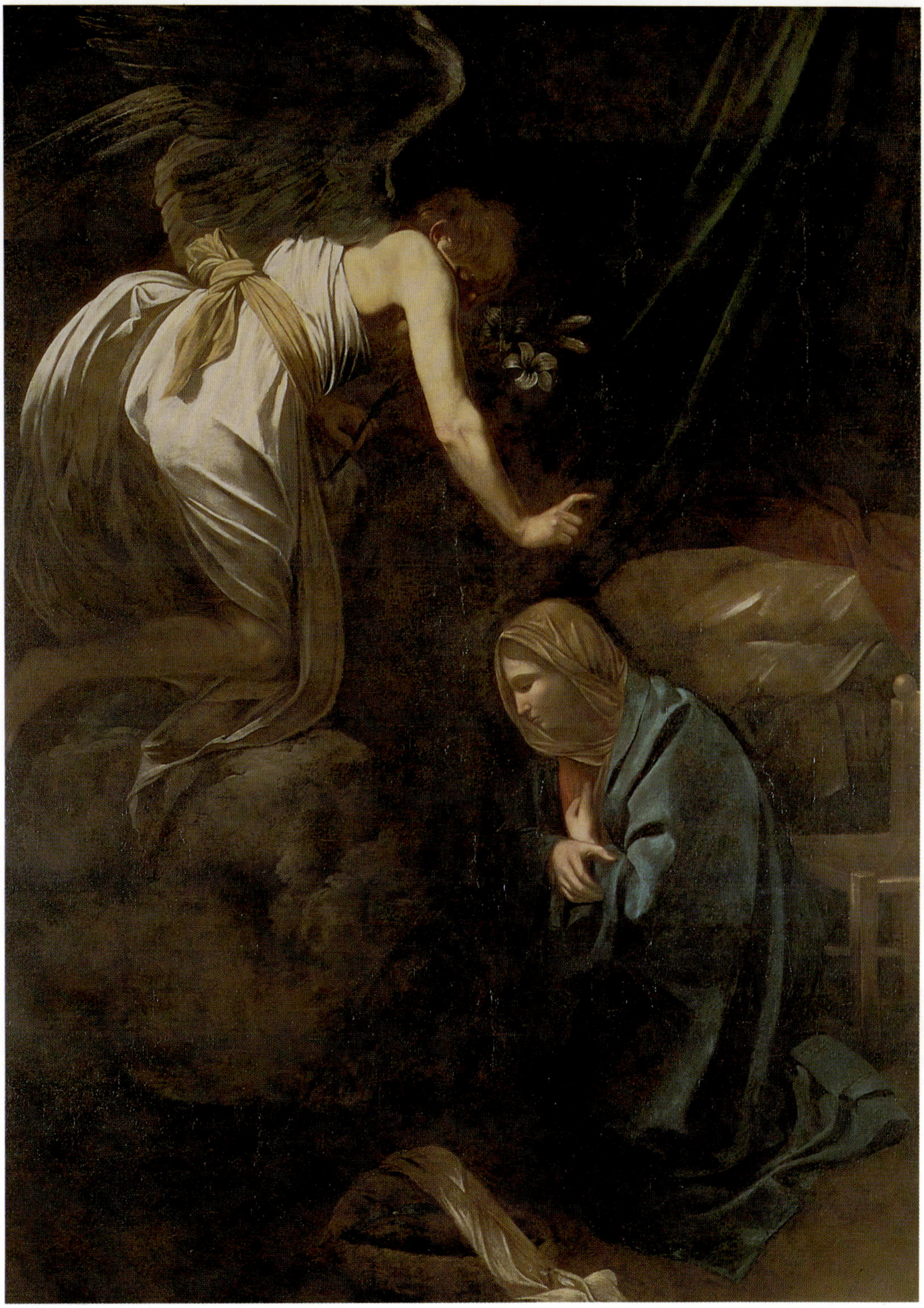

83

1610, overcome by fever on the Tyrrhenian coast at Porto Ercole (while waiting for a pardon that would have permitted him to return to Rome), he was already very famous, and younger artists were painting pictures in his "maniera." Some of his followers picked up only a few elements of his style, quickly changing them into conventions, and by so doing becoming as unlike Caravaggio as they could. Others were more deeply affected, and did not draw merely upon the artist's technique (the use of light and shadow) or thematic propensities (painting still-lifes, or the common people), but tapped the underlying spirit of continuous inquiry as well. Scholars, following the path marked out by Roberto Longhi, have engaged in the immense task of classifying, distinguishing, or recognizing influences; and heated discussions between those who wish to enlarge the sphere of Caravaggio's followers and those who prefer to restrict it, have not been uncommon. Whereas for some critics (Bellori, for instance, or the advocates of classicism) Caravaggio was a constant source of trouble (and traces of this attitude, which sees Caravaggio as a corruptive influence, survived until very recently), certain great artists saw him as a brilliant source of inspiration. We have mentioned Rubens in this connection; but it must be pointed out that, contrary to the restrictive theories that have been advanced, especially outside Italy, without Caravaggio the three great painters of the seventeenth century — Velasquez, Rembrandt, and Vermeer — would not have been the same. Velasquez saw the artist's works first hand, in Rome. Rembrandt and Vermeer saw what Caravaggio's Dutch followers brought back to Holland. The great multitude of foreign artists who turned to Caravaggio for inspiration from a very early date spread the characteristics of his style throughout France, the Low Countries, and the Iberian Peninsula. And in Italy, Caravaggio influenced all great painting of the seventeenth and eighteenth centuries, either positively or negatively, and we presuppose his importance even when we fail to mention it. Here we have followed only his own path of creative development. Along this path we have highlighted the most fascinating stages. From the boldness of the early works, through the splendid maturity of the central ones, up to the solitary monologue of the late paintings, we have acknowledged the regenerating creativity that animated a life otherwise characterized by a lucid desire for self-destruction.

New attributions and additions

When this short book appeared in the book review section of the prestigious journal 'The Burlington Magazine' it was described as "well informed and well illustrated". For a book aimed at the general reader one could not have hoped for a better appraisal. As space permits only the briefest of updates of this monograph, which was first published some years ago, I propose to leave unaltered both my interpretation of Caravaggio's work and the stylistic analysis of his paintings. I will, therefore, limit myself to two areas: brief indications of my reconsideration of some paintings and of specific problems; and the addition of at least some of those recently discovered paintings whose attribution to Caravaggio has met with sufficient critical acceptance.

It was a mistake not to include in the first edition of
84 the book the only mural painting by Caravaggio. This
is the ceiling painted in oils for the small "alchemy
room" of Cardinal del Monte (Zandri, 1969) situated in
what is now a corridor of the Villa Boncompagni Lu-
dovisi. Mentioned by Bellori and datable between 1597
and 1600, this is a work of exceptional importance. Of
85 slightly earlier date (c. 1595-6) is the painting I Bari, or
the Cardsharps, which had once belonged to the Sciar-
ra branch of the Barberini family and which was still un-
traced at the time of the first edition (see p. 14). Happi-
ly, it has now found its way to the Kimbell Art Museum,
Fort Worth — a truly epoch-making rediscovery.

Caravaggio had painted for Cardinal del Monte an
8 earlier version of the Lute Player, now at Leningrad and
86 formerly in the Giustiniani Collection. This first version
is now owned by Wildenstein's of New York who have
given it on loan to the Metropolitan Museum, New
York. Denis Mahon has published both the Cardsharps
(1988) and the Lute Player (1990) with the addition of
excellent technical appendices by Keith Christiansen.

87 There is now a reproduction of the Martyrdom of

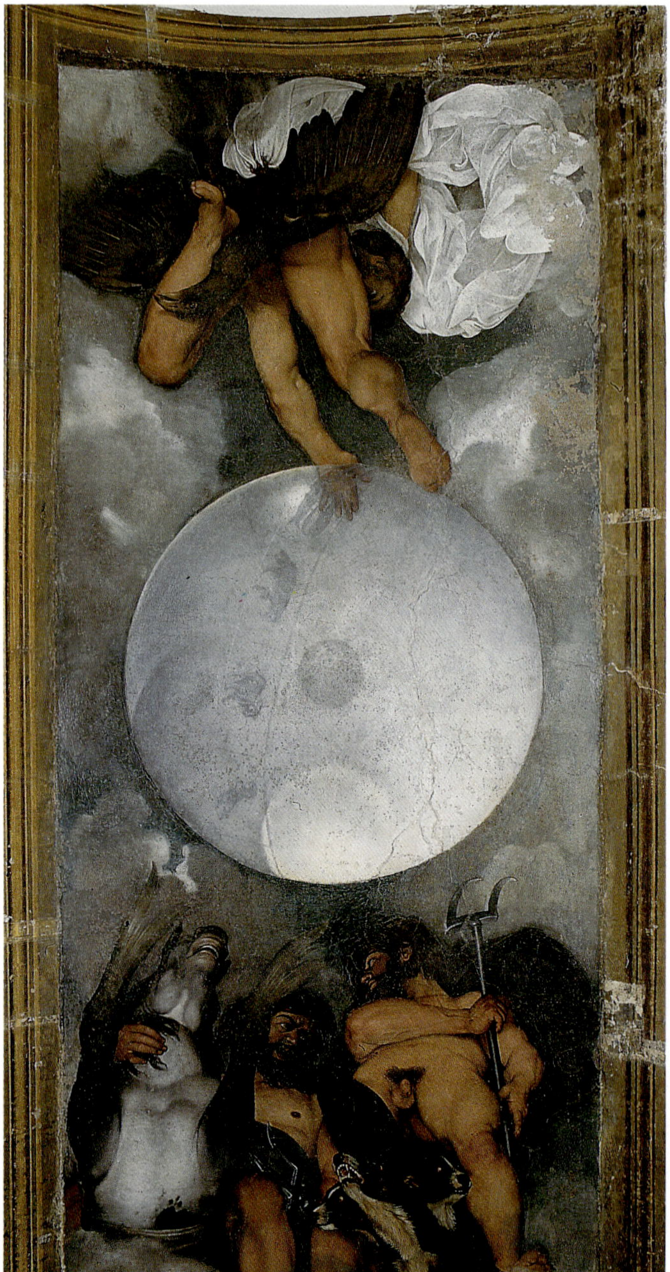

84

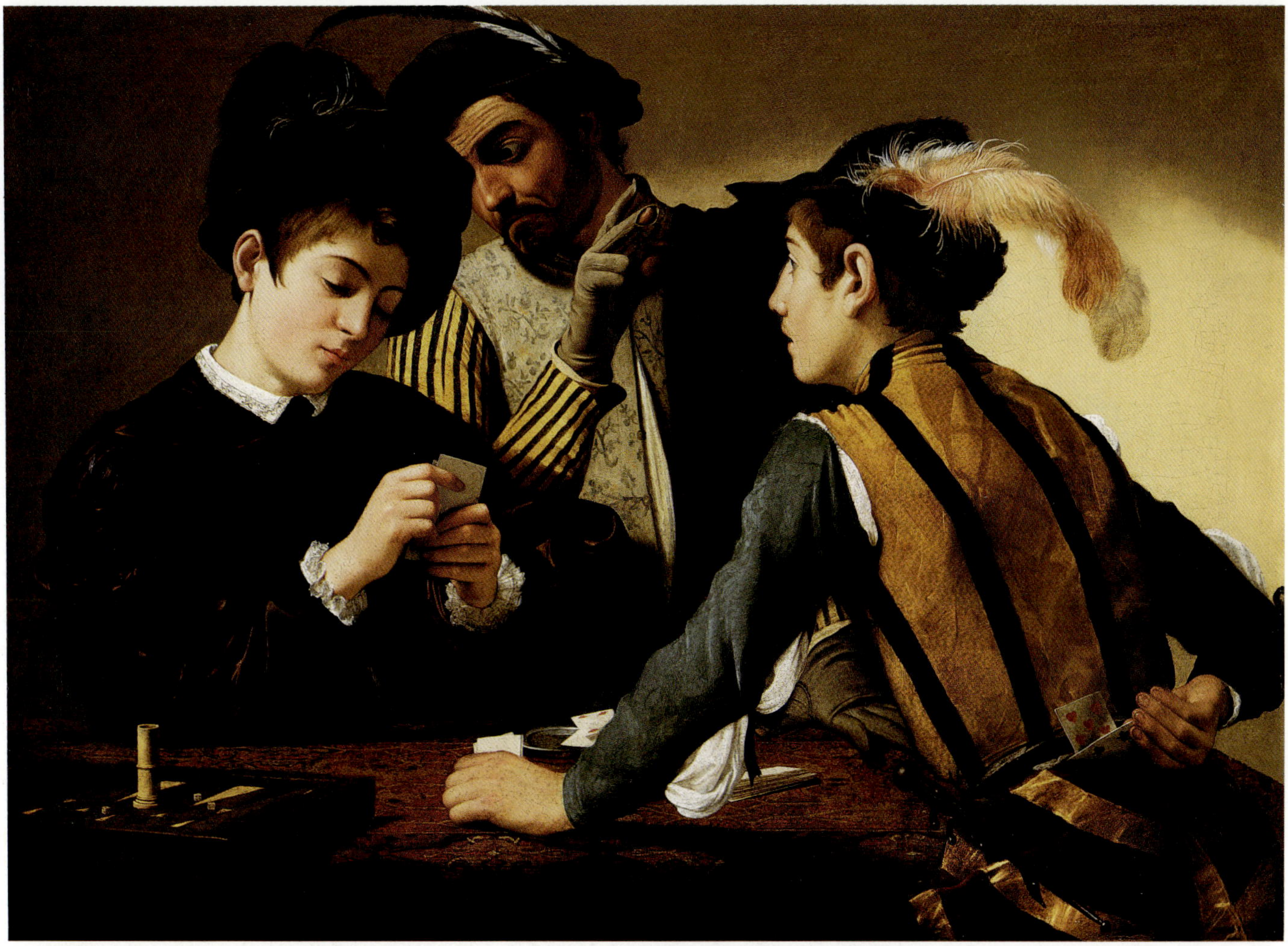

85

84. Jupiter, Neptune and Pluto
Rome, Casino Boncompagni Ludovisi

85. The Cardsharps
cm. 94x131
Fort Worth, Kimbell Art Museum

St. Ursula, of the Banca Commerciale Italiana, Naples, which was not possible to illustrate in the first edition (see p. 73). In addition, a chronological error needs
82 correction: the Crowning with Thorns in Prato is datable
to around 1603 (recently discovered documentary evidence seems to confirm the attribution to Caravaggio). Once more, the restricted length of this volume does not allow for any consideration of some much debated works such as the Vienna Crowning with Thorns and the St. Francis paintings in Carpineto Romano, in the Church of the Capuchins, Rome and in Cremona. Another St. Francis, in the Barbara Johnson Collection, has been published by Bologna. Mina Gregori has attributed to Caravaggio a Sacrifice of Isaac from the same collection; judgement should be reserved on these works until they have received further careful examination. Also, it is not possible to discuss here those numerous Still-lifes attributed to the young Caravaggio.

One aspect of Caravaggio's output which we know considerably more about today is his production of autograph duplicates (but I am not entirely convinced that the London version of the Youth Bitten by a Lizard is by his hand; therefore I refer here only to the Longhi
Collection painting). In any case, it is clear that 4
Caravaggio produced an impressive number of paintings during his short life and that the great majority of them have survived — a truly rare phenomenon.

Finally, Testori has published (1984) what is perhaps the only surviving drawing by Caravaggio: a study of a head for the Adoration of the Shepherds, stolen in 1969 from the Oratory of San Lorenzo, Palermo and which, sadly, has still not come to light.

86

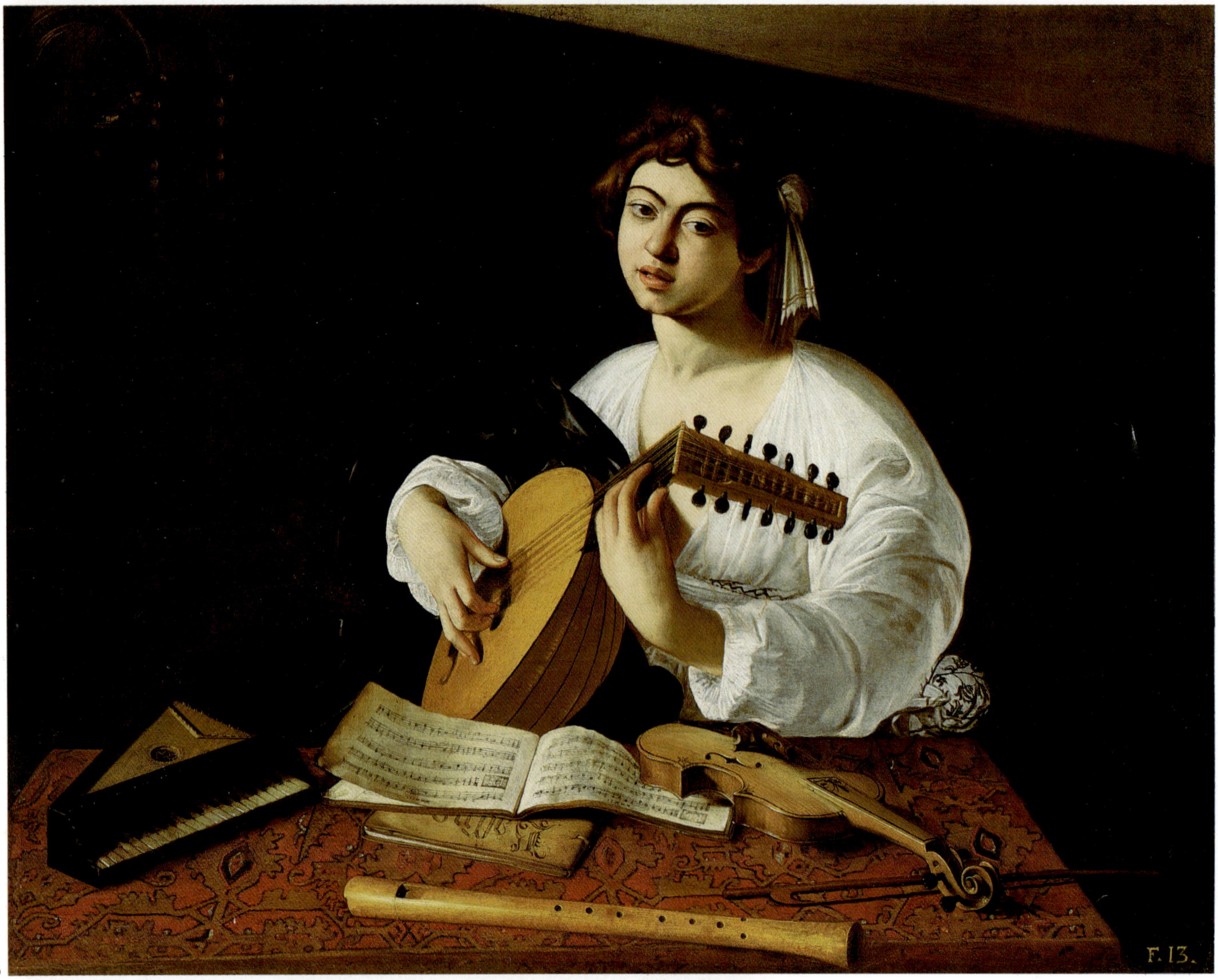

87

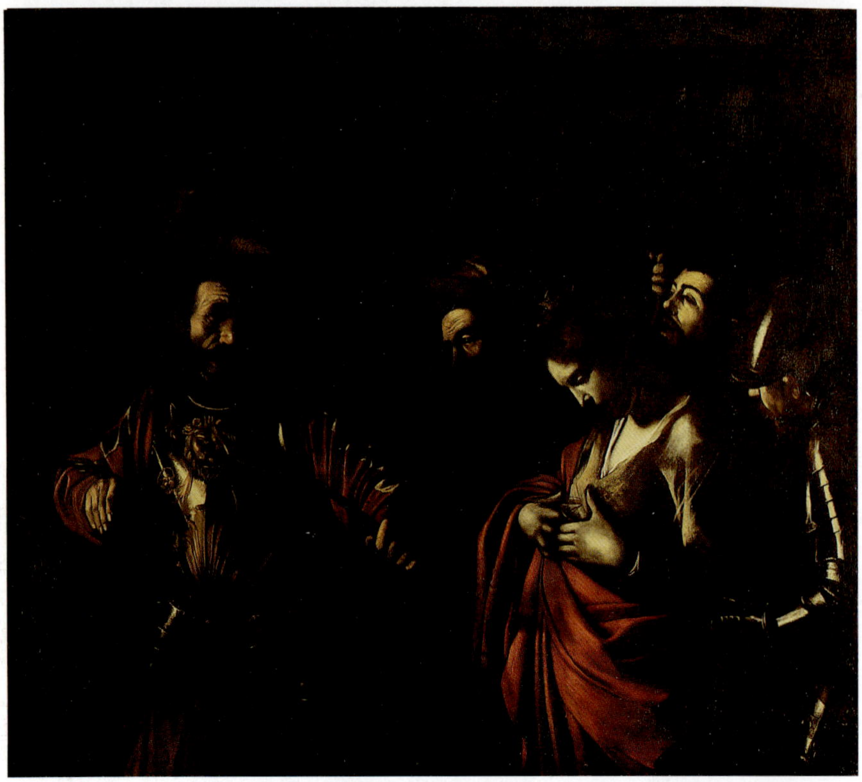

86. Lute Player
cm. 100x126.5
New York, private collection

87. Martyrdom of St. Ursula
cm. 154x178
Naples, Banca Commerciale Italiana